GROUPING AND ACCELERATION PRACTICES IN GIFTED EDUCATION

ESSENTIAL READINGS IN GIFTED EDUCATION

SERIES EDITOR

SALLY M. REIS

Linda E. Brody
EDITOR

GROUPING AND ACCELERATION PRACTICES IN GIFTED EDUCATION

A Joint Publication of Corwin Press and the National Association for Gifted Children

ESSENTIAL READINGS IN GIFTED EDUCATION
Sally M. Reis, SERIES EDITOR

CORWIN PRESS
A Sage Publications Company
Thousand Oaks, California

For information:

Corwin Press
A Sage Publications Company
2455 Teller Road
Thousand Oaks, California 91320
www.corwinpress.com

Sage Publications Ltd
1 Oliver's Yard
55 City Road
London EC1Y 1SP
United Kingdom

Sage Publications India Pvt. Ltd.
B-42, Panchsheel Enclave
Post Box 4109
New Delhi 110 017 India

Printed in the United States of America

Library of Congress Cataloging-in-Publication Data

Grouping and acceleration practices in gifted education / Linda E. Brody, editor.
    p. cm. — (Essential readings in gifted education ; 3)
"A joint publication of Corwin Press and the National Association for Gifted Children."
Includes bibliographical references and index.
ISBN 1-4129-0429-3 (pbk.)
    1. Gifted children—Education—United States. 2. Educational acceleration—United States.
I. Brody, Linda. II. National Association for Gifted Children (U.S.) III. Series.
LC3993.9.G76 2004
371.95′6—dc22

                                        2004001094

This book is printed on acid-free paper.

04   05   06   07   08   10   9   8   7   6   5   4   3   2   1

Acquisitions Editor:	Kylee Liegl
Editorial Assistant:	Jaime Cuvier
Production Editor:	Sanford Robinson
Typesetter:	C&M Digitals (P) Ltd.
Cover Designer:	Tracy E. Miller
NAGC Publications Coordinator:	Jane Clarenbach

Contents

About the Editors

Sally M. Reis is a professor and the department head of the Educational Psychology Department at the University of Connecticut where she also serves as principal investigator of the National Research Center on the Gifted and Talented. She was a teacher for 15 years, 11 of which were spent working with gifted students on the elementary, junior high, and high school levels. She has authored more than 130 articles, 9 books, 40 book chapters, and numerous monographs and technical reports.

Her research interests are related to special populations of gifted and talented students, including: students with learning disabilities, gifted females and diverse groups of talented students. She is also interested in extensions of the Schoolwide Enrichment Model for both gifted and talented students and as a way to expand offerings and provide general enrichment to identify talents and potentials in students who have not been previously identified as gifted.

She has traveled extensively conducting workshops and providing professional development for school districts on gifted education, enrichment programs, and talent development programs. She is co-author of *The Schoolwide Enrichment Model, The Secondary Triad Model, Dilemmas in Talent Development in the Middle Years*, and a book published in 1998 about women's talent development titled *Work Left Undone: Choices and Compromises of Talented Females*. Sally serves on several editorial boards, including the *Gifted Child Quarterly*, and is a past president of the National Association for Gifted Children.

Linda E. Brody directs the Study of Exceptional Talent and co-directs the Diagnostic and Counseling Center at the Johns Hopkins University Center for Talented Youth (CTY). She has over 25 years' experience counseling gifted students and their families and conducting research on this population. Having earned her doctorate in the Education of the Gifted from Johns Hopkins, she has taught graduate courses in gifted education there for many years. Her research interests focus on special populations, especially highly gifted students, gifted females, and gifted students with learning disabilities. She is also interested in identifying strategies and programs that facilitate talent development and supervises the publication of *Imagine,* a magazine for academically talented students. Linda has published numerous articles in professional journals and co-edited two books: *Women and the Mathematical Mystique* and *Learning Disabled Gifted Students: Identification and Programming.* She presents papers on a regular basis at national and international conferences and reviews articles for numerous journals in the field including *Gifted Child Quarterly, Journal of Secondary Gifted Education*, and *Roeper Review.*

Series Introduction

Sally M. Reis

The accomplishments of the last 50 years in the education of gifted students should not be underestimated: the field of education of the gifted and talented has emerged as strong and visible. In many states, a policy or position statement from the state board of education supports the education of the gifted and talented, and specific legislation generally recognizes the special needs of this group. Growth in our field has not been constant, however, and researchers and scholars have discussed the various high and low points of national interest and commitment to educating the gifted and talented (Gallagher, 1979; Renzulli, 1980; Tannenbaum, 1983). Gallagher described the struggle between support and apathy for special programs for gifted and talented students as having roots in historical tradition—the battle between an aristocratic elite and our concomitant belief in egalitarianism. Tannenbaum suggested the existence of two peak periods of interest in the gifted as the five years following *Sputnik* in 1957 and the last half of the decade of the 1970s, describing a valley of neglect between the peaks in which the public focused its attention on the disadvantaged and the handicapped. "The cyclical nature of interest in the gifted is probably unique in American education. No other special group of children has been alternately embraced and repelled with so much vigor by educators and laypersons alike" (Tannenbaum, 1983, p. 16). Many wonder if the cyclical nature to which Tannenbaum referred is not somewhat prophetic, as it appears that our field may be experiencing another downward spiral in interest as a result of current governmental initiatives and an increasing emphasis on testing and standardization of curriculum. Tannenbaum's description of a valley of neglect may describe current conditions. During the late 1980s, programming flourished during a peak of interest and a textbook on systems and models for gifted programs included 15 models for elementary and secondary programs (Renzulli, 1986). The Jacob Javits Gifted and Talented Students Education Act passed by Congress in 1988 resulted in the creation of the National Research Center on the Gifted and Talented, and dozens of model programs were added to the collective knowledge in the field in areas related to underrepresented populations and successful practices. In the 1990s, reduction or elimination of gifted programs occurred, as budget pressures exacerbated by the lingering recession in the late 1990s resulted in the reduction of services mandated by fewer than half of the states in our country.

Even during times in which more activity focused on the needs of gifted and talented students, concerns were still raised about the limited services provided to these students. In the second federal report on the status of education for our nation's most talented students entitled *National Excellence: A Case for Developing America's Talent* (Ross, 1993), "a quiet crisis" was described in the absence of attention paid to this population: "Despite sporadic attention over the years to the needs of bright students, most of them continue to spend time in school working well below their capabilities. The belief espoused in school reform that children from all economic and cultural backgrounds must reach their full potential has not been extended to America's most talented students. They are under-challenged and therefore underachieve" (p. 5). The report further indicates that our nation's gifted and talented students have a less rigorous curriculum, read fewer demanding books, and are less prepared for work or postsecondary education than the most talented students in many other industrialized countries. Talented children who come from economically disadvantaged homes or are members of minority groups are especially neglected, the report also indicates, and many of them will not realize their potential without some type of intervention.

In this anniversary series of volumes celebrating the evolution of our field, noted scholars introduce a collection of the most frequently cited articles from the premiere journal in our field, *Gifted Child Quarterly*. Each volume includes a collection of thoughtful, and in some cases, provocative articles that honor our past, acknowledge the challenges we face in the present, and provide hopeful guidance for the future as we seek the optimal educational experiences for all talented students. These influential articles, published after a rigorous peer review, were selected because they are frequently cited and considered seminal in our field. Considered in their entirety, the articles show that we have learned a great deal from the volume of work represented by this series. Our knowledge has expanded over several decades of work, and progress has been made toward reaching consensus about what is known. As several of the noted scholars who introduce separate areas explain in their introductions, this series helps us to understand that some questions have been answered, while others remain. While we still search for these answers, we are now better prepared to ask questions that continue and evolve. The seminal articles in this series help us to resolve some issues, while they highlight other questions that simply refuse to go away. Finally, the articles help us to identify new challenges that continue to emerge in our field. Carol Tomlinson suggests, for example, that the area of curriculum differentiation in the field of gifted education is, in her words, an issue born in the field of gifted education, and one that continues to experience rebirth.

Some of the earliest questions in our field have been answered and time has enabled those answers to be considered part of our common core of knowledge. For example, it is widely acknowledged that both school and home experiences can help to develop giftedness in persons with high potential and that a continuum of services in and out of school can provide the greatest likelihood that this development will occur. Debates over other "hot" issues such as grouping and acceleration that took place in the gifted education community 30 years ago are now largely unnecessary, as Linda Brody points out in her introduction to a series of articles in this area. General agreement seems to have been reached, for example, that grouping, enrichment and acceleration are all necessary to provide appropriate educational opportunities for gifted and talented learners. These healthy debates of the past helped to strengthen our field but visionary and reflective work remains to be done. In this series, section editors summarize what has been learned and raise provocative questions about the future. The questions alone are some of the most thoughtful in our field, providing enough research opportunities for scholars for the next decade. The brief introductions below provide some highlights about the series.

DEFINITIONS OF GIFTEDNESS (VOLUME 1)

In Volume 1, Robert Sternberg introduces us to seminal articles about definitions of giftedness and the types of talents and gifts exhibited by children and youth. The most widely used definitions of gifts and talents utilized by educators generally follow those proposed in federal reports. For example, the Marland Report (Marland, 1972) commissioned by the Congress included the first federal definition of giftedness, which was widely adopted or adapted by the states.

The selection of a definition of giftedness has been and continues to be the major policy decision made at state and local levels. It is interesting to note that policy decisions are often either unrelated or marginally related to actual procedures or to research findings about a definition of giftedness or identification of the gifted, a fact well documented by the many ineffective, incorrect, and downright ridiculous methods of identification used to find students who meet the criteria in the federal definition. This gap between policy and practice may be caused by many variables. Unfortunately, although the federal definition was written to be inclusive, it is, instead, rather vague, and problems caused by this definition have been recognized by experts in the field (Renzulli, 1978). In the most recent federal report on the status of gifted and talented programs entitled *National Excellence* (Ross, 1993), a newer federal definition is proposed based on new insights provided by neuroscience and cognitive psychology. Arguing that the term *gifted* connotes a mature power rather than a developing ability and, therefore, is antithetic to recent research findings about children, the new definition "reflects today's knowledge and thinking" (p. 26) by emphasizing talent development, stating that gifted and talented children are children and youth with outstanding talent performance or show the potential for performing at remarkably high levels of accomplishment when compared with others of their age, experience, or environment. These children and youth exhibit high performance capability in intellectual, creative, and/or artistic areas, possess an unusual leadership capacity, or excel in specific academic fields. They require services or activities not ordinarily provided by the schools. Outstanding talents are present in children and youth from all cultural groups, across all economic strata, and in all areas of human endeavor. (p. 26)

Fair identification systems use a variety of multiple assessment measures that respect diversity, accommodate students who develop at different rates, and identify potential as well as demonstrated talent. In the introduction to the volume, Sternberg admits, that just as people have bad habits, so do academic fields, explaining, "a bad habit of much of the gifted field is to do research on giftedness, or worse, identify children as gifted or not gifted, without having a clear conception of what it means to be gifted." Sternberg summarizes major themes from the seminal articles about definitions by asking key questions about the nature of giftedness and talent, the ways in which we should study giftedness, whether we should expand conventional notions of giftedness, and if so, how that can be accomplished; whether differences exist between giftedness and talent; the validity of available assessments; and perhaps most importantly, how do we and can we develop giftedness and talent. Sternberg succinctly summarizes points of broad agreement from the many scholars who have contributed to this section, concluding that giftedness involves more than just high IQ, that it has noncognitive and cognitive components, that the environment is crucial in terms of whether potentials for gifted performance will be realized, and that giftedness is not a single thing. He further cautions that the ways we conceptualize giftedness greatly influences who will have opportunities to develop their gifts and reminds readers of our responsibilities as educators. He also asks one of the most critical questions in our field: whether gifted and talented individuals will use their knowledge to benefit or harm our world.

IDENTIFICATION OF HIGH-ABILITY STUDENTS (VOLUME 2)

In Volume 2, Joseph Renzulli introduces what is perhaps the most critical question still facing practitioners and researchers in our field, that is how, when, and why should we identify gifted and talented students. Renzulli believes that conceptions of giftedness exist along a continuum ranging from a very conservative or restricted view of giftedness to a more flexible or multi-dimensional approach. What many seem not to understand is that the first step in identification should always be to ask: identification for what? For what type of program or experience is the youngster being identified? If, for example, an arts program is being developed for talented artists, the resulting identification system must be structured to identify youngsters with either demonstrated or potential talent in art.

Renzulli's introductory chapter summarizes seminal articles about identification, and summarizes emerging consensus. For example, most suggest, that while intelligence tests and other cognitive ability tests provide one very important form of information about one dimension of a young person's potential, mainly in the areas of verbal and analytic skills, they do not tell us all that we need to know about who should be identified. These authors do not argue that cognitive ability tests should be dropped from the identification process. Rather, most believe that (a) other indicators of potential should be used for identification, (b) these indicators should be given equal consideration when it comes to making final decisions about which students will be candidates for special services, and (c) in the final analysis, it is the thoughtful judgment of knowledgeable professionals rather than instruments and cutoff scores that should guide selection decisions.

Another issue addressed by the authors of the seminal articles about identification is what has been referred to as the distinction between (a) convergent and divergent thinking (Guilford, 1967; Torrance, 1984), (b) entrenchment and non-entrenchment (Sternberg, 1982), and (c) schoolhouse giftedness versus creative/productive giftedness (Renzulli, 1982; Renzulli & Delcourt, 1986). It is easier to identify schoolhouse giftedness than it is to identify students with the potential for creative productive giftedness. Renzulli believes that progress has been made in the identification of gifted students, especially during the past quarter century, and that new approaches address the equity issue, policies, and practices that respect new theories about human potential and conceptions of giftedness. He also believes, however, that continuous commitment to research-based identification practices is still needed, for "it is important to keep in mind that some of the characteristics that have led to the recognition of history's most gifted contributors are not always as measurable as others. We need to continue our search for those elusive things that are left over after everything explainable has been explained, to realize that giftedness is culturally and contextually imbedded in all human activity, and most of all, to value the value of even those things that we cannot yet explain."

ACCELERATION AND GROUPING, CURRICULUM, AND CURRICULUM DIFFERENTIATION (VOLUMES 3, 4, 5)

Three volumes in this series address curricular and grouping issues in gifted programs, and it is in this area, perhaps, that some of the most promising practices have been implemented for gifted and talented students. Grouping and curriculum interact with each other, as various forms of grouping patterns have enabled students to work on advanced curricular opportunities with other talented students. And, as is commonly known now about instructional and ability grouping, it is not the way students are grouped that matters most, but rather, it is what happens within the groups that makes the most difference.

In too many school settings, little differentiation of curriculum and instruction for gifted students is provided during the school day, and minimal opportunities are offered. Occasionally, after-school enrichment programs or Saturday programs offered by museums, science centers, or local universities take the place of comprehensive school programs, and too many academically talented students attend school in classrooms across the country in which they are bored, unmotivated, and unchallenged. Acceleration, once a frequently used educational practice in our country, is often dismissed by teachers and administrators as an inappropriate practice for a variety of reasons, including scheduling problems, concerns about the social effects of grade skipping, and others. Various forms of acceleration, including enabling precocious students to enter kindergarten or first grade early, grade skipping, and early entrance to college are not commonly used by most school districts.

Unfortunately, major alternative grouping strategies involve the reorganization of school structures, and these have been too slow in coming, perhaps due to the difficulty of making major educational changes, because of scheduling, finances, and other issues that have caused schools to substantially delay major change patterns. Because of this delay, gifted students too often fail to receive classroom instruction based on their unique needs that place them far ahead of their chronological peers in basic skills and verbal abilities and enable them to learn much more rapidly and tackle much more complex materials than their peers. Our most able students need appropriately paced, rich and challenging instruction, and curriculum that varies significantly from what is being taught in regular classrooms across America. Too often, academically talented students are "left behind" in school.

Linda Brody introduces the question of how to group students optimally for instructional purposes and pays particular concern to the degree to which the typical age-in-grade instructional program can meet the needs of gifted students—those students with advanced cognitive abilities and achievement that may already have mastered the curriculum designed for their age peers. The articles about grouping emphasize the importance of responding to the learning needs of individual students with curricular flexibility, the need for educators to be flexible when assigning students to instructional groups, and the need to modify those groups when necessary. Brody's introduction points out that the debate about grouping gifted and talented learners together was one area that brought the field together, as every researcher in the field supports some type of grouping option, and few would disagree with the need to use grouping and accelerated learning as tools that allow us to differentiate content for students with different learning needs. When utilized as a way to offer a more advanced educational program to students with advanced cognitive abilities and achievement levels, these practices can help achieve the goal of an appropriate education for all students.

Joyce VanTassel-Baska introduces the seminal articles in curriculum, by explaining that they represent several big ideas that emphasize the values and relevant factors of a curriculum for the gifted, the technology of curriculum development, aspects of differentiation of a curriculum for the gifted within core subject areas and without, and the research-based efficacy of such curriculum and related instructional pedagogy in use. She also reminds readers of Harry Passow's concerns about curriculum balance, suggesting that an imbalance exists, as little evidence suggests that the affective development of gifted students is occurring through special curricula for the gifted. Moreover, interdisciplinary efforts at curriculum frequently exclude the arts and foreign language. Only through acknowledging and applying curriculum balance in these areas are we likely to be producing the type of humane individual Passow envisioned. To achieve balance, VanTassel-Baska recommends a full set of curriculum options across domains, as well as the need to nurture the social-emotional needs of diverse gifted and talented learners.

Carol Tomlinson introduces the critical area of differentiation in the field of gifted education that has only emerged in the last 13 years. She believes the diverse nature of the articles and their relatively recent publication suggests that this area is indeed, in her words, "an issue born in the field of gifted education, and one that continues to experience rebirth." She suggests that one helpful way of thinking about the articles in this volume is that their approach varies, as some approach the topic of differentiation of curriculum with a greater emphasis on the distinctive mission of gifted education. Others look at differentiation with a greater emphasis on the goals, issues, and missions shared between general education and gifted education. Drawing from an analogy with anthropology, Tomlinson suggests that "splitters" in that field focus on differences among cultures while "lumpers" have a greater interest in what cultures share in common. Splitters ask the question of what happens for high-ability students in mixed-ability settings, while lumpers question what common issues and solutions exist for multiple populations in mixed-ability settings.

Tomlinson suggests that the most compelling feature of the collection of articles in this section—and certainly its key unifying feature—is the linkage between the two areas of educational practice in attempting to address an issue likely to be seminal to the success of both over the coming quarter century and beyond, and this collection may serve as a catalyst for next steps in those directions for the field of gifted education as it continues collaboration with general education and other educational specialties while simultaneously addressing those missions uniquely its own.

UNDERREPRESENTED AND TWICE-EXCEPTIONAL POPULATIONS AND SOCIAL AND EMOTIONAL ISSUES (VOLUMES 6, 7, 8)

The majority of young people participating in gifted and talented programs across the country continue to represent the majority culture in our society. Few doubts exist regarding the reasons that economically disadvantaged, twice-exceptional, and culturally diverse students are underrepresented in gifted programs. One reason may be the ineffective and inappropriate identification and selection procedures used for the identification of these young people that limits referrals and nominations and eventual placement. Research summarized in this series indicates that groups that have been traditionally underrepresented in gifted programs could be better served if some of the following elements are considered: new constructs of giftedness, attention to cultural and contextual variability, the use of more varied and authentic assessments, performance-based identification, and identification opportunities through rich and varied learning opportunities.

Alexinia Baldwin discusses the lower participation of culturally diverse and underserved populations in programs for the gifted as a major concern that has forged dialogues and discussion in *Gifted Child Quarterly* over the past five decades. She classifies these concerns in three major themes: *identification/selection, programming,* and *staff assignment and development.* Calling the first theme **Identification/Selection**, she indicates that it has always been the Achilles heel of educators' efforts to ensure that giftedness can be expressed in many ways through broad identification techniques. Citing favorable early work by Renzulli and Hartman (1971) and Baldwin (1977) that expanded options for identification, Baldwin cautions that much remains to be done. The second theme, **Programming**, recognizes the abilities of students who are culturally diverse but often forces them to exist in programs designed "for one size fits all." Her third theme relates to **Staffing and Research,** as she voices concerns about the diversity of teachers in these programs as well as the attitudes or mindsets of researchers who develop theories and conduct the research that addresses these concerns.

Susan Baum traces the historical roots of gifted and talented individuals with special needs, summarizing Terman's early work that suggested the gifted were healthier, more popular, and better adjusted than their less able peers. More importantly, gifted individuals were regarded as those who could perform at high levels in all areas with little or no support. Baum suggests that acceptance of these stereotypical characteristics diminished the possibility that there could be special populations of gifted students with special needs. Baum believes that the seminal articles in this collection address one or more of the critical issues that face gifted students at risk and suggest strategies for overcoming the barriers that prevent them from realizing their promise. The articles focus on three populations of students: twice-exceptional students—gifted students who are at risk for poor development due to difficulties in learning and attention;

gifted students who face gender issues that inhibit their ability to achieve or develop socially and emotionally, and students who are economically disadvantaged and at risk for dropping out of school. Baum summarizes research indicating that each of these groups of youngsters is affected by one or more barriers to development, and the most poignant of these barriers are identification strategies, lack of awareness of consequences of co-morbidity, deficit thinking in program design, and lack of appropriate social and emotional support. She ends her introduction with a series of thoughtful questions focusing on future directions in this critical area.

Sidney Moon introduces the seminal articles on the social and emotional development of and counseling for gifted children by acknowledging the contributions of the National Association for Gifted Children's task forces that have examined social/emotional issues. The first task force, formed in 2000 and called the Social and Emotional Issues Task Force, completed its work in 2002 by publishing an edited book, *The Social and Emotional Development of Gifted Children: What Do We Know?* This volume provides an extensive review of the literature on the social and emotional development of gifted children (Neihart, Reis, Robinson, & Moon, 2002). Moon believes that the seminal studies in the area of the social and emotional development and counseling illustrate both the strengths and the weaknesses of the current literature on social and emotional issues in the field of gifted education. These articles bring increased attention to the affective needs of special populations of gifted students, such as underachievers, who are at risk for failure to achieve their potential, but also point to the need for more empirical studies on "what works" with these students, both in terms of preventative strategies and more intensive interventions. She acknowledges that although good counseling models have been developed, they need to be rigorously evaluated to determine their effectiveness under disparate conditions, and calls for additional research on the affective and counseling interventions with specific subtypes of gifted students such as Asian Americans, African Americans, and twice-exceptional students. Moon also strongly encourages researchers in the field of gifted education to collaborate with researchers from affective fields such as personal and social psychology, counseling psychology, family therapy, and psychiatry to learn to intervene most effectively with gifted individuals with problems and to learn better how to help all gifted persons achieve optimal social, emotional, and personal development.

ARTISTICALLY AND CREATIVELY TALENTED STUDENTS (VOLUMES 9, 10)

Enid Zimmerman introduces the volume on talent development in the visual and performing arts with a summary of articles about students who are talented in music, dance, visual arts, and spatial, kinesthetic, and expressive areas. Major themes that appear in the articles include perceptions by parents, students, and teachers that often focus on concerns related to nature versus nurture in arts talent development; research about the crystallizing experiences of artistically talented students; collaboration between school and community members about identification of talented art students from diverse backgrounds; and leadership issues related to empowering teachers of talented arts students. They all are concerned to some extent with teacher, parent, and student views about educating artistically talented students. Included also are discussions about identification of talented students from urban, suburban, and rural environments. Zimmerman believes that in this particular area, a critical need exists for research about the impact of educational opportunities, educational settings, and the role of art teachers on the development of artistically talented students. The impact of the standards and testing movement and its relationship to the education of talented students in the visual and performing arts is an area greatly in need of investigation. Research also is needed about students' backgrounds, personalities, gender orientations, skill development, and cognitive and affective abilities as well as cross-cultural contexts and the impact of global and popular culture on the education of artistically talented students. The compelling case study with which she introduces this volume sets the stage for the need for this research.

Donald Treffinger introduces reflections on articles about creativity by discussing the following five core themes that express the collective efforts of researchers to grasp common conceptual and theoretical challenges associated with creativity. The themes include **Definitions** (how we define giftedness, talent, or creativity), **Characteristics** (the indicators of giftedness and creativity in people), **Justification** (Why is creativity important in education?), **Assessment** of creativity, and the ways we **Nurture** creativity. Treffinger also discusses the expansion of knowledge, the changes that have occurred, the search for answers, and the questions that still remain. In the early years of interest of creativity research, Treffinger believed that considerable discussion existed about whether it was possible to foster creativity through training or instruction. He reports that over the last 50 years, educators have learned that deliberate efforts to nurture creativity are possible (e.g., Torrance, 1987), and further extends this line of inquiry by asking the key question, "What works best, for whom, and under what conditions?" Treffinger summarizes the challenges faced by educators who try to nurture the development of creativity through effective teaching and to ask which experiences will have the greatest impact, as these will help to determine our ongoing lines of research, development, and training initiatives.

EVALUATION AND PUBLIC POLICY (VOLUMES 11, 12)

Carolyn Callahan introduces the seminal articles on evaluation and suggests that this important component neglected by experts in the field of gifted education for at least the last three decades can be a plea for important work by both evaluators and practitioners. She divides the seminal literature on evaluation, and in particular the literature on the evaluation of gifted programs into four categories, those which (a) provide theory and/or practical guidelines, (b) describe or report on specific program evaluations, (c) provide stimuli for the discussion of issues surrounding the evaluation process, and (d) suggest new research on the evaluation process. Callahan concludes with a challenge indicating work to be done and the opportunity for experts to make valuable contributions to increased effectiveness and efficiency of programs for the gifted.

James Gallagher provides a call-to-arms in the seminal articles he introduces on public policy by raising some of the most challenging questions in the field. Gallagher suggests that as a field, we need to come to some consensus about stronger interventions and consider how we react to accusations of elitism. He believes that our field could be doing a great deal more with additional targeted resources supporting the general education teacher and the development of specialists in gifted education, and summarizes that our failure to fight in the public arena for scarce resources may raise again the question posed two decades ago by Renzulli (1980), looking toward 1990: "Will the gifted child movement be alive and well in 2010?"

CONCLUSION

What can we learn from an examination of our field and the seminal articles that have emerged over the last few decades? First, we must **respect the past** by acknowledging the times in which articles were written and the shoulders of those persons upon whom we stand as we continue to create and develop our field. An old proverb tells us that when we drink from the well, we must remember to acknowledge those who dug the well, and in our field the early articles represent the seeds that grew our field. Next, we must **celebrate the present** and the exciting work and new directions in our field and the knowledge that is now accepted as a common core. Last, we must **embrace the future** by understanding that there is no finished product when it comes to research on gifted and talented children and how we are best able to meet their unique needs. Opportunities abound in the work reported in this series, but many questions remain. A few things seem clear. Action in the future should be based on both qualitative and quantitative research as well as longitudinal studies, and what we have completed only scratches the surface regarding the many variables and issues that still need to be explored. Research is needed that suggests positive changes that will lead to more inclusive programs that recognize the talents and gifts of diverse students in our country. When this occurs, future teachers and researchers in gifted education will find answers that can be embraced by educators, communities, and families, and the needs of all talented and gifted students will be more effectively met in their classrooms by teachers who have been trained to develop their students' gifts and talents.

We also need to consider carefully how we work with the field of education in general. As technology emerges and improves, new opportunities will become available to us. Soon, all students should be able to have their curricular needs preassessed before they begin any new curriculum unit. Soon, the issue of keeping students on grade-level material when they are many grades ahead should disappear as technology enables us to pinpoint students' strengths. Will chronological grades be eliminated? The choices we have when technology enables us to learn better what students already know presents exciting scenarios for the future, and it is imperative that we advocate carefully for multiple opportunities for these students, based on their strengths and interests, as well as a challenging core curriculum. Parents, educators, and professionals who care about these special populations need to become politically active to draw attention to the unique needs of these students, and researchers need to conduct the experimental studies that can prove the efficacy of providing talent development options as well as opportunities for healthy social and emotional growth.

For any field to continue to be vibrant and to grow, new voices must be heard, and new players sought. A great opportunity is available in our field; for as we continue to advocate for gifted and talented students, we can also play important roles in the changing educational reform movement. We can continue to work to achieve more challenging opportunities for all students while we fight to maintain gifted, talented, and enrichment programs. We can continue our advocacy for differentiation through acceleration, individual curriculum opportunities, and a continuum of advanced curriculum and personal support opportunities. The questions answered and those raised in this volume of seminal articles can help us to move forward as a field. We hope those who read the series will join us in this exciting journey.

REFERENCES

Baldwin, A.Y. (1977). Tests do underpredict: A case study. *Phi Delta Kappan, 58,* 620-621.

Gallagher, J. J. (1979). Issues in education for the gifted. In A. H. Passow (Ed.), *The gifted and the talented: Their education and development* (pp. 28-44). Chicago: University of Chicago Press.

Guilford, J. E. (1967). *The nature of human intelligence.* New York: McGraw-Hill.

Marland, S. P., Jr. (1972). *Education of the gifted and talented: Vol. 1. Report to the Congress of the United States by the U.S. Commissioner of Education.* Washington, DC: U.S. Government Printing Office.

Neihart, M., Reis, S., Robinson, N., & Moon, S. M. (Eds.). (2002). *The social and emotional development of gifted children: What do we know?* Waco, TX: Prufrock.

Renzulli, J. S. (1978). What makes giftedness? Reexamining a definition. *Phi Delta Kappan, 60*(5), 180-184.

Renzulli, J. S. (1980). Will the gifted child movement be alive and well in 1990? *Gifted Child Quarterly, 24*(1), 3-9. **[See Vol. 12.]**

Renzulli, J. (1982). Dear Mr. and Mrs. Copernicus: We regret to inform you . . . *Gifted Child Quarterly, 26*(1), 11-14. **[See Vol. 2.]**

Renzulli, J. S. (Ed.). (1986). *Systems and models for developing programs for the gifted and talented.* Mansfield Center, CT: Creative Learning Press.

Renzulli, J. S., & Delcourt, M. A. B. (1986). The legacy and logic of research on the identification of gifted persons. *Gifted Child Quarterly, 30*(1), 20-23. **[See Vol. 2.]**

Renzulli J., & Hartman, R. (1971). Scale for rating behavioral characteristics of superior students. *Exceptional Children, 38,* 243-248.

Ross, P. (1993). *National excellence: A case for developing America's talent.* Washington, DC: U.S. Department of Education, Government Printing Office.

Sternberg, R. J. (1982). Nonentrenchment in the assessment of intellectual giftedness. *Gifted Child Quarterly, 26*(2), 63-67. **[See Vol. 2.]**

Tannenbaum, A. J. (1983). *Gifted children: Psychological and educational perspectives.* New York: Macmillan.

Torrance, E. P. (1984). The role of creativity in identification of the gifted and talented. *Gifted Child Quarterly, 28*(4), 153-156. **[See Vols. 2 and 10.]**

Torrance, E. P. (1987). Recent trends in teaching children and adults to think creatively. In S. G. Isaksen (Ed.), *Frontiers of creativity research: Beyond the basics* (pp. 204-215). Buffalo, NY: Bearly Limited.

Introduction to Grouping and Acceleration Practices in Gifted Education

Linda E. Brody

Johns Hopkins University

The question of how to group students optimally for instructional purposes has stimulated debate within the educational community ever since the primary responsibility for educating children moved from the home to the community, and schools were formed. While most schools today group students into grades on the basis of age, educators keep moving birthday cut-offs, contemplating exceptions to those cut-offs, and worrying about students whose needs may not be met by age-in-grade instruction. Of particular concern is the degree to which the typical instructional program can meet the needs of gifted students—those students with advanced cognitive abilities and achievement who may already have mastered the curriculum designed for their age peers.

In order to provide access to more challenging coursework, grouping gifted students with age peers who are also academically advanced (ability or instructional grouping), or placing them with older students or otherwise providing access to advanced content (acceleration), are among the options that have been widely implemented. These intervention strategies have generated considerable controversy, however.

While the development of special programs for gifted students sometimes pits educators of the gifted against those more concerned about other groups of students, the debates over grouping and acceleration have also taken place within the gifted education community. Acceleration versus enrichment became highly debated in the 70s and 80s, while ability grouping versus cooperative learning was an issue during the late 80s and much of the 90s. The good news about these debates is that they spurred a great deal of research as advocates sought support for their positions. They also stimulated compromise, creative solutions, and the development of a variety of new program models. Today, the field is stronger because of the questions that were asked and answered about grouping and acceleration. We have come to expect research-based validation of new program models and curricula, and there are many more options available to serve gifted students.

Because so much of the discussion and research on acceleration and grouping took place within the gifted education community, publications over the years in the *Gifted Child Quarterly* are highly representative of the concerns, research findings, and programmatic initiatives that resulted. The articles that follow, all of which were published in the *Gifted Child Quarterly*, represent some of the most important and widely cited works on these topics. Several of them were included in a special Spring 1992 issue on Grouping and Acceleration.

The articles on acceleration dispel many common misconceptions about the practice and make a strong case for utilizing acceleration as a strategy for serving gifted students who need more challenge than the typical age-in-grade curriculum can provide. In particular, a number of the authors counter the belief that acceleration equates with skipping grades by describing a wide variety of ways to accelerate students. Several of these articles also offer strong research evidence that refutes the prevailing concern that students who are accelerated will experience social and emotional maladjustment.

The articles on ability or instructional grouping describe the issues that have made the practice controversial. In particular, the effectiveness and fairness of grouping students have been questioned. Research findings in support of grouping students for instructional purposes are presented, along with suggestions for utilizing grouping in a fair and flexible way.

The common theme that emerges from all of these articles, whether on acceleration or grouping, is that curricula designed for average students needs to be modified to address the needs of academically advanced students. Evidence is presented that acceleration and grouping are effective strategies for achieving this goal. A summary of the major points in these articles follows, along with references to selected other publications on these topics.

ACCELERATION

In spite of continuing concern by educators about the social and emotional adjustment of accelerated students, allowing advanced students to skip grades has been a fairly common practice in American education (Daurio, 1979). When seeking to identify the brightest students for his study, Terman (1925) found that they were frequently the youngest in a class because they had been accelerated in grade placement. In past generations, the solution for challenging an exceptionally bright child was often to place him or her in the next grade.

When Julian Stanley established the Study of Mathematically Precocious Youth (SMPY) at Johns Hopkins University in 1971, he turned to acceleration as a vehicle for serving students with exceptionally advanced academic abilities. Although a variety of accelerative strategies were used, including subject acceleration and academic summer programs, SMPY's work with the radical accelerants who entered Johns Hopkins University several years early gained the greatest attention (Stanley, Keating, & Fox, 1974). Fear of possible social and emotional maladjustment among these radical accelerants helped fuel the controversy and debate over acceleration as a mechanism for serving gifted learners. The proceedings of a 1977 symposium on acceleration and enrichment provide a glimpse into the issues in this debate (George, Cohn, & Stanley, 1979).

Stanley and his colleagues studied the progress of the students they worked with, finding support for acceleration as an appropriate strategy for gifted students. Stanley's article (1985) that is reprinted in this volume investigates the achievements of six exceptionally young college graduates. He finds that, at the time this study was conducted, five of them had earned Ph.D. degrees and were working in prestigious positions, while the sixth was an 18-year-old graduate student. Clearly, these students have done exceptionally well, and the study reports no ill-effects resulting from their radical acceleration.

In spite of consistent research findings that groups of early college entrants have done well academically and socially (Brody & Stanley, 1991), anecdotal reports of poor adjustment among individual accelerated students persist. The study by Brody, Assouline, and Stanley (1990) in this volume confirms the success of a group of young college entrants but also seeks to identify the factors that are most important for success within that group. Interestingly, the students with the highest level of academic success also had earned the greatest number of College Board Advanced Placement Program credits before entering college. Thus, though they entered college young, they were advanced in their mastery of subject matter. This study links subject acceleration to grade acceleration and supports the view that a variety of factors, including content knowledge, should be evaluated before students enroll in college at younger-than-typical ages.

The importance of considering students' individual needs and providing appropriate assessment and counseling before making decisions about acceleration is also affirmed in the articles by Gross (1992), and by Rimm and Lovance (1992), who present case studies of students who accelerated in subject and/or grade placement. Gross compares radically accelerated students with other extremely bright students who were given little opportunity to go beyond the regular curriculum. She finds that the accelerated students were academically superior, more motivated, and had healthier social relationships than the non-accelerants. The study by Rimm and Lovance (1992) also presents compelling case studies of students whose academic successes were enhanced by opportunities to accelerate in subject matter and/or grade placement. In fact, a reversal of underachievement was observed in some cases.

One response to concerns about early entrants' readiness for college has been the establishment of Early College Entrance Programs at a number of

xxvi   Grouping and Acceleration Practices in Gifted Education

universities. These programs bring young students to college as a cohort and provide greater academic counseling and social and emotional support than is typically available for college students. The article by Lupkowski, Whitmore, and Ramsey (1992) evaluates students at the end of their first semester at the Texas Academy of Mathematics and Science, a program at the University of North Texas. While some minor negative impact on self-esteem common to many college students was observed, the authors conclude that no serious adjustment difficulties were found among the students in this program. Studies of students enrolling in special Early Entrance Programs at other universities are also well represented in the gifted education literature (e.g., Gregory & March, 1985; Janos & Robinson, 1985; Sethna, Wickstrom, Boothe, & Stanley, 2001).

Proponents of acceleration never intended early college entrance to be the only, or even the primary, model for accelerating gifted students, and many ways to accelerate in subject matter without having to skip grades have been identified and/or developed in recent years and are described in the literature. These include such options as telescoped programs, compacted curricula, credit by examination, mentorships, distance education, part-time college enrollment, Advanced Placement courses, and academic summer programs (Rogers, 2001; Southern & Jones, 1991; Southern, Jones, & Stanley, 1993). Brody and Benbow's (1987) article in this volume investigates the academic success and social and emotional adjustment of students who used a variety of accelerative options. Regardless of the degree or type of acceleration the students pursued, positive academic effects are reported without concomitant social and emotional difficulties.

The article by VanTassel-Baska (1992) presents an overview of research and practice on acceleration. She makes a strong case for utilizing this strategy to provide content at a level and pace that is appropriate for gifted learners. Readers should also see the important research findings reported by Kulik and Kulik (1984), Rogers (1992), and Swiatek and Benbow (1991) that demonstrate the overall positive effects of acceleration.

GROUPING

While acceleration and ability grouping have often been treated as separate issues in much of the gifted education literature, they are actually very much related. Grouping students together who are ready for an advanced curriculum can provide a vehicle for accelerating their learning. On the other hand, when a lack of grouping results in no differentiation of content for advanced learners, these students may be more likely to turn to skipping grades as the only way to have their needs addressed. Unfortunately, a lack of any prior exposure to advanced content could impede their success in the higher grade.

Grouping students into classes on the basis of age was largely a response to mandatory education laws and the consequent dramatic increase in school enrollment. To accommodate the academic needs of the diverse student populations that enrolled, "tracking" became a common practice, i.e., students were organized into groups for instructional purposes, usually on the basis of IQ scores. Critics of tracking questioned the fairness of the tests used to assign students and the relative lack of mobility between the "tracks" over time. School reform efforts intensified the battle cry over what was seen as poor instruction in the groups consisting of lower scoring students, and many schools responded by abandoning any grouping of students within grades in favor of inclusive classes composed of students of all ability and achievement levels. The articles by Feldhusen and Moon (1992), Mills and Durden (1992), and VanTassel-Baska (1992) summarize these concerns, but they also describe the difficulties inherent in trying to meet the educational needs of advanced students if ability grouping is eliminated.

With ability grouping under attack, the challenge of serving students with different backgrounds and abilities has led educators to seek other ways to group students within classes. One strategy that was developed was cooperative learning (Slavin, 1988). Instead of putting students into instructional groups based on similar levels of ability or achievement, cooperative learning encourages the formation of small heterogeneous groups of students who work together. The expectation is that the brighter, more advanced students might contribute to the learning of students who are having more difficulty in mastering skills and knowledge. As cooperative learning gained in popularity, many gifted education advocates became concerned that the method often results in limiting the access of gifted students to advanced content. Eventually, an ongoing debate ensued, pitting advocates of ability grouping against supporters of cooperative learning (Robinson, 1990). Many viewed these two strategies as mutually exclusive and incompatible with each other. The articles by Feldhusen and Moon (1992), and by Mills and Durden (1992), provide insight into the issues behind the debate over ability grouping versus cooperative learning.

While strong opinions surfaced early in this debate, the research results on the effects of ability grouping were less clear because there appeared to be contradictory findings. Kulik and Kulik's (1992) meta-analysis of studies of research on ability grouping, the results of which are summarized in their article in this volume, proved to be very important in shedding light on this issue. Their results show that grouping can be very positive for high-ability students, *as long as an appropriate adjustment is made in the curriculum*. While their research suggests that grouping by itself will not impact on achievement if the curriculum is not changed in any way, they conclude that grouping facilitates making the curricular adjustments that will serve students in an optimal way. In their study, accelerated classes made the greatest gains of the groups investigated, an important finding. In a more recent paper, Kulik (2003) evaluates current research and practice with regard to ability grouping.

But if grouping is effective when done well, is it also fair, particularly to low achievers who were often left unchallenged in low tracks in the past? This was the concern of many critics of ability grouping. The article by Mills and Durden (1992) describes how grouping can facilitate achieving an optimal match between students' educational needs and their educational programs for students of all levels of abilities, and VanTassel-Baska's article (1992) comments on the benefits of utilizing grouping and acceleration to serve high-ability minority students. In their article, Feldhusen and Moon (1992) demonstrate how grouping, unlike tracking, can be sensible, flexible, and based on students' achievement as well as ability. In fact, the term "ability grouping" is probably an unfortunate one, since achievement as well as ability should always be considered when assigning students to instructional groups.

A variation of flexible grouping is "cluster grouping," a strategy that was developed as a way to offer differentiated learning opportunities to high achievers within a heterogeneous classroom. This practice assigns small groups of students with similar educational needs together in classes to meet these needs. For example, if students across a grade are identified as reading on any of six levels, students representing no more than two or three of these levels might be assigned to one classroom teacher. Most importantly, all of the very top readers would be assigned to one class so that they could be taught as a group. In their article, Gentry and Owens (1999) describe the beneficial effects on achievement they observed for students of all skill levels when cluster grouping was used in a school during a three-year period. As with any method of grouping students, the effectiveness of cluster grouping is dependent on adjusting the curriculum to meet the needs of the students in the groups.

IMPLICATIONS FOR POLICY AND PRACTICE

The articles in this section strongly support the use of a variety of forms of acceleration, when appropriate for individual students, and ability grouping, when implemented with flexibility and accompanied by appropriate adjustment to the curriculum, as effective strategies for meeting the needs of gifted students. Utilizing both quantitative and qualitative research methodologies, drawing on theory as well as practice, and offering new ideas for implementing these practices more effectively, the body of literature represented here is compelling in its arguments. For those seeking research evidence to validate grouping and acceleration as practices to serve gifted students, the debates should be over, and within much of the gifted community they are.

Acceleration and enrichment are both widely accepted as appropriate options for gifted learners, rather than being viewed as mutually exclusive, and a wide variety of program models have been developed that fall under both categories. With regard to grouping, the gifted community is focusing more on *how* to group students, rather than whether to group them at all. It is understood that grouping gifted students together is effective and defensible only when the curriculum is also adjusted to meet their academic needs.

But the larger educational community remains less supportive and still suspicious of these practices. In their articles, Feldhusen and Moon (1992), Mills and Durden (1992), and VanTassel-Baska (1992) describe the social-political climate that has influenced school systems' decisions about grouping and acceleration. It appears that equity/excellence issues are still impacting decisions about these practices for gifted students (Gallagher, 2003). Although school reform initiatives have tried to address the importance of both excellence and equity in American education, concern about the lowest-performing students has received the most attention. Consequently, ability grouping, which separates high from low achievers and therefore can call more attention to the low achievers, and acceleration, which allows high achievers to go faster and could create an even larger gap between high and low achievers, have received relatively little support from the larger educational community.

Of course, not all schools have abandoned these strategies. In their article in this volume, Jones and Southern (1992) report that both accelerative and grouping practices were in operation in the schools they studied, though these practices were more prevalent in urban than rural districts. The dramatic rise of the Advanced Placement Program in high schools suggests that advanced work is available in many schools. Other practices have emerged, such as cluster grouping and enrichment in the regular classroom. A number of very rigorous magnet schools have been also established, including several state-funded residential high schools for academically talented students (Koloff, 2003; Stanley, 1991). It is ironic, however, that a school system that lacks support for an accelerated reading group in a first grade class due to its concern about equity may send students to a magnet high school that groups advanced students together on a full-time residential basis.

Universities and a number of private organizations have also established a wide variety of opportunities and programs for advanced students who want to accelerate their educational progress, including summer programs, Saturday programs, distance education, mentorships, internships, and Early College Entrance programs. The work by Stanley and others in identifying many different ways to accelerate, along with demand by parents and students for services, has generated much programmatic development. Similarly, proponents of enrichment responded to the debate over the value of enrichment by creating more and better opportunities for students to broaden their knowledge through extracurricular activities, special programs, and other opportunities. There are more educational options available for gifted students than ever before, many of them created in response to having to seek alternatives to traditional grouping and school-based acceleration.

Many of these programs exist outside of school, however, and limited financial resources may impede some students' participation. In addition, students returning to school from these programs need opportunities to continue to learn at a pace and level appropriate for their abilities and achievement levels. Schools need to be made aware of the strong and persuasive research evidence that supports ability grouping and various forms of acceleration as effective pedagogical practices to further the educational achievement of gifted learners.

CONCLUSION

Providing an appropriate educational program for all students is a goal that is universally agreed upon; what is less clear is how to achieve it. Students with advanced academic abilities and achievement need an educational program that matches their instructional needs, and often this requires some form of acceleration. While grouping is not an essential component of acceleration, bringing together students with similar instructional needs facilitates delivery of more advanced curricula in an efficient way.

In reviewing the articles included herein, what is emphasized throughout is the importance of responding to the learning needs of individual students with curricular flexibility. Educators need to be flexible when assigning students to instructional groups and must modify those groups when necessary. They need to be flexible in determining the age at which a student is ready to learn something or the pace at which it should be taught. They must also be willing to look beyond the school offerings to consider other program options to meet students' needs and give them credit for these learning experiences when warranted.

Acceleration and grouping are tools that allow us to differentiate content for students with different learning needs. When utilized as a way to offer a more advanced educational program to students with advanced cognitive abilities and achievement levels, these practices can help achieve the goal of an appropriate education for all students.

REFERENCES

Brody, L. E., & Stanley, J. C. (1991). Young college students: Assessing factors that contribute to success. In W. T. Southern & E. D. Jones (Eds.), *The academic acceleration of gifted children* (pp. 102-131). New York: Teachers College Press.

Brody, L. E., & Benbow, C. P. (1987). Accelerative strategies: How effective are they for the gifted? *Gifted Child Quarterly, 3*(3), 105-110. **[See Vol. 3, p. 57.]**

Brody, L. E., Assouline, S. G., & Stanley, J. C. (1990). Five years of early entrants: Predicting successful achievement in college. *Gifted Child Quarterly, 34*(4), 138-142. **[See Vol. 3, p. 3.]**

Daurio, S. P. (1979). Educational enrichment versus acceleration: A review of the literature. In W. C. George, S. J. Cohn, & J. C. Stanley (Eds.), *Educating the gifted: Acceleration and enrichment* (pp. 3-63). Baltimore: Johns Hopkins University Press.

Feldhusen, J. F. & Moon, S. M. (1992). Grouping gifted students: Issues and concerns. *Gifted Child Quarterly, 36*(2), 63-67. **[See Vol. 3, p. 81.]**

Gallagher, J. J. (2003). Issues and challenges in gifted education. In N. Colangelo & G. A. Davis (Eds.), *Handbook of gifted education* (3rd ed.) (pp. 11-23). Boston: Allyn & Bacon.

Gentry, M. & Owen, S. V. (1999). An investigation of the effects of total school flexible cluster grouping on identification, achievement, and classroom practices. *Gifted Child Quarterly, 43*(4), 224-243. **[See Vol. 3, p. 115.]**

George, W. C., Cohn, S. J., & Stanley, J. C. (Eds.) (1979). *Educating the gifted: Acceleration and enrichment*. Baltimore: Johns Hopkins University Press.

Gregory, E., & March, E. (1985). Early entrance program at California State University, Los Angeles. *Gifted Child Quarterly, 29*(2), 83-86.

Gross, M. U. M. (1992). The use of radical acceleration in cases of extreme intellectual precocity. *Gifted Child Quarterly, 36*(2), 91-99. **[See Vol. 3, p. 13.]**

Janos, P. M., & Robinson, N. M. (1985). The performance of students in a program of radical acceleration at the university level. *Gifted Child Quarterly, 29*(4), 175-179.

Jones, E. D., & Southern, W. T. (1992). Programming, grouping, and acceleration in rural school districts: A survey of attitudes and practices. *Gifted Child Quarterly, 36*(2), 112-117. **[See Vol. 3, p. 147.]**

Koloff, P. B. (2003). State-supported residential high schools. In N. Colangelo & G. A. Davis (Eds.), *Handbook of gifted education* (3rd ed.) (pp. 238-246). Boston: Allyn & Bacon.

Kulik, J. A. (2003). Grouping and tracking. In N. Colangelo & G. A. Davis (Eds.), *Handbook of gifted education* (3rd ed.) (pp. 268-281). Boston: Allyn & Bacon.

Kulik, J. A., & Kulik, C. C. (1984). Effects of accelerated instruction on students. *Review of Education Research, 54*, 409-425.

Kulik, J. A., & Kulik, C. C. (1992). Meta-analytic findings on grouping programs. *Gifted Child Quarterly, 36*(2), 73-77. **[See Vol. 3, p. 105.]**

Lupkowski, A. E., Whitmore, M., & Ramsay, A. (1992). The impact of early entrance to college on self-esteem: A preliminary study. *Gifted Child Quarterly, 36*(2), 87-90. **[See Vol. 3, p. 47.]**

Mills, C. J., & Durden, W. G. (1992). Cooperative learning and ability grouping: An issue of choice. *Gifted Child Quarterly, 36*(1), 11-16. **[See Vol. 3, p. 91.]**

Rimm, S. B., & Lovance, K. J. (1992). The use of subject and grade skipping for the prevention and reversal of underachievement. *Gifted Child Quarterly, 36*(2), 100-105. **[See Vol. 3, p. 33.]**

Robinson, A. (1990). Cooperation or exploitation? The argument against cooperative learning for talented students. *Journal for the Education of the Gifted, 14*(3), 9-27.

Rogers, K. B. (1992). A best-evidence synthesis of the research on acceleration options for gifted learners. In N. Colangelo, S. G. Assouline, & D. L. Ambroson (Eds.), *Talent development: Proceedings from the 1991 Henry B. and Jocelyn Wallace national symposium on talent development* (pp. 406-409). Unionville, NY: Trillium Press.

Rogers, K. B. (2001). *Re-forming gifted education.* Scottsdale, AZ: Great Potential Press.

Sethna, B. N., Wickstrom, C. D., Boothe, D., & Stanley, J. C. (2001). The Advanced Academy of Georgia: Four years as a residential early-college-entrance program. *Journal of Secondary Gifted Education, 13*(1), 11-21.

Slavin, R. (1988). *Cooperative learning: Theory, research, and practice.* Englewood Cliffs, NJ: Prentice Hall.

Southern, W. T., & Jones, E. D. (Eds.) (1991). *The academic acceleration of gifted children.* New York: Teachers College Press.

Southern, W. T., Jones, E. D., & Stanley, J. C. (1993). Acceleration and enrichment: The context and development of program options. In K. A. Heller, F. J. Monks, & A. H. Passow (Eds.), *International handbook of research and development of giftedness and talent* (pp. 387-409). Oxford, England: Pergamon Press.

Stanley, J. C. (1985). How did six highly accelerated gifted students fare in graduate school? *Gifted Child Quarterly, 29*(4), 180. **[See Vol. 3, p. 1.]**

Stanley, J. C. (1991). A better model for residential high schools for talented youths. *Phi Delta Kappan, 72*, 471-473.

Stanley, J. C., Keating, D. P., & Fox, L. H. (Eds.) (1974). *Mathematical talent: Discovery, description, and development.* Baltimore: Johns Hopkins University Press.

Swiatek, M., & Benbow, C. P. (1991). Ten-year longitudinal follow-up study of ability-matched accelerated and unaccelerated students. *Journal of Educational Psychology, 83*, 528-538.

Terman, L. M. (1925). *Mental and physical traits of a thousand gifted children. Genetic studies of genius*, Vol. I. Stanford, CA: Stanford University Press.

VanTassel-Baska, J. (1992). Educational decision making on acceleration and grouping. *Gifted Child Quarterly, 36*(2), 68-72. **[See Vol. 3, p. 69.]**

How Did Six Highly Accelerated Gifted Students Fare in Graduate School?

Julian C. Stanley

The Johns Hopkins University

This article reports follow-up information on six very young college graduates. The myth of "early ripe, early rot" is clearly refuted by the outstanding success of each of these six young accelerants.

I n the October, 1977, issue of the *Smithsonian* magazine, seven unusually young college graduates were featured (Nevin, 1977; *Time,* 1977). Six of them

Editor's Note: From Stanley, J. C. (1985). How did six highly accelerated gifted students fare in graduate school? *Gifted Child Quarterly*, 29(4), 180. © 1985 National Association for Gifted Children. Reprinted with permission.

had begun graduate work that fall at five different universities. Five of them have their doctorates, and the sixth is still in progress. As the following information indicates, that is a remarkable record:

Colin Farrell Camerer, a graduate of Johns Hopkins the month he became 17 years old, received his M.B.A. degree from the University of Chicago's School of Business at age 19 and his Ph.D. degree there in December, 1981, the month he became 22. After being an assistant professor of decision science in the School of Business of Northwestern University, 1981–83, he moved to the Wharton School of the University of Pennsylvania (see Holmes, Rin, Tremblay, & Zeldin, 1984).

Eric Robert Jablow, a summa cum laude graduate of Brooklyn College at age 15, received his Ph.D. degree in mathematics from Princeton University in December, 1982, at age 20. In the fall of 1983 he became an assistant professor of mathematics at the State University of New York at Stony Brook.

Michael Thomas Kotschenreuther, a Phi Beta Kappa graduate of Johns Hopkins at age 18, received his Ph.D. degree in theoretical plasma physics from Princeton University in December, 1982, the month after he became 24. In 1982 he became a researcher at the University of Texas (Austin).

Paul Frederick Dietz, a Phi Beta Kappa graduate of Johns Hopkins at age 17, completed work for his Ph.D. degree in computer science at Cornell University in May, 1984, at age 24. In 1981 he became an assistant professor at the University of Southern California. Currently, he is a computer scientist with the Schlumberger-Doll Company in Connecticut.

Eugene William Stark, an honors graduate of Johns Hopkins at age 17, completed his Ph.D. degree in computer science at the Massachusetts Institute of Technology in June, 1984. That fall he became an assistant professor of computer science at State University of New York at Stony Brook.

Mark Tollef Jacobson, a Phi Beta Kappa graduate of George Washington University at age 18, is a doctoral student in statistics at Stanford University.

Clearly, in this group, there is no hint of "early ripe, early rot"! Five have maintained their precocity, receiving the Ph.D. degree in difficult subjects from top-flight universities 5 to 8 years earlier than is usual and obtaining positions at excellent universities. The sixth is still young. It will be interesting to follow their professional progress.

REFERENCES

Holmes, J. S., Rin, L., Tremblay, J. M., & Zeldin, R. K. (1984, May/June). Colin Camerer: Radical educational accelerant, now well along professionally. G/C/T, 33–35.

Nevin, D. (1977, October 7). Young prodigies take off under special program. *Smithsonian, 8,* 76–82, 160.

Smorgasbord for an IQ of 150. (1977, June 6). *Time, 109* (23), 64.

Five Years of Early Entrants: Predicting Successful Achievement in College

Linda E. Brody

Johns Hopkins University

Susan G. Assouline

University of Iowa

Julian C. Stanley

Johns Hopkins University

This study evaluated the achievements of 65 young entrants as beginning undergraduates in a highly selective university. The group as a whole was found to be quite successful. Compared to nonaccelerants, the early entrants tended to graduate in a shorter period of time and earn more honors

Editor's Note: From Brody, L.E., Assouline, S. G., & Stanley, J. C. (1990). Five years of early entrants: Predicting successful achievement in college. *Gifted Child Quarterly*, 34(4), 138-142. © 1990 National Association for Gifted Children. Reprinted with permission.

at graduation. For the early entrants, starting college with a large number of Advanced Placement Program credits was found to be the best predictor of outstanding academic achievement. It seems advisable for young college entrants to have Scholastic Aptitude Test scores and content knowledge equal to or greater than that of the typical freshman at the college the student will attend.

Perceptions and stereotypes of the success or nonsuccess of early entrants to college (i.e., those who enter college several years younger than the typical college freshman) are often based on anecdotal evidence or case studies of one or a few individuals. Even more empirical attempts to study accelerated students often involve small samples since few entering freshmen at a given university are early entrants. Yet research is needed so that college admissions officers can better predict young applicants' likelihood of success in college and so that students contemplating entering college early can make every effort to prepare academically and personally for the college experience.

Many mathematically and verbally talented students who seek fast-paced, challenging courses run out of advanced coursework in high school and therefore enter college early (Brody & Stanley, in press). A study of students who were early entrants at colleges and universities throughout the United States found that the majority of students were extremely successful academically and socially during their freshman year in college (Brody, Lupkowski, & Stanley, 1988). It was concluded that achievement and adjustment are likely to be enhanced if (a) verbal reasoning and writing abilities are well developed before entering college, (b) students participate in Advanced Placement (AP) or college-level courses before leaving high school, (c) they are highly motivated to enter college early. The sample size in this study was quite small, however, including only 24 students who attended 17 different colleges.

Since colleges differ greatly in their selectivity, difficulty of coursework, and many other variables, it is useful to investigate the success rate of early entrants within one institution. Stanley studied students at least two years younger than typical college freshmen who entered a highly selective university in 1980 and 1981 (Stanley, 1985; Stanley & McGill, 1986), as well as the 32 students who received a BA at that institution before age 19 between 1976 and 1982 (Stanley & Benbow, 1983). These studies provide considerable support for the hypothesis that bright and motivated early entrants, to college can be quite successful in college and later in life, but the generalizability of the results is somewhat limited by the small samples. The present study expands on the studies by Stanley (1985) and Stanley and McGill (1986) to include a considerably larger sample of early entrants to college over a five-year period.

METHOD

Subjects: Sixty-five students, 38 males and 27 females, who entered a highly selective private university from 1980 through 1984 were designated as early entrants for the purpose of this study. Sixty students in this five-class group qualified by entering at least two years younger than is typical; that is, their 17th birthday occurred after December 31 of the fall in which they became full-time students. Five additional students were included whose 17th birthdays were a few months prior to December 31, but they entered with at least 24 semester-hour college credits, enough to be given sophomore status. The mean age of the 65 students when they entered was 16 years 2 months, with the youngest student entering at 13 years 8 months and the oldest student entering at 17 years 7 months. The average age of entering freshmen at this institution is 18 years 0 months (personal communication from the registrar of the institution). Records revealed that some students had completed all four years of high school and had accelerated earlier in their school careers, and others had skipped from one to three years of high school. These 65 students were the total number of undergraduates who entered in 1980–1984 and met the designated criteria; they represent about 2% of the undergraduate population admitted during those years.

Putting the Research to Use

Highly gifted students are often anxious to accelerate their education to obtain more challenging educational opportunities. Yet school counselors, parents, and college admissions officers may be fearful that students may not be academically or socially ready to enter college at a younger age than is typical. Although this study did not investigate social factors, some guidelines related to identifying academic readiness for college did emerge. In particular, students planning to enter college at a young age should be encouraged to take a wide variety of Advanced Placement or other advanced high school courses before leaving high school and to work hard to learn their subject matter well. It is also advisable that both of the young entrants' SAT scores be at least average for the particular college they plan to attend. If their scores are not at this level, perhaps they should choose a less selective university or reconsider entering college at such a young age.

Procedure: This study was conducted retrospectively, after the students had graduated from the university. Preadmission and college achievement data were obtained from university records. For some comparisons, data were obtained on nonaccelerated students. The comparisons did not always involve the same subjects, depending on what data were available, but the comparison students were typically some or all of the nonaccelerated students who were freshmen between 1980 and 1984, the same years that the early entrants entered the university. Chi-square analyses were used to compare the accelerated students with nonaccelerated ones on selected preadmission and college achievement variables. Within the early entrant group, stepwise multiple regressions were used to assess the predictability of high achievement in college from preadmission variables.

COMPARISONS WITH NONACCELERATED STUDENTS

Preadmission Characteristics: The accelerated students were a highly able group. Table 1 shows the mean Scholastic Aptitude Test (SAT) scores of the early entrants in comparison to those of nonaccelerated students who were freshmen at the same institution in 1980–1984. Despite their younger age, the accelerated group averaged 43 points higher on SAT-M ($p = .001$) and 49 points higher on SAT-V ($p = .001$). In addition, a significantly larger proportion of the accelerants than of the nonaccelerants entered with credit earned through the Advanced Placement Program ($p = .05$), in spite of the fact that many of them did not attend four years of high school. (This university does not require its entrants to be high school graduates. Credit is awarded for scores of 4s or 5s on AP examinations except that a 3 on Calculus BC results in credit for one course of Calculus.) Thus, it appears that in terms of aptitude and advanced high school coursework, measures typically used to predict success in college, the early entrants were well equipped to be successful college students. A chi-square test comparing the proportion of students in each group who had attended a public versus a private high school was not statistically significant.

College Achievement: Of the 65 early entrants, 57 remained and graduated, all but three of these in four years or less. Thus, from the entering group, 83% graduated from this university in four years or less. This percentage is similar to the 78% of the nonaccelerated students in the class who entered in the fall of 1983 and graduated in four years or less (see Table 1). Graduating in 3½ years or less was a more common occurrence among the early entrants, 32% of whom finished that quickly compared to 12% of the nonaccelerated students in the entering class of 1983 (see Table 1, $p = .001$). Students who completed college in fewer than four years did so through a variety of mechanisms, including entering with AP or college credit, taking courses during summers or intersessions, and/or registering for a heavier than normal courseload during the regular school year.

The early entrants were also compared to the nonaccelerated students who graduated between 1983 and 1988 on selected honors and awards (see Table 1); the early entrants performed extremely well. Eleven percent of them earned concurrent bachelor's and master's degrees, compared to only 1% of the nonaccelerated students (p = .001). To be eligible to earn concurrent bachelor's and master's degrees, students must be doing exceptional work in their major and then be invited or apply to do additional work; this work may include additional, more advanced coursework and/or a thesis. Specific requirements vary according to the field of study.

There were also significant differences in honors at graduation: 42% of the accelerants compared to 25% of the nonaccelerants (p = .01) were awarded general honors based on their cumulative grade-point averages (=3.50 on a 4-point scale), and 35% of the accelerants versus 16% of the nonaccelerants (p = .001) received departmental honors. Approximately twice the percentage of accelerants as compared to nonaccelerants (26% versus 12%) were elected to either Phi Beta Kappa or the national engineering honor society Tau Beta Pi (p = .01).

PREDICTING ACADEMIC SUCCESS FROM PREADMISSION VARIABLES

In spite of the fact that all of the students in the early entrant group could be considered quite able by virtue of having been admitted at a young age to a highly selective university, and that the group as a whole was quite successful, there was considerable range evidenced in both preadmission characteristics and the degree of success in college. Table 2 shows minimum, maximum, and average scores for selected preadmission and achievement variables for the 57 accelerated students who graduated from the college they originally entered. For example, SAT-M scores averaged 721.23, but the range was from 530 to 800. The range was even greater on SAT-V, 360 to 770. Students in the early entrant group entered college with as few as zero AP credits or as many as 30; the total credits from AP plus part-time college courses with which they entered ranged from 0 to 49.

There was also considerable range in the performance of the students. Grade-point averages (GPA) during the first semester of the freshman year ranged from 1.24 to 4.00: at graduation, the GPA range was still considerable, 2.29 to 3.97. This variability in grades also affected other measures of achievement, such as qualifying for the Dean's List, being elected to a national honor society, or receiving general and departmental honors at graduation.

Stepwise multiple regression analyses were used to predict the degree of academic success from preadmission factors. The dependent variables studied were grade-point average during the first semester, cumulative grade-point average at graduation, percentage of semesters on the Dean's List, and honors at graduation (for which a possible three-point scale was used, based on whether the student graduated with general honors, departmental honors, or was inducted into either Phi Beta Kappa or Tau Beta Pi). The predictor variables used were sex, SAT-M scores, SAT-V scores, number of Advanced Placement (AP) credits, age at entry to college, and the number of credits at entry from both AP and part-time college courses.

For all four achievement measures, the only significant predictor was AP courses ($p = .01$ for freshman GPA, GPA, and Dean's List, $p = .05$ for honors). The percentage of variance accounted for by the Advanced Placement variable was 16% for predicting freshman GPA, 12% for cumulative GPA at graduation, 14% for Dean's List, and 6% for honors at graduation. In other words, for this fairly large group of students whose age at entry as well as amount of high school completed varied considerably and whose SAT scores, while impressive, nonetheless exhibited considerable range, the common denominator in predicting high achievement in college was having successfully completed a significant number of Advanced Placement courses. A contributing factor may be that schools that offer AP courses are likely to provide high quality coursework throughout their curriculum; however, the data necessary to evaluate the overall quality of the high schools these students attended were not available for this study.

EARLY ENTRANTS WHO DID NOT GRADUATE FROM THE SCHOOL THEY ENTERED

Eight (12%) of the 65 accelerated students withdrew before graduating, a smaller percentage than withdrew from the entire class that entered in 1983. Of the eight students, four transferred to other universities and have since graduated, one of them *magna cum laude*. A fifth transferred into the college's evening division and graduated with honors. Another student was enrolled part-time in college, but to the best of our knowledge never received his degree. The whereabouts of the other two students are unknown. Gender did not seem to be a factor, since four of the accelerants who withdrew were male and four were female. Since we do not have any way of tracing the nonaccelerated students who withdrew, it is difficult to draw comparisons. However, it is evident that almost all of the early entrants did complete at least a bachelor's degree.

DISCUSSION

In spite of increasing empirical evidence that acceleration in elementary and/or high school is quite beneficial for many highly gifted students (e.g., Brody & Benbow, 1987; Daurio, 1979; Janos, Robinson, & Lunneborg, 1989; Southern & Jones, in press), much concern about the practice exists because people often know (sometimes via hearsay) of a specific case in which an accelerated student encountered academic or social problems. It is thus important to identify the particular factors that contribute to successful acceleration.

This study of students who entered college two or more years early found them as a group to be highly successful. Compared to nonaccelerants, they tended to graduate in a shorter period of time and earned more honors at graduation. Although we do not have systematic data on the whole group about their activities after college, we know that one accelerated student won a Rhodes Scholarship, and several others have received fellowships or assistantships to attend graduate school in the United States. Forty-nine of the 57 students who graduated from the original university earned GPAs of at least 3.0 during their undergraduate career, and the mean GPA was 3.4. Of the few who left, most transferred to other universities and graduated. Only one student in the group is known not to have completed college.

The early entrants appeared to have an advantage over other students in terms of higher SAT scores and better preparation in high school (as evidenced by successful completion of AP coursework) prior to college entry. While it may seem obvious that students with high SATs, AP courses, and motivation (presumably, early entrants are motivated to move ahead) are likely to succeed in college, there is still concern about and resistance to students' entering college early, and some accelerated students are not succeeding academically in college.

Thus, the main focus of this study, after verifying that the group as a whole was relatively successful compared to students in general, was to identify the specific factors that make a difference; that is, what preadmission factors might predict *exceptional* academic success. We consider it undesirable to accelerate students only to have them become relatively average college students, and there was a range of achievement in the group. One hopes that highly gifted students will achieve well in college; acceleration should encourage, not diminish, this prospect.

Of a variety of preadmission variables studied, the number of Advanced Placement credits students earned in high school was found to predict high achievement in college. The Advanced Placement Program, sponsored by the College Board, offers curricula in a wide variety of subject areas and 29 examinations for advanced high school students. The course content is designed to be equivalent to that offered college freshmen at selective colleges and universities; successful scores on the AP tests can result in the awarding of college credit for the courses taken in high school.

While we strongly support the benefits of the Advanced Placement Program for talented students, this finding does not necessarily suggest that students who do not enroll in Advanced Placement courses cannot be successful in college. We did not evaluate the program for regular nonaccelerated students, and even within the accelerated group there were examples of students without AP credits who did well. However, students who enter college early often skip a considerable amount of high school coursework. The results of this study suggest that the background provided by that coursework may be important. Students need not get it at the regular pace at the typical age, but those who plan to enter college young should be advised that it is desirable to get advanced high school coursework in a variety of subject areas as preparation for college and proof that the student can handle rigorous college courses. Mastery of 12th grade content in stimulating courses with excellent teachers, even though not in an AP-designated class, may provide the background

Table 1   Comparison of Early Entrants with Nonaccelerated Undergraduates

Preadmission Characteristics:	Early Entrants (N = 65)	1980–1984 Nonaccelerated Freshmen (N = 3055)	Significance Test Statistic
Average SAT-M	718	675	4.67***[1]
Average SAT-V	672	623	4.86***[1]
% Public High School	75	66	2.59[2]
% Earning AP Credit	66	53	4.76*[2]

Graduation Statistics:

	Early Entrants (N = 65)	1983 Nonaccelerated Freshmen (N)	Chi-Square Value
% Graduated 4 years or less	83	78	98
% Graduated 3½ years or less	32	12	16.29***

	Early Entrants Who Graduated (N = 57)	Nonaccelerants Graduating 1983–1988 (N = 3670)	Chi-Square Value
% Earning Concurrent BA/MA	11	1	37.86***
% Graduated with General Honors	42	25	8.75***
% Graduated with Departmental Honors	35	16	14.45***
% Graduated with Phi Beta Kappa or Tau Beta Pi	26	12	10.04**

[1]To determine the significance of the difference between the two groups on SAT-M and SAT-V scores, t tests were conducted. Since standards deviations for the 1980–1984 group were not available, we used the SD for the 1989 entering class, which was 74 for SAT-V and 70 for SAT-M, the best estimate available. For the accelerants, the SD was 80 for SAT-V and 72 for Sat-M.
[2]These values were computed from Chi-square tests of significance.
* $p \le .05$
** $p \le .01$
*** $p \le .001$

needed. The AP program serves to document what the students have learned, and a large number of AP credits suggests a strong background in a wide variety of subject areas.

The word "variety" is important here. Part-time college courses did not prove to be as relevant, possibly because students often take them in only one subject

Table 2   Means, Standard Deviations, and Ranges of Variables Used in the Multiple Regression Analysis (Early Entrants Graduating from the University, N = 57)

	Mean	Standard Deviation	Minimum	Maximum
Predictor Variables:[1]				
SAT-M	721.23	59.55	530	800
SAT-V	668.77	80.40	360	770
Number of AP Credits	9.04	9.27	0	30
Age of Entry (years)	16.14	0.57	13.67	17.25
Credits Earned Upon Entry	15.58	12.06	0	49
Dependent Variables:				
Freshman GPA	3.21	0.72	1.24	4.00
GPA at Graduation	3.37	0.39	2.29	3.97
% Semesters on Dean's List	40.83	32.18	0	100
Honors at Graduation[2]	1.04	1.22	0	3

[1]Gender was one of the predictor variables. There were 38 male and 27 female early entrants. In the multiple-regression analysis, the mean value for gender was .60 and the standard deviation was .49.
[2]Includes Departmental Honors, General Honors, and/or Phi Beta Kappa or Tau Beta Pi, each contributing one point for a maximum score of 3 on this variable.

area, for example, mathematics, and perhaps at less selective colleges, for example, evening courses or courses in a community college. A large number of Advanced Placement courses seems to be indicative of a breadth of knowledge at an advanced level and probably of having attended a high-quality high school.

While SAT scores were not significant in the multiple regression, perhaps because so many students had such high scores, the accelerated students as a group had SAT scores significantly higher than typical freshmen at the university studied. We believe that it is important that students who plan to enter college early have SAT scores, both Verbal and Mathematical, at least at the mean for the freshman class of the college they plan to enter. Thus, they would need to have higher scores if they attend a more selective college than if they attend a less selective college.

Our conclusion, then, is that young accelerated students can be successful, even outstanding, college students. In selecting students as candidates for early admission, however, it is advisable that students have the ability (as measured by SAT scores) and content background (as measured by successful completion of the equivalent of advanced high school coursework) equal to or greater than that of typical freshmen at the college the student will attend.

REFERENCES

Brody, L. E., & Benbow, C. P. (1987). Accelerative strategies: How effective are they for the gifted? *Gifted Child Quarterly, 3*, 105–110.

Brody, L. E., Lupkowski, A. E., & Stanley, J. C. (1988). Early entrance to college: A study of academic and social adjustment during freshman year. *College and University, 63,* 347–359.

Brody, L. E., & Stanley, J. C. (in press). Young college students: Assessing factors that contribute to success. In W. T. Southern and E. D. Jones (Eds.), *Academic acceleration of gifted children.* New York: Teachers College Press.

Daurio, S. P. (1979). Educational enrichment versus acceleration: A review of the literature. In W. C. George, S. J. Cohn, & J. C. Stanley (Eds.), *Educating the gifted: Acceleration and enrichment* (pp. 13–63). Baltimore: Johns Hopkins University Press.

Janos, P. M., Robinson, N. M., & Lunneborg, C. E. (1989). Markedly early entrance to college. *Journal of Higher Education, 60,* 495–518.

Stanley, J. C. (1985). Young entrants to college: How did they fare? *College and University, 60,* 219–228.

Stanley, J. C., & Benbow, C. P. (1983). Extremely young college graduates: Evidence of their success. *College and University, 58,* 361–372.

Stanley, J. C., & McGill, A. M. (1986). More about "Young entrants to college: How did they fare?" *Gifted Child Quarterly, 30,* 70–73.

Southern, W. T., & Jones, E. D. (Eds.). (in press). *Academic acceleration of gifted children.* New York: Teachers College Press.

3

The Use of Radical Acceleration in Cases of Extreme Intellectual Precocity

Miraca U. M. Gross

University of New South Wales

This paper reviews the school histories of five extremely gifted children, of IQ 160–200, who have been radically accelerated. Prior to their acceleration, the children were retained in the regular classroom in a lockstep curriculum based on their chronological age and grade placement. They suffered severe intellectual frustration, boredom, lack of motivation, and social rejection by age-peers, and displayed significantly lowered levels of social self-esteem. A combination of grade-skipping and radical subject matter acceleration has given the children access to curricula commensurate with their academic-achievement

Editor's Note: From Gross, M. U. M. (1992). The use of radical acceleration in cases of extreme intellectual precocity. *Gifted Child Quarterly*, 36(2), 91-99. © 1992 National Association for Gifted Children. Reprinted with permission.

levels and the intellectual and social companionship of children who share their abilities and interests. The young accelerands are more stimulated intellectually, enjoy closer and more productive social relationships, and display healthier levels of social self-esteem than do equally gifted children who have been retained with age-peers of average ability.

> *"Someone has said that genius is of necessity solitary, since the population is so sparse at the higher levels of mental ability. However, adult genius is mobile and can seek out its own kind. It is in the case of the child with extraordinarily high IQ that the social problem is most acute. If the IQ is 180, the intellectual level at 6 is almost on a par with the average 11-year-old, and at 10 or 11 is not far from that of the average high school graduate. . . The inevitable result is that the child of IQ 180 has one of the most difficult problems of social adjustment that any human being is ever called upon to meet."*
>
> —Burks, Jensen, and Terman (1930, p. 264)

It is ironic that although the research of Terman and his colleagues is rightly credited with refuting the myth that intellectual giftedness is linked to nervous instability and emotional maladjustment (Tannenbaum, 1983; Grinder, 1985), the education community has largely ignored their associated warning that extraordinarily gifted young people are nonetheless at serious risk of social isolation and rejection by age-peers.

In a comprehensive review of the research on the psychosocial development of the intellectually gifted. Janos and Robinson (1985) showed that the research findings most often referenced regarding favorable social adjustment emanate from studies of moderately gifted children. The few studies which have investigated the social and emotional development of the extremely gifted suggest that exceptionally gifted (IQ 160–179) and profoundly gifted (IQ 180+) children tend to have greater problems of social acceptance (Hollingworth, 1942; Gallagher, 1958; DeHaan & Havighurst, 1961; Barbe, 1964; Janos, 1983).

Hollingworth (1926) defined the IQ range 125–155 as "socially optimal intelligence." She found that children scoring within this range were well-balanced, confident and socially effective individuals. She claimed, however, that above the level of IQ 160 the difference between exceptionally gifted children and their age-mates is so great that it leads to special problems of development which are correlated with social isolation.

Research both in the United States and in Australia has noted the decrease in motivation among extremely gifted children confined to the regular classroom

(Janos, 1983; Silverman, 1989; Gross, 1989a). After many years of studying the extremely gifted, Hollingworth became convinced that enrichment alone was not a sufficient response to their academic and social needs. She became a persuasive advocate of full-time, self-contained classes for exceptionally gifted children (Hollingworth, 1926, 1936, 1942; Hollingworth & Cobb et al., 1923; Hollingworth & Cobb, 1928). Terman and Oden (1947) argued forcefully that for extremely gifted children the more conservative accelerative procedures, such as a single grade-skip, are not sufficient; they advised radical acceleration through several grade-skips spaced appropriately throughout the student's school career.

Putting the Research to Use

Exceptionally gifted children appear in the population at a ratio of fewer than 1 in 10,000. Research has repeatedly found that these children differ quite significantly from moderately gifted age-peers on many cognitive and affective variables. Because of this, it is not enough to place them in part-time programs, such as resource room or pull-out, which are designed for moderately gifted students; they require full-time grouping with children closer to their own mental age and levels of socio-affective development. Research suggests that exceptionally and profoundly gifted students are best served by a program of radical acceleration incorporating a number of grade-skips appropriately spaced through the student's school career, supplemented with subject acceleration where it is required. It is important that the student is also provided with lateral enrichment at each stage. Radical acceleration provides the extremely gifted child with the intellectual and social companionship of children at similar stages of cognitive and affective development. Exceptionally gifted children retained with age-peers, or accelerated by only one year, are at serious risk of peer rejection and social isolation.

These recommendations were strongly supported by the subsequent research of Sheldon (1959), Janos (1983), and Silverman (1989) which suggested that the social isolation experienced by exceptionally gifted children is not the clinical isolation of emotional disturbance, but rather a condition imposed on the child by the absence of a peer group with whom to relate. When extremely gifted children who have been socially rejected by age-peers are removed from the inappropriate grade placement and placed with intellectual peers, then social difficulties disappear (Hollingworth, 1942; Silverman, 1989).

THE PRESENT STUDY

Since the early 1980s I have conducted a longitudinal study of the intellectual, academic, social, and emotional development of 40 children who have scored IQ 160 or above on the Stanford-Binet Intelligence Scale (L-M). The children live in six of the eight states of Australia and are presently aged between 6 and 16. This study has followed the children's development over several years and will continue until the youngest child graduates from high school. Aspects of the children's academic and psychosocial development have already been reported (Gross, 1989b, 1990; Gross & Feldhusen, 1990; Gross & Start, 1991; Gross, in press), and the early years of the study were reported in depth in my doctoral dissertation (Gross, 1989a).

The study employs a wide range of qualitative and quantitative observation techniques, triangulated to increase the validity and reliability of the study (Kidder & Fine, 1987). The children take standardized tests of achievement in several academic subject areas, and their tested levels of achievement are compared with the levels of work they are permitted to undertake in class. This enables the researcher to judge the degree of "fit" between the children's demonstrated achievement and the programs provided for them by their schools. In addition, since Australian schools generally communicate with the parents of students through written reports on the child's academic progress, the children's school reports from different grade levels are examined to analyse their teachers' perceptions of their levels of ability and achievement.

Many educators and psychologists studying the gifted and talented have emphasized the significance of a positive self-concept in the realization of intellectual potential (Hollingworth, 1926; Carroll, 1940; DeHaan & Havighurst, 1961; Feldhusen & Hoover, 1986). Self-esteem, an affective aspect of self-concept, is largely derived from the positive or negative feedback individuals receive from significant others about the value or effectiveness of their actions (Foster, 1983). Particularly in a society such as Australia, where the highly egalitarian social ethos is based, in large part, on "cutting down the tall poppies" (Ward, 1958; Goldberg, 1981; Start, 1986), there is the danger that extremely gifted students will receive deliberately misleading feedback about their abilities and potential not only from classmates but also from teachers. The Coopersmith Self-Esteem Inventory (SEI) is used in this study to measure the children's general self-esteem and their self-esteem in social relationships, relationships with family, and in their academic work.

Surveys of the reading interests of extremely gifted children reveal that they often read, with full comprehension and enjoyment, literature written for young people 5–7 years older (Burks, Jensen, & Terman, 1930; Hollingworth, 1942; Gross, 1989a). At 2-year intervals, surveys are made of the hours each child spends daily in voluntary reading over a 21-day period; the title, author, and subject classification of all materials read; the books which the children class as current favorites; and their reasons for preferring these particular books. Regular surveys are also made, over several weeks, of the nature and extent of television viewing, computer usage, hobbies and play interests, and interest in or participation in sports.

Developmental and demographic data have been acquired from many sources including questionnaires, medical records, parent diaries, and family documents. Semistructured interviews are held, at regular intervals, with the parents of each child and with the children themselves. These interviews follow up, clarify, and expand on the material gathered through the questionnaires, the achievement and personality testing, the school reports, and all other sources of information. The interviews also elicit the parents' opinions on more sensitive issues, such as the children's educational program, their relationships with teachers and classmates, and their social and emotional development. Similarly, the student interviews elicit the children's own views on their progress at school, their feelings about their school experiences, their social relationships, and their perceptions of themselves and their own abilities.

Of the 40 children in this study, a minority have been recognized by their schools as being young people of truly remarkable intellectual potential. In the considerable majority of cases, however, the children's teachers have remained unaware of their extraordinary intellectual potential or, where psychometric evidence of this has been made available, the school has refused, on ideological grounds, to develop any form of differentiated curriculum for the gifted child (Gross, 1989a). The majority of the extremely gifted children in this study have spent, or are spending, their elementary school years working through a lock-step curriculum in a heterogeneous classroom without access to other gifted, even moderately gifted, students.

However, 9 of the 40 children in this study have been radically accelerated and are undertaking part or all of their schooling with students 3 years older. This paper reports on the school histories of 5 of these children and discusses the factors that have contributed to the success of the individualized programs. The names by which the children and their families are identified in this paper are pseudonyms chosen by the children themselves.

It should be noted that the Australian school system is based on the British system. Accordingly, Australian children enter preschool or kindergarten at age 4, and formal schooling at age 5, one year earlier than their American counterparts.

Ian Baker

Ian Baker taught himself to read, write, and count before the age of 2. At age 4, he was assisting his kindergarten teacher by reading stories to the other children. By the time he entered school at age 5, he was reading, with great enjoyment, E.B. White's *Charlotte's Web*. He took an equal delight in mathematical problem solving, having taught himself to add, subtract, multiply, and divide.

The teacher's response to Ian's remarkable abilities was to place him, along with the other 5-year-olds, in a reading readiness program and a math program which involved recognising the numbers 1 through 10.

Six months into his first year at school Ian's parents were called for an emergency conference with the school vice-principal, who informed them that the school wished to have an psychometrically tested as a preliminary to referring him to a special school for behaviorally disturbed children. According to the vice-principal, Ian had become uncontrollable in class and was displaying frightening bouts of physical violence toward other children.

The school psychologist assessed Ian on the Stanford-Binet Intelligence Scale (L-M) as having an IQ of 170+. On a standardized test of reading achievement, the Neale Analysis of Reading, he was found to have reading accuracy and comprehension ages of 12. He was just over 5 years old.

The psychologist was appalled at the school's mismanagement of Ian's education and informed the principal that the child's behavioral difficulties arose not from emotional disturbance but from severe intellectual and social frustration. He advised the school that Ian desperately required an educational program adapted to his needs and regular access to other intellectually gifted students.

For a short time, the school made curricular adaptations for Ian. He was permitted to do Grade 7 math (but without leaving his Grade 1 classroom) and a small pull-out program was established. His intellectual frustration abated somewhat and his behavior improved. However, the appointment of a new building principal, whose extremely egalitarian ideological views precluded any special provision for the gifted, ended the pull-out program and put Ian back into a lock-step curriculum based on his chronological age and grade placement rather than his mental age and levels of achievement. This led to astonishing mismatches between Ian's levels of tested achievement and the curriculum prescribed for him. At the age of 9, while in Grade 4, Ian took the Scholastic Aptitude Test–Mathematics (SAT-M) as part of the data collection procedures for this study. He made a scaled score of 560, .6 of a standard deviation above the mean, on this test standardized on 17- and 18-year-old American students planning to enter college. Meanwhile, in his Grade 4 classroom, Ian was required to work lock-step with his 9-year-old classmates on Grade 4 math. The antisocial behaviors returned, together with psychosomatic disturbances such as migraines, bouts of nausea, and abdominal cramps. The mornings became a battle to get Ian "well enough" and subdued enough to go to school.

At the age of 9 years 3 months, Ian was again assessed on the Stanford-Binet (L-M). On this occasion, he achieved a mental age of 18 years 6 months. Psychologists with a special interest in the profoundly gifted advocate that, in cases such as this, when the child scores significantly beyond the ceiling of even the Stanford-Binet, a ratio IQ should be computed (Silverman & Kearney, 1989). A ratio computation places Ian's IQ at approximately 200.

At the end of Ian's Grade 4 year, his parents withdrew him from this state (government) elementary school and enrolled him in an independent (private) school whose principal has a special interest in the gifted and talented. Here, Ian has been permitted to flourish. He has an individualized program that incorporates radical subject matter acceleration, grade-skipping, "relevant academic enrichment" (Stanley, 1979), and mentorship. In 1991, aged 11, he was based in Grade 8 with 13-year-olds, but took math and computer science with 11th grade, and science, history, and geography with 10th graders. He is popular with his teachers and warmly accepted by the other students, and he is beginning to accept that although he is different, this need not prove a barrier to warm and supportive social relationships, as it did when he was isolated from intellectual peers in the regular classroom. He enjoys his accelerated and enriched curriculum and is thinking of taking some university math courses in 2 or 3 years.

Christopher Otway

Christopher, currently aged 14, is, like Ian, a profoundly gifted young man. Tested on the Stanford-Binet (L-M) at the age of 10 years 11 months, he achieved a mental age of 22 years, and thus a ratio IQ of approximately 200. At the age of 11 years 4 months, he achieved the remarkable score of 710 on the SAT-M.

From his earliest years Chris displayed prodigious talent in math and language. He taught himself to read at 2 years of age, and by age 4 he was reading children's encyclopedias and had acquired a level of general knowledge that would be unmatched by the majority of Grade 5 or 6 students. His math ability developed almost as precociously. Shortly after his 3rd birthday he spontaneously began to devise simple addition and subtraction sums, and by the time he entered kindergarten at the usual age of 4, he was capable of working at Grade 4 level in math. A psychometric assessment established that shortly after his 4th birthday, Chris had a mental age of at least 7.

In contrast to the debacle which greeted Ian Baker's arrival in school, the principal and teachers of Chris's primary school recognized his remarkable abilities within a few days of his enrollment and were willing to ensure that he received an appropriate education. Chris's parents had studied the literature on giftedness and were aware of the educational and psychosocial benefits of acceleration. Accordingly, they suggested to the building principal that Chris might be a suitable candidate for subject matter acceleration or grade-skipping, and the principal, after some thought, agreed to the experiment. By a fortunate chance he had visited Stanley and Benbow of the Study of Mathematically Precocious Youth at Johns Hopkins University while on study leave and was aware of the advantages of acceleration.

At first, Chris was withdrawn from his Grade 1 class for a few hours each day to join Grade 2 for English and Grade 5 for math. It soon became evident, however, that even this intervention did not address the full extent of Chris's advancement, and the following year, as a Grade 2 student, he attended the Grade 7 class each day for math. At the end of this year Chris was permitted to skip directly into Grade 4, and his subject matter acceleration continued, with Chris attending 8th grade for math and starting flute lessons with his 8th grade classmates in recognition of his obvious aptitude for music. Several of the highly gifted young mathematicians in this Australian study also display high levels of musical precocity (Gross, 1990).

Christopher's program of grade-skipping and subject acceleration has been extremely successful. At the age of 12 he was based in Grade 9 with students 2 and 3 years older but took physics, chemistry, English, math, and economics with the 11th grade classes. He entered Grade 10 in 1990, a few weeks after his 13th birthday, but rather than accelerate to Grade 12 for individual subjects, he himself chose to "repeat" Grade 11 in different curriculum areas, this time taking humanities and foreign language subjects. He plans to "repeat" Grade 12 in the same way. By the time he completes the final grade of high school at age 15 (rather than the usual age of 18), he will have undertaken a remarkable range of subjects from which he can choose those he will study at university.

It is of concern, however, that despite being permitted both acceleration and enrichment in English, Chris still had an unrealistically low perception of his abilities in this subject. Tested on the SAT-V at the age of 11 years 4 months, he was astonished by his score of 580 and requested that the test be rescored. "I couldn't have done as well as that," he told me in genuine concern. "The teachers reckon I'm just average in English." It is disturbing to note that many of the children in this study have received extremely inaccurate and negative feedback from their class teachers about their abilities and achievement levels.

Roshni Singh

Roshni Singh, aged 7, has a Stanford-Binet IQ of 162. Sarah, Roshni's mother, is Australian. Juspreet, her father, is of the Sikh religion and was born in Singapore. Roshni is a delicately beautiful child with dark, expressive eyes which are alive with intelligence. She is intensely aware of her identity as a "Punjabi person" and her adherence to the Sikh faith. Roshni was reading at age 3, and by 4 was writing letters to her relatives in Singapore on the family's personal computer. At 5 years 5 months old, she scored at the 84th percentile for 8-year-olds on the Leicester Number Test, a standardized test of math achievement commonly used in Britain and Australia.

Roshni's exceptional abilities were recognized in early childhood and she was permitted early entrance to kindergarten at the age of 3, and to primary school at the age of 4, on the grounds of her accelerated reading capacities. Yet neither the kindergarten nor the school was at first prepared to modify the curriculum in response to the very talents which had prompted them to offer her early entrance. Despite being able to read as well as the average second grader, Roshni was presented by the kindergarten with large cut-out letters as an introduction to the alphabet. Picture books were freely available, but no books with printed text. Not surprisingly, Roshni stopped reading. She was receiving from the kindergarten the unequivocal message that 3- and 4-year-olds were not supposed to read and that to do so was somehow "wrong." So, to conform to her teacher's wishes and her classmates' expectations, she did her best to pretend to be a "normal" 3-year-old. With tact, loving encouragement, and a great deal of patience, Sarah and Juspreet were able to reassure Roshni that she should not be ashamed of her reading capacity, and after a few weeks she began to read again. The following year, however, when Roshni entered formal schooling, the pattern was repeated. She entered an environment in which all knowledge and learning was assumed to flow to the children through the teacher. The teacher believed that reading should be taught at age 5, not age 4, and was disturbed by Roshni's self-acceleration. Obediently, Roshni stopped reading again.

This time, the setback was more serious, and Roshni's deliberate under-achievement became more difficult to reverse. She had no one in her class of 5-year-olds who shared her ability or interests, and she became very bored, lonely, and depressed. After some months of unsuccessful negotiation with Roshni's teacher, Sarah and Juspreet expressed their concern to the principal and asked whether, since the school seemed unwilling to extend her academically within the regular classroom, they might be willing to consider some form of acceleration. Fortunately, both the psychologist attached to the school and one of the primary school teachers knew something of gifted education, and the school somewhat reluctantly agreed. Roshni was permitted to move from the reception class into Grade 1 eight weeks before the end of the school year, and since this intervention was highly successful, she moved to Grade 2 with her new classmates at the start of the following year. She entered Grade 2 at the age of 5 years 4 months, fully 2 years younger than is customary.

At the time of writing Roshni has just passed her 7th birthday and is in Grade 4 with children 2 and 3 years her senior. The class is grouped by ability, and Roshni is in the top group in every subject. Nonetheless, Roshni admits that the math which she is doing is still considerably below her ability. However, she thoroughly enjoys school. She is liked by her teachers and extremely popular with her classmates. As noted earlier, most Australian schools send home regular written reports on the children's progress. On Roshni's most recent report, the principal wrote: "Roshni has applied herself diligently to all tasks and maintained her high position. She is very settled in her peer relationships despite the age difference, and this allows her to use the opportunities presented to develop and extend her own knowledge. I do enjoy Roshni's lively personality with her mischievous sense of humour!"

One disadvantage of Roshni's school program is that it includes little planned enrichment and no opportunity for work with other gifted children. In Roshni's Grade 2 year the school considered introducing a pull-out program for gifted students but this plan was abandoned for political reasons because of the school's fear of possible accusations of elitism and potential objections from parents of children not selected for the program. Roshni's parents are aware that acceleration by itself will not provide a balanced educational and social diet for their daughter, and they are investigating the possibility of transferring her to another school which will maintain her acceleration program and also facilitate her interaction with other gifted students.

Fred Campbell

Fred Campbell is a small, wiry, continuously alert young man with an eager, inquiring mind. Fred entered 11th grade 2 weeks after his 14th birthday. His school has combined grade-skipping, subject matter acceleration, and enrichment in an individualized program designed to foster Fred's exceptional abilities in math and science. Unfortunately, his elementary school was less concerned about his abilities.

Fred is an extremely able and multitalented student. He has a Stanford-Binet IQ of 163. At the age of 12 years I month he scored 640 on the SAT-M and 500 on the SAT-V (Verbal). He taught himself to read before his 3rd birthday and his remarkable math skills developed soon afterwards. He is, furthermore, a highly gifted artist.

Fred was bitterly unhappy in elementary school. Like many exceptionally gifted children, he read deeply in many fields, burying himself in a subject until he had exhausted the resources available, then moving on to another topic which he absorbed with equal enthusiasm. At the age of 9, he developed a keen interest in psychology and devoured adult texts in this discipline which he borrowed from libraries in the large city in which he lives. In his school, however, he was a social outcast, derided and rejected for being different. Fred's classmates could not understand his interest in psychology, philosophy, and music. They were unable to understand his passion for mathematics. His actions, reactions, and opinions, when he tried to express them, were utterly alien to their system of values. They taunted, derided, and attacked him mercilessly and made his life a misery. The school refused to offer Fred any form of differentiated curriculum. "He is a rather independent person who likes to be allowed to set his own goals and to take responsibility for his own learning, and this was not accepted at his elementary school," says Fred's mother, Eleanor. "Their attitude was that he should be like the other 9-year-olds, take more interest in sport, and work at the level of the class."

Finally, in desperation, during Fred's Grade 5 year, his parents approached the local high school (in most Australian states, high schools take children from Grade 7 through Grade 12) and asked the principal whether they would consider admitting Fred a year early. After meeting Fred, the principal agreed enthusiastically. Consequently, at age 10 Fred entered 7th grade, an immediate grade-skip of one year, and the following year he was based in Grade 8 but took math and chemistry with Grade 11. This program proved so successful that he was next permitted to skip Grade 9 while continuing his subject acceleration in math, science, and computing. Both academically and socially, acceleration is, in Fred's own words, "the best thing that has ever happened to me. " For the first time he was able to associate with children whose ways of thinking and viewing the world were like his own. His classmates, who are 2 and 3 years older than he, accept him as one of them, and he has made a number of warm and continuing friendships.

Hadley Bond

Hadley Bond is 9 years old, is in 7th grade, and has a Stanford-Binet ratio IQ of 178. His phemonenal mathematical ability was evident from very early childhood. At 18 months of age he was already fascinated by the math drill programs used by his two older brothers on the family's home computer. He delighted in simple addition problems. He would work out the answer to a question using plastic beads, and type it into the computer, laughing with pleasure when the response was verified. He was reading small books before the age of two, and at 3 he had the reading skills of a child of 8.

Like Roshni, Hadley was permitted early entrance to school on the basis of his remarkable abilities in math and language, which had been identified and assessed in preschool. Unfortunately, Hadley's school was similarly unwilling to adapt the curriculum to his needs. Three years after teaching himself to add and subtract, Hadley, along with the other 5-year-olds, was being invited to place in order the numbers 1–10. Hadley was bored and resentful, and announced frankly to his parents that school was a waste of time. Concerned that such a negative experience, if it continued, might leave the child with a lasting dislike for school, his parents removed him. A few months later, at the "proper" age, they enrolled him in a different school a few miles away. The principal of this second school recognized Hadley's remarkable abilities and placed him in Grade 1, an immediate grade-skip of 12 months.

Extremely gifted children often realize at a very early age that their abilities and interests differ radically from those of other children, and they may come to blame or denigrate themselves for being out of step (Hollingworth, 1926; Gross, 1989a). At his second school Hadley took care to disguise, as much as possible, the fact that he was "different" from other 5-year-olds. He carefully modeled his behavior on his classmates, even mimicking them by selecting, from the classroom bookshelves, picture books or books with only a few words of text. Despite the psychologist's assessment which placed his full-scale IQ on the WPPSI at 150, the classroom teacher took his reading performance at face value, and some months passed before the school recognized and responded to his exceptional reading abilities. Fortunately, subject matter acceleration formed part of this response, and Hadley was permitted to go to Grade 2 for math and Grade 3 for computer instruction.

Hadley responded much more positively to acceleration than he had to the attempts at individualized instruction and in-class enrichment which the school had tried initially. He was much happier in his relations with the Grade 3 students with whom he worked in computer class than with his own classmates who were only 12 months older than he. Accordingly, at the end of Grade 1, Hadley was advanced into Grade 3, to be with children 2 years his senior. "It was a social wonderland for Hadley," says his mother. "For the first time he was fully accepted by the other children in his grade and he made lots of good friends. It was then that he started to talk about how bad the previous years had been and how lonely and isolated he had felt" (Gross, in press). Hadley's new-found happiness led to a surge in his motivation to achieve, and at the end of his Grade 4 year the principal, Hadley, and his parents decided that he should skip directly to Grade 6. This grade-skip, like the previous two, proved extremely successful, and at the start of 1991 Hadley, aged 9, moved with his

12-year-old classmates into Grade 7. To his surprise and delight he topped his class of 125 students in the math placement test.

Examples of Inappropriate Educational Provision

Of the 40 exceptionally and profoundly gifted children in this study, 31 have been retained in the regular classroom or have been offered token grade-skips of one year. The school programs of several of these children are textbook cases of educational mismanagement.

At age 4, Richard amazed a professor of mathematics at a major Australian university by doing arithmetic mentally in binary, octal, and hexadecimal. At the age of 12 years 6 months, he scored 780 on the SAT-M. He is a gifted musician and composer and has won two state-wide elementary school chess championships. Throughout his school career, Richard has been retained with age-peers both in math and in all other school subjects.

Anastasia has a Stanford-Binet ratio IQ of 173. At age 6, her favorite out-of-school reading was *National Geographic*. Aged 7, she was reading Richard Adams' *Watership Down*. At age 8 she read an English translation of *Les Misérables*; having seen the show, she wanted to read the book. Anastasia has been grade-skipped by one year. It is doubtful whether placing an 8-year-old who reads adult novels with 9-year-olds would provide anything more than a temporary alleviation of her boredom and social isolation.

Adam, IQ 162, was a competent and enthusiastic reader by the age of 3. He spent his earliest years of schooling in a small country school where the first three grades were contained in the same classroom. His teacher, who stated that he was the brightest child she had encountered in her teaching career, permitted him to complete the work of the three grades in 18 months. At 6 years 10 months, he was reading Charles Kingsley's classic, The *Water Babies* and his reading accuracy and comprehension were assessed at Grade 7 level.

The building principal, however, shared the concern of many school administrators that acceleration would lead to social or emotional damage (Southern, Jones, & Fiscus, 1989). Adam's accelerated progress was halted, and his 3rd grade teacher insisted that he read, and study, the same materials as the other students. This necessitated him repeating much of the work he had already covered in previous grades. Adam's consequent boredom, depression, and intellectual frustration manifested itself both at school and at home. His teachers reported him as arrogant, disruptive, and unmannerly. At home, he was aggressive and short-tempered. However, as the year progressed, he lost even the will to rebel. He began to conform to the requirements of his teachers and the academic standards of his classmates. His teachers were delighted with the "improvement" in Adam's behavior and expressed their approval to his parents. Half-way through the school year, Adam's father expressed his fears in a letter to the author.

What I find it hard to tell them, because I can't define it, is that he has lost, or rather is no longer able to display, the "spark" that he always had. This was the sharpness; the quick, often humorous, comment; the sudden bubbling over of enthusiasm when he starts following through a series of ideas. It is rather like a stone with many sharp edges; they have knocked these edges off and as a result he is rolling more smoothly in class and they are happy about that. I feel that they have caused him to bury an important part of himself. It is still there; it bursts out at home now and again, but he has learned to keep it hidden. I hope you know what I mean, because I have tried to explain it to the teachers and I fail every time. They believe they have had great success, but I know they are depressing some vital spark. (Gross, 1989a, p. 228)

FACTORS IN THE SUCCESS OF THE ACCELERATION PROGRAMS

Program Design and Planning

Nine of the 40 children in this study have been radically accelerated. In each case the grade-skips and subject matter acceleration have been carefully planned and monitored, addressing the children's social and emotional maturity as well as their academic achievement. No child has skipped more than one grade at a time; as recommended by Terman and Oden (1947), the skips have been spaced appropriately as the child progressed through school, with at least one year of consolidation between each skip. As advised by Feldhusen, Proctor, and Black (1986) in their guidelines for grade advancement of precocious children, each student was psychometrically assessed to establish his or her intellectual capacity and to ensure that the child would be able to perform at a level considerably beyond the average for the receiving grade. In each case, it was understood that acceleration would be undertaken on a trial basis, and the children knew that they had the option, at any time, to return to their earlier placement. In every case, however, the acceleration has proven overwhelmingly successful.

In each instance the children's parents and the children themselves were involved in the planning and monitoring of the acceleration program. Indeed in the majority of cases the initial grade-skip was proposed not by the teachers but by the parents who had familiarized themselves with the research literature on appropriate educational provision for the gifted. In several cases the school was extremely reluctant to permit any form of acceleration and concurred only when it had become obvious that retaining the child with age-peers, with a token provision of in-class enrichment or pull-out, was proving quite inadequate to the child's academic and social needs (Gross, 1989a).

The relative merits of acceleration and enrichment have been much debated. Many researchers (Goldberg, Passow, Camm, & Neill, 1966; Sisk, 1979; Feldhusen, 1983) conclude that the most effective intervention structure for highly gifted students is a combination of both procedures enhanced by other provisions such as individual study and mentorships. With the exception of Roshni, the children's acceleration has been supplemented with enrichment and ability grouping in the form of pull-out programs, mentorships, or tracking in academic subjects. Further extension has been provided for Chris and Ian by permitting them to enter state and national math competitions at ages much younger than is usually permitted. Even with radical acceleration, the mental ages of these children are still considerably higher than the average student in the classes they have entered, and additional educational adaptations have been necessary to ensure that they are, indeed, provided with academic challenge and intellectual peers.

Enhancement of Social Self-Esteem

The Coopersmith Self-Esteem Inventory, used to measure the self-esteem of the children in this study, consists of four subscales, each measuring a different aspect of self-esteem: these are social self-peers, home-parents, school-academic, and general self (Coopersmith, 1981). Marked contrasts appear between the academic and social self-concept scores of the radical accelerands and the other students.

It might be anticipated that exceptionally gifted children who have been radically accelerated would score highly on the index of academic self-esteem. By contrast, they display positive but modest scores, between the mean for their age groups and .7 of a standard deviation above. These students compare their academic performance with that of their classmates who are several years their senior. They still outperform their classmates and they enjoy the intellectual and academic challenge, but they have to work to achieve their success. These results contradict the popular belief that children who have been accelerated will become conceited about their academic ability.

Interestingly, it is the children who have not been radically accelerated whose academic self-esteem is unusually inflated. The schoolwork presented to these exceptionally gifted children demands little effort, their performance is generally far beyond that of their classmates, and they have no contact with other children whose achievement levels approach their own and with whom they could realistically compare themselves.

In this study, as in previous studies of the extremely gifted (Hollingworth, 1942; DeHaan & Havighurst, 1961; Janos, 1983), the majority of children retained in the regular classroom have experienced extreme difficulty in establishing positive social relationships with their classmates. The strongly negative perceptions which they develop both of their own social skills and of their image in the eyes of other children are reflected in extremely low levels of social self-esteem. Over half the children in the study have social self-esteem scores *at least one* standard deviation below the mean. The social self-esteem scores of Anastasia and Richard, expressed in z-scores, are -2.59 and -1.14 respectively, Ian Baker's social self-esteem z-score, before being permitted early entrance to high school, was a disturbingly low -1.97.

Significantly, the only children scoring more than one standard deviation above the mean on the social self-peers subscale of the SEI are children who have been radically accelerated. These young people are able to work and socialize with other children who share, or can at least empathize with, their interests, their delight in intellectual enquiry, and their ways of viewing the world. These children are confident in their relationships with classmates. They are enjoying the social pleasures of childhood while, at the same time, experiencing the intellectual satisfaction of challenging academic work.

Provision of an Intellectual Peer Group

It is now generally understood and accepted that a child's level of social and emotional development is more highly correlated with his mental age than with his chronological age (Hallahan & Kauffman, 1982; Tannenbaum, 1983; Janos & Robinson, 1985). The significance of this is immense when dealing with the extremely gifted since the higher the IQ, the greater the discrepancy between chronological and mental age, and thus the wider the gap between the psychosocial development of the gifted child and that of his age-peers. Children tend to make friendship choices on the basis of mental, rather than chronological age (Hubbard, 1929; O'Shea, 1960), and researchers over the last 60 years have noted that, as a rule, intellectually gifted children seek out, as preferred companions, children somewhat older than themselves (Davis, 1924; Terman, 1926; Hollingworth, 1931; Janos & Robinson, 1985). Christopher, Ian, Fred, and the other radical accelerands in this study have been given access to a group of children who are at similar stages of intellectual and emotional development.

Extremely gifted children may be hampered in socialization by the fact that their reading interests and preferred leisure activities tend to lie completely outside the realm of capability or interest of the average child (Zorbaugh & Boardman, 1936; Hollingworth, 1942; Gross, 1989b). This can lead to severe problems of salience and possible social rejection should the extremely gifted child try to share his reading interests with age peers. Few 8-year-olds choose, like Anastasia, to read *Les Misérables*. Fred, aged 9 and in Grade 4, had no access to friends who would understand his passionate interest in psychology and the history of art. By contrast, Hadley, also aged 9 but in Grade 7, has teenage classmates who share his enjoyment of science fantasy; the novels he prefers would be completely above the heads of his age-peers. Christopher, who at age 12 was enthralled by Dickens and the Brontës, could share his enthusiasm with his 11th grade classmates.

The Reversal of Underachievement

The common perception of the extremely gifted as eager, academically successful young people who display high levels of task commitment has been refuted by research which demonstrates that many highly gifted children underachieve seriously in the regular classroom, and that, by the end of elementary school, many have almost completely lost the motivation to excel (Pringle, 1970; Painter, 1976; Whitmore, 1980; Gross & Feldhusen, 1990).

The majority of the extremely gifted young people in this study state frankly that for substantial periods in their school career they have deliberately concealed their abilities or significantly moderated their scholastic achievement in an attempt to reduce their classmates' and teachers' resentment of them. Generally, the radical accelerands admit that even the considerably advanced curriculum they are now offered does not challenge their intellectual abilities to the fullest; however, they state uniformly that the emotional security they now experience through being placed with intellectual peers has alleviated or completely removed the pressure to underachieve for social acceptance.

There may, however, be a temporal limit to the reversability of underachievement. Attempts to reverse academic underachievement in gifted high school students who have been working significantly below their potential for several years meet with variable success (Tannenbaum, 1983). Ian Baker's father recognizes how close Ian came to losing, perhaps irretrievably, his motivation to learn. "He has had to start all over again and learn to work in school," wrote Brock when Ian was first permitted radical subject acceleration in math. "It's years since he had to think about anything that was presented to him in class, and it has come as quite a shock to him to have to apply himself. At first, he even resented it. However, his attitude towards school has definitely improved. A few times in the last few weeks he has come home with the gleam in his eye that we remember from when he was little. Only now have we realized how much he had turned off. I think we've arrested the slide, but I also think we went very close to him switching off altogether."

The exceptionally gifted children who have not been permitted radical acceleration are not so fortunate. In almost every case, the parents of children retained in the regular classroom with age-peers or grade-skipped by only 12 months report, like the parents of Adam, that the drive to achieve, the delight in intellectual exploration and the joyful seeking after new knowledge which had characterized their children in the early years has seriously diminished or disappeared completely. Unfortunately, rather than investigating the cause of this, the schools attended by these children have tended to view their decreased motivation, with the attendant drop in academic attainment, as indicators that the child has "leveled out" and is no longer gifted.

SUMMARY

The study reported here is the only longitudinal study of exceptionally or profoundly gifted children conducted outside the United States. The findings support the conclusions of American researchers such as Stanley and Benbow (1983), Pollins (1983), and Janos et al. (1988) that radical acceleration is a practical and effective response to the intellectual and psychosocial needs of the extremely gifted.

In every case, the students who have been radically accelerated, and their teachers and parents, believe strongly that they are now much more appropriately placed, both academically and socially. These students display higher levels of motivation, they report that pressure to underachieve for peer acceptance has significantly diminished or disappeared completely, and, although the curriculum which they are offered does not completely address their academic needs, it provides a challenging and stimulating intellectual environment when enhanced with ability grouping, enrichment, or mentoring. The radical accelerands have positive attitudes toward school and believe that they are warmly regarded by their teachers. They have a greater number of friends and enjoy closer and more productive social relationships than they did prior to their acceleration. They have significantly higher levels of social and general self-esteem than do children of equal intellectual ability who have been retained with age-peers or grade-skipped by a single year.

Prior to their acceleration, many of the accelerands displayed the negative attitudes and behaviors which still characterize the extremely gifted students who have not been radically accelerated. These children display disturbingly low levels of motivation and social self-esteem, are more likely to report social rejection by their classmates, and state that they frequently underachieve in attempts to gain acceptance by age-peers and teachers. Several of these children are required to work, in class, at levels 7 or more years below their tested achievement.

In Australia, as in the United States, many teachers argue that acceleration may jeopardize the child's social and emotional development. This study finds no evidence to suggest that social or emotional problems arise through well-planned and carefully monitored programs of radical acceleration and suggests that we should concern ourselves rather with the maladjusting effects of prolonged educational misplacement. Accelerating exceptionally or profoundly gifted children by a single year is no more effective than retaining them in the regular classroom with age-peers.

REFERENCES

Barbe, W. B. (1964). One in a thousand: *A comparative study of highly and moderately gifted elementary school children*. Columbus, OH: F. J. Heer.

Burks, B. S., Jensen, D. W., & Terman, L. S. (1930). *Genetic studies of genius: Vol. 3: The promise of youth*. Stanford, CA: Stanford University Press.

Carroll, H. A. (1940). *Genius in the making*. New York: McGraw Hill.

Coopersmith, S. (1981). *Self-esteem inventories:* Manual. Palo Alto, CA: Consulting Psychologists Press.

Davis, H. (1924). Personal and social characteristics of gifted children. In G. M. Whipple (Ed.), *Report on the Society's Committee on the Education of Gifted Children* (pp. 123–144). The Twenty-Third Yearbook of the National Society for the Study of Education. Bloomington, IL: Public School Publishing Company.

DeHaan, R. F., & Havighurst, R. J. (1961). *Educating gifted children*. Chicago: University of Chicago Press.

Feldhusen, J. F. (1983). Eclecticism: A comprehensive approach to education of the gifted. In C. P. Benbow & J. C. Stanley (Eds.), *Academic precocity: Aspects of its development* (pp. 192–204). Baltimore, MD: Johns Hopkins University Press.

Feldhusen, J. F., & Hoover, S. M. (1986). A conception of giftedness: Intelligence, self-concept and motivation. *Roeper Review, 8*(3), 140–143.

Feldhusen, J. F., Proctor, T. B., & Black, K. N. (1986). Guidelines for grade advancement of precocious children. *Roeper Review, 9*(1), 25–27.

Foster, W. (1983). Self-concept, intimacy and the attainment of excellence. *Journal for the Education of the Gifted, 6*(1), 20–27.

Gallagher, J. J. (1958). Peer acceptance of highly gifted children in elementary school. *Elementary School Journal, 58*, 465–470.

Goldberg, M. L. (1981). *Issues in the education of gifted and talented children in Australia and the United States.* Canberra, Australia; Commonwealth Schools Commission.

Goldberg, M. L., Passow, A. H., Camm, D. S., & Neill, R. D. (1966). *A comparison of mathematics programs for able high school students* (Vol. 1). Washington, DC: U.S. Office of Education, Bureau of Research.

Grinder, R. E. (1985). The gifted in our midst: By their divine deeds, neuroses and mental test scores we have known them. In F. D. Horowitz & M. O'Brian (Eds.), *The gifted and talented: Developmental perspectives* (pp. 5–36). Washington, DC: American Psychological Association.

Gross, M. U. M. (1989a). *Children of exceptional intellectual potential: Their origin and development.* Unpublished doctoral dissertation, Purdue University, West Lafayette, IN.

Gross, M. U. M. (1989b). The pursuit of excellence or the search for intimacy? The forced-choice dilemma of gifted youth. *Roeper Review, 11*(4), 189–194.

Gross, M. U. M. (1990). Relationships between musical precocity and high intellectual potential. *Australian String Teacher, 12*(1), June, 7–11.

Gross, M. U. M., & Feldhusen, J. F. (1990). The exceptionally gifted child. *Understanding Our Gifted, 2*(5), 1, 7–10.

Gross, M. U. M., & Start, K. B. (1991). "Not waving but drowning": The exceptionally gifted child in Australia. In S. Bailey, E. Braggett, & M. Robinson (Eds.), *The challenge of excellence: A vision splendid* (pp. 25–36). Wagga Wagga, Australia: Australian Association for the Education of the Gifted and Talented.

Gross, M. U. M. (in press). The early development of three profoundly gifted young boys of IQ 200+. In A. J. Tannenbaum and P. N. Klein (Eds.), *To be young and gifted.* New York: Ablex.

Hallahan, D. P., & Kauffman, J. (1982). *Exceptional children.* Englewood Cliffs, NJ: Prentice Hall.

Hollingworth, L. S. (1926). *Gifted children: Their nature and nurture.* New York: Macmillan.

Hollingworth, L. S. (1931). The child of very superior intelligence as a special problem in social adjustment. *Mental Hygiene, 15*(1), 3–16.

Hollingworth, L. S. (1936). The founding of Public School 500, Speyer School. *Teachers College Record, 38*, 119–128.

Hollingworth, L. S. (1942). *Children above IQ 180.* New York: World Books.

Hollingworth, L. S., Cobb, M. V., et al. (1923). The special opportunity class for gifted children, Public School 165, Manhattan. *Ungraded, 8*, 121–128.

Hollingworth, L. S., & Cobb, M. V. (1928). Children clustering at 165 IQ and children clustering at 145 IQ compared for three years in achievement. In G. M. Whipple (Ed.), *Nature and nurture: Their influence upon achievement.* The Twenty-Seventh Yearbook of the National Society for the Study of Education, Part 2 (pp. 3–33). Bloomington, IL: Public School Publishing Company.

Hubbard, R. (1929). A method of studying spontaneous group formation. In *Some new techniques for studying social behavior*, Child Development Monograph 1 (pp. 55–61). New York: Bureau of Publications, Teachers College, Columbia University.

Janos, P. M. (1983). *The psychological vulnerabilities of children of very superior intellectual ability*. Unpublished doctoral dissertation, Ohio State University, Columbus, OH.

Janos, P. M., & Robinson, N. M. (1985). Psychosocial development in intellectually gifted children. In F. D. Horowitz and M.O'Brien (Eds.), *The gifted and talented: Developmental perspectives*. Washington, DC: American Psychological Association.

Janos, P. M. (1988). A cross-sectional developmental study of the social relations of students who enter college early. *Gifted Child Quarterly 32*, 210–215.

Kidder, L. H., & Fine, M. (1987). Qualitative and quantitative methods: When stories converge. In M. M. Mark & R. L. Shotland (Eds.), *Multiple methods in program evaluation* (pp. 105–139). San Francisco: Jossey-Bass.

O'Shea, H. (1960). Friendship and the intellectually gifted child. *Exceptional Children, 26*(6), 327–335.

Painter, F. (1976). *Gifted children: A research study*. Knebworth, UK: Pullen Publications.

Pollins, L. D. (1983). The effects of acceleration on the social and emotional development of gifted students. In C. P. Benbow & J. C. Stanley (Eds.), *Academic precocity: Aspects of its development* (pp. 160–178). Baltimore, MD: Johns Hopkins University Press.

Pringle, M. L. K. (1970). *Able misfits*. London: Longman.

Sheldon, P. M. (1959). Isolation as a characteristic of highly gifted children. *The Journal of Educational Sociology, 32*, 215–221.

Silverman, L. K. (1989). The highly gifted. In J. F. Feldhusen, J. Van Tassel-Baska & K. R. Seeley (Eds.), *Excellence in educating the gifted* (pp. 71–83). Denver, CO: Love.

Silverman, L. K., & Kearney, K. (1989). Parents of the extraordinarily gifted. *Advanced Development, 1*, 1–10.

Sisk, D. (1979). Acceleration versus enrichment: A position paper. In W. C. George, S. J. Cohn, & J. C. Stanley (Eds.), *Educating the gifted: Acceleration and enrichment* (pp. 236–238). Baltimore, MD: Johns Hopkins University Press.

Southern, W. T., Jones, E. D., & Fiscus, E. D. (1989). Practitioner objections to the academic acceleration of gifted children. *Gifted Child Quarterly, 33*, 29–35.

Stanley, J. C. (1979). Identifying and nurturing the intellectually gifted. In W. C. George, S. J. Cohn, & J. C. Stanley (Eds.), *Educating the gifted: Acceleration and enrichment* (pp. 172–180). Baltimore, MD: Johns Hopkins University Press.

Stanley, J. C., & Benbow, C. P. (1983). Extremely young college graduates: Evidence of their success. *College and University, 58*, 219–228.

Start, K. B. (1986). A deprived group thought too clever by half. *Sydney Morning Herald*, p. 14.

Tannenbaum, A. J. (1983). *Gifted children: Psychological and educational perspectives*. New York: Macmillan.

Terman, L. M. (1926). *Genetic studies of genius: Vol. 1. Mental and physical traits of a thousand gifted children*. Stanford, CA: Stanford University Press.

Terman, L. M., & Oden, M. H. (1947). *Genetic studies of genius: Vol. 4. The gifted child grows up*. Stanford, CA: Stanford University Press.

Ward, R. (1958). *The Australian legend*. Melbourne, Australia: Oxford University Press.

Whitmore, J. (1980). *Giftedness, conflict and underachievement*. Boston: Allyn and Bacon.

Zorbaugh, H. W., & Boardman, R. K. (1936). Salvaging our gifted children. *Journal of Educational Sociology, 10*, 100–108.

4

The Use of Subject and Grade Skipping for the Prevention and Reversal of Underachievement

Sylvia B. Rimm and Katherine J. Lovance

Family Achievement Clinic, Oconomowoc, Wisconsin

Acceleration, including early entrance to kindergarten, grade skipping, and subject skipping, has been used as a strategy to prevent and reverse underachievement in a selected group of gifted students. Fourteen sets of parents and 11 students were interviewed to determine their perceptions of the effectiveness of the acceleration strategy. All the parents and all the students indicated they would make the same decision again.

Only two of the school administrators and six of the receiving teachers were initially positive about the skipping but most of them changed their positions with the child's success, at least in regard to the specific accelerated

Editor's Note: From Rimm, S. B., & Lovance, K. J. (1992). The use of subject and grade skipping for the prevention and reversal of underachievement. *Gifted Child Quarterly, 36*(2), 100-105. © 1992 National Association for Gifted Children. Reprinted with permission.

child. There appeared to be a period (between one quarter and a semester) during which teachers expressed concern over the students' adjustment, but students did not perceive themselves as having adjustment difficulties.

Acceleration has long been used as a strategy to permit gifted students to progress at a rate appropriate to their intellectual capabilities and prevent them from needing to conform to the slower pace of typical students. There is continuous debate among leaders in gifted education about the value of acceleration versus enrichment (Davis & Rimm. 1989); advocates of acceleration (Stanley & Benbow, 1986) proclaim enrichment "busywork dad irrelevant" and even consider it "potentially dangerous if not accompanied or followed by acceleration" (Stanley, 1978, page 181).

A longitudinal study (Swiatek & Benbow, 1991) and a meta-analysis of accelerative, research (Rogers, 1990) confirm the academic advantages and even the social advantages of acceleration. However, there are no studies we are aware of in which acceleration has been used specifically as a technique to reverse underachievement.

Family Achievement Clinic uses acceleration strategies as part of the TRI-FOCAL Model (Rimm, 1986) in the treatment plan for gifted children who are underachieving. The TRIFOCAL Model is a six-step plan which takes into consideration the following three arenas: (a) students self-perceptions, (b) parenting strategies, and (c) school curriculum. Underachievement is defined globally at the Clinic as a discrepancy between the child's performance and some index of his or her ability, such as intelligence, achievement, or creativity scores, or observational data (Davis & Rimm, 1989). Although subject and grade skipping are only part of the treatment, they are viewed by students, parents, and psychologists as important factors in the reversal of the problem. A description of the components of the TRIFOCAL Model which involve providing a more challenging curriculum by grade or subject skipping follows.

Awareness of lack of academic challenge is the initiating factor in the exploration of the use of an accelerative strategy at Family Achievement Clinic. This lack may be brought to the Clinic's attention by parents or by teacher referral. Individual tests of academic ability (IQ) and achievement continue to be the most important evaluative measures used for acceleration decision making. Despite the many documented problems of IQ tests, they do provide good predictors for successful acceleration.

The academic makeup of the child's present class, as well as that of the class to which the child could be accelerated, are always considered. Peer academic environment can vary from grade to grade, and sometimes a challenging peer group can provide more appropriate learning in a lower grade. The availability and quality of school enrichment programs may also affect decision making.

Other variables which are considered, but rarely affect actual decisions, are motivation or lack thereof, social adjustment, physical size and maturity, grades, and attitude of the receiving teacher. These are of lesser importance because (a) acceleration often improves motivation; (b) studies indicate that acceleration has no negative effect on social adjustment (Swiatek & Benbow, 1991) and may actually help it (Rogers, 1990); (c) physical size, maturity, and grades don't appear to make a difference (Lueck, 1989); and (d) although attitude of the receiving teacher appears to make a dramatic, immediate difference, it does not seem to have any long-term effect (Lueck, 1989).

Putting the Research to Use

Parents, teachers, and administrators tend to be extremely hesitant about grade and subject skipping or entering children into kindergarten early. This fear persists despite a plethora of research which documents that these forms of acceleration are excellent strategies for motivating gifted students to achieve. Interviews with parents and students provide specific case examples that should assure those who must make these difficult educational decisions that grade and subject skipping, with brief therapy as an adjunct, can actually prevent and reverse some kinds of under-achievement. Subject and grade skipping can even be considered for children who are nonproductive in school if test scores are extremely high. Parents of gifted students may wish to share these case studies with teachers as they consider possible decisions about the appropriateness of acceleration for their own children. This study emphasizes, however, that a professional psychologist or school psychologist who is knowledgeable about research in giftedness should conduct a psychoeducational evaluation to guide parents and teachers in this important decision.

In reviewing the variables considered for academic acceleration, it becomes clear that the most important criteria relate to an academically challenging environment, and all other variables are of much lesser importance. It is also relatively clear that test scores are the best indicators for grade or subject skipping, despite their limitations.

With this framework in mind, the purpose of this study is twofold. It summarizes and describes case study examples of grade- or subject-skipped students, whose stories can be used concretely to supplement empirical research already available on acceleration. It also introduces the need to do further empirical research on the effectiveness of grade skipping for underachieving students whose classroom production is so poor that they would not ordinarily be viewed by teachers or parents as potential candidates for grade skipping consideration.

METHOD

The parents of 14 children who have been subject- or grade-skipped during the past 7 years were recently interviewed by the second author using a structured interview schedule.[1] The children were also interviewed, except the kindergartners and first graders. Although many more than 14 children have been accelerated by Clinic recommendation, families were difficult to find because of geographic mobility or limited research resources. These 14 were selected based only on the immediate recall of the first author, who was also their therapist. For the most part, the parents of these students stay in contact with the Clinic to verify that their children continue to be appropriately challenged. Although it is obvious that this data may be biased and cannot be used to draw actual research conclusions, case studies can provide important information to guide parents, teachers, and psychologists in decision making for students they may wish to consider for subject or grade skipping.

RESULTS

Kindergarten and First-Grade Accelerants

Ten of the sample children had their first acceleration by early entrance to kindergarten, skipping first grade, or subject skipping in first grade. Some of these are recent accelerants (3); the others are now between ages 8 and 14. Of the 10 children with some acceleration at kindergarten and first-grade level, 3 were entered early into kindergarten, 2 skipped first grade, and 5 were subject-skipped in first grade.

All parents of the three early entrants and two first-grade "skippers" feel certain that their decision was correct. Only one early kindergarten entrant, who is now in sixth grade, has needed further subject acceleration to keep her challenged. All five of the early subject skippers were eventually grade-skipped, and two thought that perhaps skipping first grade entirely would have been more beneficial than the gradual subject acceleration.

Test scores were a major consideration for these acceleration decisions. Average Wechsler (Wechsler, 1974) IQ[2] test scores for the group when they were first tested were Verbal—144, Performance—129, and Full Scale—140. Tasks of speed and small muscle coordination tended to have a lowering effect on performance scores. Average Peabody Individual Achievement Test scores for these children were 92nd percentile for Reading Recognition, 97th percentile for Reading Comprehension, and 88th percentile for Mathematics. Although height or gender were not primary considerations, 9 of the 10 children were tall for their age, and one was of medium height. There were 6 girls and 4 boys in the group.

The 10 children were enrolled in eight different schools, two of which were private, the other six public. Teacher and administrator attitudes toward early entrance and early grade skipping were consistently hesitant and negative.

Receiving teachers were all nonbelievers in the appropriateness of grade skipping. However, teachers were mainly positive about subject acceleration only in the early years. Occasionally there was some hesitation, but principals and teachers had recommended that children remain in their grade for their age and only skip a grade for a particular subject. However, if the child had already skipped one grade, teachers seemed much less comfortable when further subject acceleration was requested. A sample case is described below:

Danny

Danny's parents came to the Clinic at the recommendation of his school principal. His parents had indicated to the principal that they were concerned about lack of challenge in first grade while Danny was still in kindergarten. He had been reading since age two and read aloud to his kindergarten classmates. He had two years of kindergarten, was tall, and was one of the oldest boys in his class.

Socially, Danny was not advanced and missed his mother while he was away at school. In kindergarten and day care, he had not had many friends, only one good friend at a time. Danny's parents were hesitant about coming in for the evaluation because of Danny's difficult social adjustment, but they feared that Danny would be bored in first grade.

Since Danny is now a fourth grader, he has been tested regularly since kindergarten. His kindergarten WISC-R IQ test scores were: Verbal—155+, Performances—128, and Full Scale—147+. His verbal scores were all perfect 19s on a scale of 1–19. His Peabody Individual Achievement Test scores were fourth grade, first month for Reading Recognition; third grade, first month for Reading Comprehension; and fourth grade, second month for Mathematics. His GIFT (Group Inventory for Creative Talent; Rimm, 1980) creativity score was 98th percentile. In third grade, when he was tested again, his Stanford-Binet IQ test score was 185; his reading was at seventh grade, sixth month, and his mathematics at eleventh grade, third month.

The recommendation that Danny skip first grade was made after his parents assured the first author that they would not worry about his being too young for competitive sports. The principal who had referred the child to the Clinic was hesitant, citing her own personal experience that grade skipping caused severe problems later. The kindergarten teacher cautiously recommended skipping grade one for academic reasons, but indicated her concern about his social immaturity. The first-grade teacher thought it was a difficult grade to skip, and the second-grade receiving teacher was certain that it would be an impossible transition. However, the test scores were sufficiently convincing. All were willing to give Danny the opportunity to try. The psychologist advised the parents to give him practice writing brief stories during the summer and to teach him the printing that he would miss in first grade.

Six weeks into second grade, the teacher and principal invited the parents and the psychologist (and first author) to an emergency conference. The teacher was convinced Danny was wrongly placed and recommended he be sent back to first grade immediately. His writing was poor, his social skills were immature, and he seldom volunteered in class. She considered him lacking in imagination because he preferred nonfiction reading to fiction. Moreover, the teacher pointed out that the school attracted many very bright children and that the curriculum was very advanced. The teacher observed that his actual reading and math skills did fit with her top students. During the conference, the psychologist explained that some of Danny's personality characteristics might not change, such as his preference for science over imaginary stories and his pattern of playing with only one or two children. She felt sure that Danny would adjust academically to the teacher's high expectations. The psychologist assured the teacher that Danny had reported to his parents and to her that he loved second grade and his teacher. Her best guess, at that time, was that he would be adjusted by the end of first semester. At the end of first semester, she received a call from Danny's parents saying that teacher and principal were pleased with Danny's progress.

Now, in the second semester of fourth grade, Danny has adjusted comfortably to his peers and talks about his five best friends. Danny works independently in fifth-grade math with teacher guidance. The teacher preferred grouping him with another girl who said, "I can't work with Danny; he's a math wizard." His parents look back at grade skipping and believe it was the correct decision. The next concern is how to provide a continuously challenging program in mathematics. Subject compacting and skipping are likely in the future, especially in mathematics and science.

Skipping Later Grades

Five[3] students in the sample skipped grades or parts of grades beyond Grade one. Three of those skipped second, one skipped third, and one skipped sixth grade. They are presently in sixth (1), seventh (1), eighth (2), and ninth (1) grade, respectively. All five children and their parents agree that skipping grades was the right thing to do at the time of the decision. Three of the girls indicated that they were worried or hesitant at the time. All have adjusted well both academically and socially, although all experienced some unpleasant peer comments because of the skipping.

There was actually considerable academic improvement for three of the five. They became mainly A students. Two girls had underachieved dramatically in first grade before they were accelerated. One made immediate improvement; the second needed a little counseling and some adjustment time. The boy who skipped third grade initially had some difficulty with organizational skills and writing and had been described earlier as academically "at sea." A year after grade skipping, his mother reported that he had "just taken off" and had won a writing contest. His parents attributed the change to a combination of his excellent receiving teacher, a little counseling, and, primarily, the grade skipping.

The five children attended four different schools. In one public school where two sisters were grade-skipped, the principal and teachers recommended and favored the skip. In the other three, administration and teachers were initially opposed. Once the decision had been made, one receiving teacher was extremely supportive and helpful; acceptance by the other two teachers was questionable. Three of these students were tall for their age, and two were of medium height. A sample case is described below:

Sally

Sally had already entered kindergarten early when her parents brought her to the Clinic for help. She had refused to do assignments in first grade and was coming home from school terribly unhappy. She complained to her parents about "boring" work that was far too easy. Her parents had already explored with the teacher some further acceleration," but the teacher did not see good achievement in the classroom and assumed that Sally's parents were pushing her.

At age 6, Sally's WISC-R IQ test scores were Verbal—150+, Performance—135, and Full Scale—147+. Sally's Reading Recognition and Comprehension scores were at fourth-grade, fifth-month level, and her Mathematics was at second-grade, fourth-month level. Her GIFT (creativity test) was at the 84th percentile. A later testing showed her Stanford-Binet IQ scores to be 160+.

Sally's parents preferred moving her to a private school because of their personal frustration with the unwillingness of the public school to provide for, or even see, Sally's giftedness. After meeting with the teachers and principal, it was decided to begin Sally in first grade and permit her to go to reading with the third grade. Staff found that arrangement comfortable and needed no urging. However, they advised against any further acceleration.

By the end of first grade, Sally voiced impatience with the unchallenging math curriculum. After academic testing, the teachers reluctantly agreed to permit her to skip second grade. The third-grade teacher did not concur with the decision. Although Sally's third-grade school achievement was excellent, the parents believed that the third-grade teacher never accepted Sally's skip as appropriate for her socially, and Sally did not feel accepted by her teacher. Subject skipping was further required several times in reading, math, and science. Some teachers encouraged subject skipping; other teachers seemed to wish to hold Sally back because of her age and her already dramatic acceleration.

In Sally's interview, she indicated that she felt that many of her teachers did not like her acceleration and that some of the students had difficulty accepting her. In her words, "The ones who were going to accept me, accepted me. The ones who didn't, never will"; but when asked if she had any social problems, her answer was a definitive, "No; I wouldn't want to be friends with kids who don't accept me." Sally indicated that she was glad she was skipped and will want to be skipped further because of her wish for challenge. She also indicated that she had always found it "hard to do work that was too easy for her."

Sally is 13, in ninth grade, but taking mainly eleventh-grade courses. She is considering a career in medicine. She expects to graduate from high school at age 14 but has not yet decided whether to enter college immediately or to study in a 1-year pre-college program in Germany.

Subject Acceleration

All 14 children have had some subject skipping, but 3 students in the sample experienced no grade skipping and only subject skipping. One of these 3 is planning to graduate a year early, and another is likely to skip a high school grade. Subject skipping is the type of acceleration used most frequently at Family Achievement Clinic. It can be used comfortably for children with specific academic aptitudes, for children whose social maturity is questionable, and for experimentally determining if the child can adjust to grade skipping. Both parents and teachers seem to find it more acceptable then grade skipping. The Clinic usually recommends only one grade of subject skipping at a time in order to provide a period of adjustment for the child. However, further acceleration is often recommended at a later date.

The small number of "subject-skipped only" students in this sample is not indicative of the numbers that are recommended. Since it is done so frequently, it is more difficult to single out and remember which students have skipped a subject. Until recently, subject skipping has almost always been found acceptable to teachers. The new emphasis on whole-class instruction and cooperative learning and the de-emphasis on grouping seem to have caused teachers to be much more resistant to subject skipping. A case example is described below:

Steve

Steve came to the Clinic toward the end of fifth grade. He was underachieving and was a behavior problem. He was not actually disrespectful to his teachers; he just seemed to get into minor "class-clown" problems. His actual school performance was far below his tested abilities. Steve's WISC-R Verbal score was 152+, his Performance score was 131, and his Full Scale score 145+. His reading and mathematics scores were at the ceiling of the test, twelfth grade, ninth month on each.

Public school teachers and administrators were opposed to any acceleration because of his poor school performance. Steve's parents decided to enroll him in an independent school which indicated a willingness to provide a more flexible curriculum for Steve. Despite his high test scores, the school was hesitant about having him skip a grade because of his poor school record. However, the school tested him in mathematics and science and immediately skipped him in these subjects. Later he was further skipped in these two subjects, as well as in Latin, French, and history. The school took the initiative for the subject skips each time, although there were yearly consultation meetings. There were no problems of teacher acceptance since teachers had made the recommendations.

Steve is 15 now and a sophomore. He plans to graduate a year early. He has "used up" almost all the curriculum at this advanced high school. Although there were token remnants of his underachieving symptoms at first, that is, an occasional missed assignment, his problems almost completely disappeared with his new challenges. He and his parents had only three or four counseling sessions.

Steve indicates that he was somewhat lacking in confidence and felt "mildly out of place" at first. He found the class work more difficult, but the challenge only encouraged him to want to do more. "Kids," Steve said, "were surprised, but I never felt cut off from my classmates because the individual classes made it a gradual adjustment." He said he'd make the same decision if he had to do it again, and his parents only added that they wished that he had been accelerated earlier.

Summary of the Interviews

The 14 children whose parents were interviewed and described are a biased sample because the children all came to the Clinic based on a parent or teacher concern that the children were already underachieving. Although some of these children appeared to be classroom achievers and had reasonably good study habits, others had mild behavior problems, were disorganized, or were not accomplishing assignments. All families involved received some counseling, but for the most part it was minimal. Table I summarizes the presenting problems, IQ scores, grades and subjects skipped, time for adjustment, and anticipated further acceleration.

Eleven of the 14 administrators were initially negative about the subject or grade skipping requests. Two were very positive, and one was positive about some parts and negative about others. Six of the receiving teachers were positive initially; eight either had mixed feelings or strongly opposed the skips. Most of them changed their position as the child adjusted, at least in regard to the specific child.

At this time, all the children have made very good academic adjustments. In retrospect, all 14 sets of parents would make the same decision again. Five parents indicated that they should have made the decision to accelerate sooner.

A theme which appeared in all parent interviews was that there was almost always an adjustment period after grade skipping. It usually took between a school quarter and a semester before teacher and parents felt comfortable with the change. Most of the children did not describe early adjustment problems; however, they did experience some uncomfortable explanations to peers. Those who were grade-skipped found explaining easier than those who were subject-skipped only, and several of the children commented on the relief that came when they could identify with a whole grade after initially being subject-skipped and later entirely skipped. When parents were asked what advice they'd give other parents who were considering skipping their children, they recommended getting test scores, facts and figures, and a professional to back them in their request.

Table 1

Summary of Case Events

Gender of Child	Presenting Problems	Wechsler FS and Binet[1] Score (if available)	Grades/Subjects Skipped to Date	Time for Adjustment (teacher perceptions)	Add'l Therapy Required	Grade[4]	Projected Future Accelerations
F	Parent concern about boredom; behavior problems at home	147+* 151	Early placed kindergarten	one semester	yes—brief[2]	1	NYD[5]
F	Parent concern about boredom	141	Early placed kindergarten Subject skipping	none	yes—brief	6	NYD[5]
F	Behavior problems in preschool	139	Early placed kindergarten	one semester	yes—brief	K	NYD[5]
M	Behavior problems at home and school	144 172	Skipped 1st grade	one quarter	yes—brief	2	Math and reading skips or computer curriculum
M	Parent concern about boredom; peer adjustment problems; dependency	151+ 185+	Skipped 1st grade; math acceleration in 4th	one semester	yes—brief	4	Further extreme math acceleration
F	Refusal to do school work	152+ 160+	Skipped 1st grade reading; 2nd grade math; other English, math, science, foreign language	one semester	yes—occasional[3]	8	Subject skips and early graduation
M	Parent concern about boredom	141+ 173	Skipped 1st and 2nd grade reading, 2nd grade math; skipped last half of 1st grade; skipped 4th grade math	none	none	4	Subject and grade skips
F	Teacher concern about boredom	133+	Skipped last half of 2nd and first half of 3rd grade	none	none	7	None likely—AP courses available in high school
F	Unfinished work; disorganization; complaints of boredom; poor peer relations	127	Skipped 2nd grade; math accelerated later	one semester	yes—1 semester	8	AP classes; NYD[5]

(Continued)

Table 1 (Continued)

Summary of Case Events

Gender of Child	Presenting Problems	Wechsler FS IQ and Binet[1] Score (if available)	Grades/Subjects Skipped to Date	Time for Adjustment (teacher perceptions)	Add'l Therapy Required	Grade[4]	Projected Future Accelerations
M	Behavior problems at home and school; disorganization, unfinished work	149 +	Skipped 3rd grade	one year	yes—occasional	6	AP classes available in high school; NYD[5]
F	Parent and child concern about boredom	126 +	Skipped 4th grade reading and math	none for reading one quarter for math	yes—brief	8	Possible grade skip in high school
F	Parent concern about boredom	139 +	Skipped 2nd grade math, 4th grade reading; skipped 6th grade science	none	yes—brief	6	Likely subject skips; NYD[5]
F	Teacher concern about boredom, perfectionism	135	Skipped 2nd grade math, 3rd grade reading; skipped 6th grade entirely	none	none	9	None likely—AP courses available in high school
M	Behavior problems, disorganization; incomplete work	149 +	Skipped subjects in math, science, French, history, and Latin	one quarter	yes—brief	10	Early graduation

*+ indicates ceiling scores

[1] Stanford-Binet, Form L-M

[2] Brief therapy refers to no more than 4 sessions

[3] Several initial sessions followed by therapy sessions 2 or 3 times during the school year

[4] Grade at time of interview

[5] Not yet determine.

CONCLUSIONS

Despite limitations, acceleration has been shown to be very effective in providing incentive to children whose underachievement was caused or exacerbated by an unchallenging curriculum. It is perhaps more obvious to those experienced in gifted education than to those who are not that the curriculum of a higher grade is more appropriate for intellectually gifted children than the curriculum used for average and above-average students of the same chronological age.

Subject and grade skipping are not panaceas for underachievement. There are many gifted underachievers who would not benefit by such dramatic acceleration. Children with high IQ scores but major skill deficits or very difficult behavior problems are unlikely candidates for acceleration. Children who are unwilling to take the risk even after parent encouragement or those who insist that they don't want to work hard or learn are not good candidates. Extremely serious cases of underachievement that are caused more by home conditions than school curriculum are not usually recommended for grade skipping until the child becomes more productive in school. An extremely negative receiving teacher or a classroom environment which might be inappropriate for the child might also postpone consideration of skipping.

A subtle additional ingredient of the success of grade skipping may come from a sense of earning "specialness" by achievement. Several of the students mentioned in their interview that skipping made them feel special. Children who skip a subject or grade automatically view themselves as intelligent, even if they are not the top achievers in their class. They have made a commitment to work harder to catch up to other students, yet they need not feel threatened if their performance is not "perfect" since parents and teachers recognize that they are younger. Thus, they may be more likely to learn to be hard workers and find out that they can accomplish the acceleration by their own efforts. It may feel like the "earned specialness" that Benjamin Bloom refers to in Developing Talent in Young People (Bloom et al., 1985; Rimm & Lowe, 1988).

NOTES

1. Interview schedule is available upon request.

2. The Wechsler IQ tests are used for initial testing because the subtest scores are viewed as important for curriculum-related decisions. When students are at or near the ceiling score on at least two subtests, the Clinic recommends further testing using the Stanford-Binet, Form L-M. Parents usually, but not always, agree to further testing.

3. Numbers in each category equal more than the total because some children have skipped in more than one category.

REFERENCES

Bloom, B. S. (Ed.).(1985). *Developing talent in young people*. New York: Ballantine Books.

Davis, G. A., & Rimm, S. B. (1989). *Education of the gifted and talented* (2nd ed.). Englewood Cliffs, NJ: Prentice Hall.

Lueck, R. (1989). Psychosocial factors in the acceleration of gifted elementary school children. In S. B. Rimm, M. Cornale, R. Manos, & J. Behrend, *Guidebook-underachievement syndrome: Causes and cures* (pp. 360–370). Watertown, WI: Apple Publishing Company.

Rimm, S. B. (1980). *GIFT: Group inventory for finding creative talent*. Watertown, WI: Educational Assessment Service, Inc.

Rimm, S. B. (1986). *Underachievement syndrome: Causes and cures*. Watertown, WI: Apple Publishing Company.

Rimm, S. B., & Lowe, B. (1988). Family environments of underachieving gifted students. *Gifted Child Quarterly, 4*(2), 353–359.

Rogers, K. B. (1990, November). *Using effect size to make good decisions about acceleration*. Paper presented at the meeting of the National Association for Gifted Children, Little Rock, AR.

Stanley, J. C. (1978). Identifying and nurturing the intellectually gifted. In R. E. Clasen & B. Robinson (Eds.), *Simple gifts* (Vol. 1, p. 181). Madison, WI: University of Wisconsin—Extension.

Stanley, J. C., & Benbow, C. P. (1986). Extremely young college graduates: Evidence of their success. *College and University, 58*, 361–371.

Swiatek, M. A., & Benbow, C. P. (1991, November). *Acceleration: Does it cause academic or psychological harm?* Paper presented at the meeting of the National Association for Gifted Children, Little Rock, AR.

Wechsler, D. (1974). *WISC-R: Wechsler intelligence scales for children—revised*. New York: Psychological Corporation.

5

The Impact of Early Entrance to College on Self-Esteem: A Preliminary Study

Ann E. Lupkowski

Carnegie Mellon University

Marjorie Whitmore

University of North Texas

Annetta Ramsay

University of North Texas

In a study investigating the effects to an early entrance to college program on self-esteem, students in the Texas Academy of Mathematics and Science (TAMS) completed the Adult Form of the Coopersmith Self-Esteem Inventory (SEI) the week they began and again after one semester of participation in the program, a time period when the greatest changes in self-esteem would be anticipated. Overall differences between TAMS

Editor's Note: From Lupkowski, A. E., Whitmore, M., & Ramsay, A. (1992). The impact of early entrance to college on self-esteem: A preliminary study. *Gifted Child Quarterly*, *36*(2), 87-90. © 1992 National Association for Gifted Children. Reprinted with permission.

pretests and posttests were nonsignificant or negligible, indicating that the students' self-esteem did not change in a meaningful way during their first semester in the program. A number of items on the SEI showed significant changes, all in a negative direction. On the pretest, TAMS students did not differ significantly from subjects in SEI normative groups on any items. On the posttest, however, there were some differences in a negative direction: Observed changes in self-esteem may be attributed to the adjustment that all college freshmen experience when they leave home for the first time, as well as to changes in social comparisons.

THE IMPACT OF EARLY ENTRANCE TO COLLEGE ON SELF-ESTEEM

The self-esteem and self-concept of gifted students has been the subject of a number of research studies (for reviews, see Janos & Robinson, 1985; Olszewski-Kubilius, Kulieke, & Krasney, 1988). Some studies show higher self-concepts for gifted students in special programs, others find slightly lower self-concepts for gifted students, and still others report no significant differences (for a meta analysis, see Kulik & Kulik, 1982).

In addition to comparing gifted students in programs to gifted students not in special programs, it is of interest to examine the changes gifted students experience in self-esteem as a result of participation in these special programs. In a study of 5th- through 10th-grade gifted students in a residential summer program, Kolloff and Moore (1989) found that self-concepts across all grade levels and programs were significantly higher at the end of the program than at the beginning. Brody and Benbow (1987) and Richardson and Benbow (1990) investigated the self-esteem of students who selected accelerative options ranging from no acceleration through grade-skipping. No differences were found among the groups' social and emotional adjustment several years later.

One accelerative option that merits investigation is early entrance to college. Students may enter college early on their own or through special programs, such as the Texas Academy of Mathematics and Science (Redding & Ramsay, 1988), the Clarkson School of Clarkson University (Kelly, 1989), the Early Entrance Program at the University of Washington (Robinson, 1985), or the Program for the Exceptionally Gifted at Mary Baldwin College (Cohn, 1987). Although few such special programs exist, entering college early is a relatively common means for intellectually talented students to pursue academically challenging course work (Brody, Lupkowski, & Stanley, 1988; Brody & Stanley, 1991; Janos et al., 1988; Stanley, 1985b). Although school personnel express concern about the social and emotional effects of early entrance to college (Daurio, 1979), research strongly supports this type of acceleration. The majority of early entrants fare well academically and socially (Brody et al., 1988; Daurio, 1979;

Janos, 1987; Janos & Robinson, 1985; Kulik & Kulik, 1984; Pollins, 1983; Robinson, 1983; Stanley, 1985a, 1985b; Stanley & Benbow, 1983; Stanley & McGill, 1986). For example, in two studies comparing early entrants to regular-age college students, National Merit finalists, and bright high school students who had elected not to participate in the early entrance program, Robinson and Janos (1986) and Janos, Robinson, and Lunneborg (1989) found no association between early entrance and psychological or social maladjustment. The researchers concluded that accelerants appeared as well adjusted as the students in all three of the comparison groups. "Indeed, in every comparison, the early entrants were virtually indistinguishable from comparably bright agemates who had elected to attend high school" (Janos, et al., 1989, p. 514). In a comprehensive review of research findings on young entrants to college, Brody and Stanley (1991) concluded, ". . . as a group young entrants to college have been extremely successful academically and professionally and have not experienced significant social or emotional problems. There is no justification for assuming that academic difficulties or social and emotional adjustment problems are likely to accompany early entrance to college" (p. 113).

Putting the Research to Use

How does early entrance to college affect self-esteem? In this study early entrants to college did not show important changes in self-esteem after one semester of participation in an early entrance program. These findings are consistent with previous research that showed that early entrance to college does not necessarily affect students negatively. Although early entrants to college are not guaranteed success, research shows that they tend to be successful both academically and socially.

Although studies show satisfactory progress for early entrants to college in both the social and academic arenas, research is still needed to investigate the specific effects of early entrance. Most studies compare early entrants to students of traditional age. Almost no empirical work has examined how early entrants mature during their college experience. For example, in what ways do social and emotional development change due to participation in an early entrance program? Janos et al. (1988) reported on changes in social relationships during the college experience and found that early entrants spent much of their time with other early entrants during their first 2 years of college, but by junior year they had established relationships with older students. Janos et al. (1989) administered the California Psychological Inventory (CPI) at 1-year intervals to early entrants and to comparison groups. An overall increase in CPI scores was found over time, but no changes were unique to early entrants. Cornell, Callahan, and Loyd (1991) administered the CPI to early entrants at the beginning of participation in the program and again after one academic year. When compared to bright age-mates living at home and attending high school, early entrants made consistent gains in personality adjustment indicative of healthy personality growth and increased maturity. Students in the control group made relatively few changes during the same period of time.

The present research study was conducted in an attempt to clarify some of these research findings. To do so, we examined the self-esteem of students entering college 2 years younger than is typical.

The University of North Texas coordinates a unique early entrance to college program, the Texas Academy of Mathematics and Science (TAMS). Talented students live on campus, take college courses, and complete the last two years of high school and the first two years of college concurrently. The study described in this paper investigated one aspect of their development, self-esteem.

The present study addressed two research questions: (a) Does the self-esteem of early entrants change significantly during their first semester in the program? and (b) Is the self-esteem of early entrants to college significantly different from that of comparison groups? To answer the first question, early entrants' responses at the beginning of the program were compared to their responses after participating in the program for a semester. The second research question was addressed by comparing the early entrants' responses on Coopersmith's Self-Esteem Index (SEI) to those of the SEI normative group.

Although it may seem that one semester is not long enough to observe changes in students' self-esteem, research shows that dramatic changes occur in college freshmen during their first 4 to 8 weeks in the college environment (see Rossi, 1964, cited in Blimling & Miltenberger, 1984). Because many changes occur in a rather short time, we elected to study the students' self-esteem after completion of one semester in the program instead of waiting an academic year or longer.

METHOD

Subjects

All first-year TAMS students, ranging in age from 14 through 17, were invited to participate in the study. They are academically talented, as evidenced by their average combined Scholastic Aptitude Test scores of 1200 at age 15. Their scores can be compared to those of the average college bound high school senior, who earns a combined score of about 930. Students participating in the program have completed 10th grade and are selected on the basis of SAT scores, high school grades, teacher recommendations, essays, and interviews. Of the 191 students entering TAMS in the fall of 1990, 190 participated in the first phase of the study. Of that group, 35% were female, 2% Black, 8% Hispanic, and 14% Asian American.

Materials

Participants' self-esteem was measured by their responses to the Adult form of the Coopersmith Self-Esteem Inventory (SEI; Coopersmith, 1990), a self-report questionnaire designed to measure self-esteem in social, academic, family, and personal areas of experience. The 25-item Adult Form of the SEI is designed for persons age 16 and older. Respondents classify each item as "Like Me" or "Unlike Me." Kuder-Richardson reliability estimates range from .71 to .80 for students in grade 12 or in college. Test-retest reliability estimates for college students taking the short form are .80 for males and .82 for females. For the TAMS students, Kuder-Richardson reliability estimates were .78 for the pretest and .80 for the posttest.

Procedure

Participants completed the SEI prior to their first semester as TAMS students and at the beginning of their second semester as TAMS students. Both administrations were conducted in a group setting.

Effect sizes were calculated by dividing the difference between pretest and posttest means by the weighted standard deviation to yield a standard score. As defined by Cohen (1977), an effect size of .20 is considered "small"; .50 is "medium"; and .80 is "large." Effect sizes below .20 are considered "unimportant."

RESULTS

Of the 190 students who completed the SEI pretest, 185 provided usable answer sheets. The mean self-esteem score for TAMS students on the pretest was 68.56 (SD = 18.49), which did not differ by gender (see Table 1).

A total of 113 students took the SEI posttest. These were matched to pretests, resulting in 109 usable matched pretests and posttests. Fifty-nine percent of the TAMS students taking the pretest took the posttest. Of the students participating in the pretest portion of the study, 21 had not returned to the program after the first semester, so they could not participate in the posttest portion of the study. Their SEI scores ranged from 48 to 100 (mean = 73.3, SD = 15.2). Of the 21 students, 19 left primarily for academic reasons and 2 for behavioral reasons. The remaining group of students who participated in the pretest but did not complete the posttest simply chose not to continue participating in the study. The pretest results for the students who took both the pretest and the posttest were compared with those of participants who did not take the posttest; no significant difference was found ($t = 1.44, p > .05$).

The mean score for TAMS students taking the posttest was 63.74 (SD = 20.08, n = 109), with no differences according to gender. Scores from the first and second administrations of the SEI were then compared using matched pairs t-tests, yielding a significant difference ($t = 2.42, p < .05$). To determine if

Table 1   SEI scores for TAMS participants

TAMS group	Mean	SD	N
All participants, pretest	68.6	18.5	190
All participants, posttest	63.7	20.1	109
Males, pretest	68.8	18.5	119
Females, pretest	68.1	18.7	65
Males, posttest	63.8	20.5	69
Females, posttest	63.7	19.5	40

this statistically significant finding also has practical significance, the effect size (d) was calculated. In this case, the observed difference, although statistically significant, can be considered "unimportant" because the effect size was d = .16. In other words, it has little practical significance.

To address the second research question, participants' responses on both the pretest and the posttest were compared to SEI normative groups using effect sizes. Effect sizes were calculated by dividing the difference between TAMS and comparison group means by the weighted standard deviation.

As shown in Table 2, TAMS pretest scores compared to normative data yielded effect sizes ranging from −.18 to .10, all of which fall below the cutoff for a "small" effect. Scores earned on the posttest were also compared to the normative groups; only one of these effect sizes was below the cutoff for a "small" effect. This effect size compared TAMS students to 16- to 19-year-old college students. The other three effect sizes were all in the "small" range ($d = .20$ to .49), and all were in a negative direction, indicating that TAMS students had lower levels of self-esteem as measured by the SEI.

The next step in the analysis was to examine individual items on the SEI. To determine whether participants changed their responses on particular items, chi-square goodness-of-fit tests were performed for each item on the pre- and posttests ($n = 109$).

For the item "Things usually don't bother me," 81 students answered "Like Me" on the pretest compared to 65 on the posttest ($\chi^2 = 12.3$, $p < .001$). Thirty-one students said "Things are all mixed up in my life" was "Like Me" on the pretest. This number increased to 42 on the posttest ($\chi^2 = 5.5$, $p < .05$). "I give in very easily" was "Like Me" for 24 students on the pretest and 34 students on the posttest ($\chi^2 = 5.3$, $p < .05$). While 37 students felt "I often feel upset with my work" was like them when they took the pretest, 49 students felt that way when they took the posttest ($\chi^2 = 5.9$, $p < .05$).

Of six questionnaire items concerning family relations, two had significant chi-square values. On the pretest, 40 students felt the statement "I get upset easily at home" described the way they usually felt, compared to 54 on the posttest ($\chi^2 = 7.7$, $p < .01$). "I usually feel as if my family is pushing me" was "Like Me" for 33 students when they took the pretest and 45 students when they took the posttest ($\chi^2 = 6.3$, $p < .05$). No other items had a significant chi-square value. It

Table 2   Effect sizes comparing normative and TAMS data

Comparison group	Mean	(SD)	n	d (pretest)	d (posttest)
TAMS students compared to 16- to 19-year-old college students	66.7	(19.2)	78	.10	−15
20- to 34-year-old college students	71.7	(18.8)	148	−.17	−.41
TAMS males compared to male college students (ages 16 to 34)	68.4	(18.5)	114	.02	−.24
TAMS females compared to female college students (ages 16 to 34)	71.6	(19.5)	112	−.18	−.41

should be noted that 36% of the items became more positive from the pretest to the posttest, although none of these changes was significant.

Changes in SEI scores were examined for each participant. These changes ranged from a decrease of 36 points to an increase of 32 points (mean change = −3.2, SD = 13.7). Scores for 58 students changed in a negative direction, 38 students showed a positive change, and 13 showed no change.

DISCUSSION

The present study was designed to help clarify the relationship between giftedness and self-esteem as well as the changes in self-esteem that result from participation in an early entrance to college program. Based upon informal observations, we anticipated that students' self-esteem would be enhanced by their participation in TAMS. Based upon previous research (e.g., Kaiser & Berndt, 1985), we hypothesized that TAMS students would show higher levels of self-esteem than their average peers.

When the levels of self-esteem were compared using t-tests before and after one semester of participation in the program, a statistically significant drop in self-esteem was noted, although that decrease had little practical significance because the effect size was below the cutoff for even a "small" effect (see Cohen, 1977). It is important to note that, even if the group differences had little practical significance, observed changes could have serious effects on an individual. Nonetheless, the self-esteem of the group of students participating in TAMS did not change in a meaningful way during their first semester in the program.

An examination of the individual items on the SEI was conducted to determine if the students' responses changed significantly in specific areas. Of the 25 items on the questionnaire, 6 showed significant changes. All of the items with a significant chi-square value showed a decrease in self-esteem.

Concerning the items on family relations, many students have noted informally that their parents have difficulty accepting the ways in which they have changed while away at school. This is a typical adjustment problem that regular-age college freshmen have. The observed changes in the TAMS students may be a result of their adjustment to college and not of their early entrance in particular. It seems important to extend this research by including a group of regular-age college freshmen and a group of gifted high school students for comparison to determine if the observed changes are due to typical freshmen adjustments or to entering college early. Not including those two control groups is a limitation of the present study.

The TAMS students' self-esteem on the pretest did not differ significantly from that of comparison groups. Thus, it appears that they have the same level of self-esteem as other college students. In contrast, on the posttest their self-esteem was at a lower level than that of comparison groups. Since TAMS students have been placed in an environment where they are being actively challenged, achievements do not come as easily as they might have previously. For students who are used to being "top of the heap," being challenged may lead to being less sure of themselves, at least for a time. Richardson and Benbow (1990) noted that gifted students may experience lowered self-esteem because of the changes in social comparisons; being placed in a grade with older students or in segregated classes for gifted students results in students comparing themselves with other advanced students, which leads to the predicted decline in self-concept.

In conclusion, this study sheds some light on the question of how early entrants change and mature during their college experience. Their self-esteem does not decline appreciably as a result of participating in a challenging program.

REFERENCES

Blimling, G. S., & Miltenberger, L. J. (1984). The resident assistant: Working with college students in residence halls. Dubuque, IA: Kendall/Hunt.

Brody, L. E., & Benbow, C. P. (1987). Accelerative strategies: How effective are they for the gifted? *Gifted Child Quarterly, 3*(3), 105–110.

Brody, L. E., Lupkowski, A. E., & Stanley, J. C. (1988). Early entrance to college: A study of academic and social adjustment during the freshman year. *College and University, 63*, 347–359.

Brody, L. E., & Stanley, J. C. (1991). Young college students: Assessing factors that contribute to success. In W. T. Southern & E. D. Jones (Eds.), *Academic acceleration of gifted children*. New York: Teachers College Press.

Cohen, J. (1977). *Statistical power for the behavioral sciences*. New York: Academic Press.

Cohn, D. (1987, May 22). Teaching "brightest of the bright": Virginia college program caters to gifted female students. *The Washington Post*, C1, C5.

Coopersmith, S. (1990). *SEI: Self-esteem inventories*. Palo Alto, CA: Consulting Psychologists Press.

Cornell, D. G., Callahan, C. M., & Loyd, B. H. (1991). Personality growth in female early college entrants: A controlled, prospective study. *Gifted Child Quarterly, 35*(3), 135–143.

Daurio, S. P. (1979). Educational enrichment versus acceleration: A review of the literature. In S. J. Cohn & J. C. Stanley (Eds.), *Educating the gifted: Acceleration and enrichment* (pp. 13–63). Baltimore: Johns Hopkins University Press.

Janos, P. M. (1987). A 50-year follow-up of Terman's youngest college students and IQ-matched agemates. *Gifted Child Quarterly, 31*(2), 55–58.

Janos, P. M., & Robinson, N. M. (1985). Psychosocial development in intellectually gifted children. In F. D. Horowitz & M. O'Brien (Eds.), *The gifted and talented: Developmental perspectives.* (pp. 149–196). Washington, DC: American Psychological Association.

Janos, P. M., Robinson, N. M., et al. (1988). A cross-sectional developmental study of the social relations of students who enter college early. *Gifted Child Quarterly, 32*(1), 210–215.

Janos, P. M., Robinson, N. M., & Lunneborg, C. E. (1989). Markedly early entrance to college: A multi-year comparative study of academic performance and psychological adjustment. *Journal of Higher Education, 60*(5), 495–518.

Kaiser, C. F., & Berndt, D. J. (1985). Predictors of loneliness in the gifted adolescent. *Gifted Child Quarterly, 29*(2), 74–77.

Kelly, G. F. (1989). The Clarkson School: Talented students enter college early. In S. M. Elam (Ed.), *Prototypes: An anthology of school improvement ideas that work.* Bloomington, IN: Phi Delta Kappa Foundation.

Kolloff, P. B., & Moore, A. D. (1989). Effects of summer programs on the self-concepts of gifted children. *Journal for the Education of the Gifted, 12*(4), 268–276.

Kulik, C. C., & Kulik, J. A. (1982). Effects of ability grouping on secondary school students. *American Educational Research Journal, 19*, 415–428.

Kulik, J. A., & Kulik, C.-L. C. (1984). Effects of accelerated instruction on students. *Review of Educational Research, 54*(3), 409–425.

Olszewski-Kubilius, P. M., Kulieke, M. J., & Krasney, N. (1988). Personality dimensions of gifted adolescents: A review of the empirical literature. *Gifted Child Quarterly, 32*(4), 347–352.

Pollins, L. D. (1983). The effects of acceleration on the social and emotional development of gifted students. In C. P. Benbow & J. C. Stanley (Eds.), *Academic precocity: Aspects of its development* (pp. 160–178). Baltimore, MD: Johns Hopkins University Press.

Redding, R., & Ramsay, A. (1988). Brand new for 1988: Texas Academy of Mathematics and Science. *Gifted Child Today, 11*(4), 40.

Richardson, T. M., & Benbow, C. P. (1990). Long-term effects of acceleration on the social-emotional adjustment of mathematically precocious youths. *Journal of Educational Psychology, 82*(3), 464–470.

Robinson, H. B. (1983). A case for radical acceleration: Programs of the Johns Hopkins University and the University of Washington. In C. P. Benbow & J. C. Stanley (Eds.), *Academic precocity: Aspects of its development* (pp. 139–159). Baltimore, MD: Johns Hopkins University Press.

Robinson, N. M. (1985). College without high school: The Early Entrance Program at the University of Washington. *Academic Talent, 2*(1), 9–10.

Robinson, N. M., & Janos, P. M. (1986). Psychological adjustment in a college-level program of marked academic acceleration. *Journal of Youth and Adolescence, 15*, 51–60.

Stanley, J. C. (1985a). How did six highly accelerated gifted students fare in graduate school? *Gifted Child Quarterly, 29*(4), 180.

Stanley, J. C. (1985b). Young entrants to college: How did they fare? *College and University, 60*, 219–228.

Stanley, J. C., & Benbow, C. P. (1983). Extremely young college graduates: Evidence of their success. *College and University, 58*(4), 361–371.

Stanley, J. C., & McGill, A. M. (1986). More about "Young entrants to college: How did they fare?" *Gifted Child Quarterly, 30*, 70–73.

6

Accelerative Strategies: How Effective Are They for the Gifted?

Linda E. Brody

The Johns Hopkins University

Camilla Persson Benbow

Iowa State University

Accelerative strategies offer gifted students the opportunity to participate in educational programs suited to their particular needs and interests. Yet, fear of possible negative effects of acceleration prevents many educators from advocating these options. The Study of Mathematically Precocious Youth (SMPY) has evaluated the long-term effects of a variety of accelerative options for a group of highly gifted students. Academic achievements, extracurricular activities, goals and aspirations, and social and emotional adjustment were considered, and no discernible negative effects of various accelerative strategies were found.

Editor's Note: From Brody, L. E., & Benbow, C. P. (1987). Accelerative strategies: How effective are they for the gifted? *Gifted Child Quarterly, 3*(3), 105-110. © 1987 National Association for Gifted Children. Reprinted with permission.

The nation's most highly gifted and talented students often have difficulty being challenged in a regular classroom. Since classroom instruction is usually designed for the benefit of students who function at the level of the majority of their age peers, this instruction, no matter how well done, may not be appropriate for the extremely gifted student whose abilities differ greatly from this group. Even special programs for gifted and talented students may be designed for a broad group of gifted students and may not meet the specific needs of the extremely talented child, especially one with a special intellectual talent.

In response to these students' special needs, the staff of the Study of Mathematically Precocious Youth (SMPY) has explored possibilities for educating students who have been identified as extremely talented in mathematical or verbal reasoning ability. They have encouraged such students to choose from a "smorgasbord" of educational alternatives to meet individual needs and interests (Stanley, 1978; Stanley & Benbow, 1982; Stanley & Benbow, 1983a). Many of the options such as grade skipping, early graduation from high school, early entrance to college, acceleration in one or more subject areas, Advanced Placement Program tests, and college courses while in high school involve some degree of acceleration. These options generally utilize existing educational programs, but they stress a flexible approach to choosing curricula that meet the educational needs of individual students.

Yet, acceleration for gifted students is controversial. Proponents argue that, in addition to providing a suitable and challenging education for gifted students, acceleration costs little to implement and may actually save school systems money if students spend fewer years in the system (e.g., Stanley & Benbow, 1982). Kulik and Kulik (1984) found that accelerated students performed as well as older students with whom they were placed and exceeded the achievement of non-accelerated students of the same age and ability by almost a year. Concern about the social and emotional effects of acceleration (Kulik & Kulik, 1984), however, is the primary reasons for bias against its use, although many studies have documented the benefits of acceleration without harmful social and emotional effects (e.g., Daurio, 1979; Fund for the Advancement of Education, 1979; Hobson, 1963; Pollins, 1983; Pressey, 1949; Robinson, 1983; Stanley, 1985a, b; Stanley & Benbow, 1983b; Stanley & McGill, 1986).

Because the controversy over the effects of acceleration continues to exist, a long-term evaluation is needed. This study assesses the academic achievements, extracurricular activities, goals and aspirations, and social and emotional development of talented students who have accelerated to varying degrees during the high school years and compares them to non-accelerates.

METHODS

The subjects were identified in talent searches conducted by SMPY in December 1976 or January 1978. Seventh grade and under-age eighth grade students who had scored in the upper three percent on the mathematical part of a standardized achievement test were eligible to participate in the talent search and take the Scholastic Aptitude Test (SAT), an examination designed chiefly for college-bound students finishing high school. Students who met certain criteria were invited for further testing, counseling, and longitudinal follow-up. For the 1976 group, the criterion was 2(SAT-M) + SAT-V = 1330. For the 1978 group, any one of the following applied: (1) SAT-M = 500 and SAT-V = 430, (2) SAT-M = 550, (3) SAT-V = 580, and (4) Test of Standard Written English = 58. Two hundred seventy-eight students from 1976 and 395 from 1978 met the eligibility criteria and came for additional testing.

When these students had completed high school, they were sent a 20-page questionnaire. For the 1976 group, 90% of the locatable females and 86% of the locatable males returned a questionnaire. Nineteen students (7%) were unlocatable. For the 1978 group, 75% of the locatable females and 77% of the locatable males responded, while 6% were unlocatable. For this study, the students identified in 1976 and 1978 were combined for statistical analysis.

The subjects were divided into four groups on the basis of the accelerative strategies they reported using in high school. Group 1 (N = 143) included students who had skipped one or more grades, graduated from high school early, or entered college early without graduating from high school. These students were considered the most accelerated, since they had gained a year or more in the process. Group 2 (N = 277) consisted of students who reported taking AP tests or college courses on a part-time basis while in high school but did not meet the criteria for Group 1. These are options that may have resulted in course credit for the student and clearly involved work beyond the high school level. We considered this group the second most accelerated. Group 3 (N = 50) were students who reported participating in subject matter acceleration, special classes or tutoring. While we did not always have information on the nature of these experiences, students in this category generally did not receive credit for the experience. Thus, this group was considered less accelerated than the first two groups. Group 4 (N = 40) included students who reported having no accelerative experiences. Approximately two-thirds of each group were males and one-third were females.

The follow-up questionnaire included items about high school experiences, post-secondary education, employment, family background, and attitudes and interests. Items relating to the specific areas of interest in this study were selected for analysis to compare the four groups. In addition, the students identified in 1976 were also administered several tests as part of the follow-up, including the Adjective Check List (ACL). The ACL consists of a list of adjectives from which particular ones may be selected to describe an individual. Scales have been developed to describe particular psychological traits (Gough & Heilbrun, 1980). Some of these scales were used in this study to assess personality characteristics and emotional adjustment.

One-way analysis of variance (ANOVA) was used to compare the groups where test scores or interval data were involved, followed (when the ANOVA was significant) by a Scheffé multiple comparison test to determine group differences. For variables involving nominal data, chi square comparisons were used. Analyses were performed using the SPSSX computer program.

RESULTS

Academic Accomplishments

Students reported their SAT scores in high school (see Table 1). On the SAT-M, Groups 1 and 2 scored significantly higher than Groups 3 and 4 ($p = .01$). This might be expected, since these groups had also scored higher on the SAT-M in the talent search. It is important to note, however, that acceleration, particularly for those who skipped a year in high school, did not adversely affect SAT scores and thereby limit possibilities for college acceptance. Moreover, there were no differences between the groups on SAT-V in high school (Table 1). Again, this was important because spending fewer years in high school apparently did not restrict growth on the SAT significantly. Group 1 did score higher than Group 3 in the verbal area in the talent search ($p = .05$), but no differences were found with the other groups. We also studied average scores on the College Board Achievement Tests. The mean scores for all four groups were quite high, and there were no significant differences (see Table 1).

Achievement in school was also investigated. Differences were found in overall grade point average (GPA) between the 8th and 12th grades using ANOVA and the Scheffé test. Groups 1 and 2 had significantly higher GPAs than Group 3, and the mean for Group 4, while not significantly different statistically from the other groups, was almost the same as for Group 3 (see Table 1). The number of semesters of all As between and including 8th grade and 12th grade was also considered. The numbers were adjusted for the number of semesters the students spent in school during that time. In Table 1 are shown the proportion of semesters attended that the students in each group received all As. No significant differences were found, using ANOVA. Students also reported their academic rank in school as being in the top ten percent, second ten percent, third to eighth ten percent, ninth ten percent, or bottom ten percent. A chi square comparison of all responses was significant ($p = .001$). The majority in all groups were in the top ten percent, but this was more frequently true for Groups 1 and 2, where 84% and 83%, respectively, were in this category, than for Groups 3 and 4, where 72% and 68% were in the top ten percent. In terms of grades in school, therefore, the accelerated students in Groups 1 and 2 had higher GPAs and class rank, and as many semesters of all As, as the non-accelerates. Clearly, achievement in high school coursework did not suffer as a result of the accelerative options selected. Since it is likely that the students in Groups 1 and 2 also took more difficult courses (e.g., Advanced Placement courses are usually the most difficult a high school offers), the achievement of these students in terms of grades is even more impressive.

Academic awards and special accomplishments were also considered. There were no significant differences between the groups in National Honor

Table 1   Means and Standard Deviations of Selected Variables by Group

Variable	Group 1			Group 2			Group 3			Group 4		
	Mean	s.d.	N	Mean	s.d.	N	Mean	s.d.	N	Mean	s.d.	N
SAT-M	743	46	132	741	48	268	705	65	44	698	59	38
SAT-V	658	71	133	666	69	268	642	68	44	632	86	38
TS SAT-M*	579	81	142	548	64	276	510	52	49	519	49	40
TS SAT-V**	467	75	142	453	71	276	433	57	49	439	85	40
College Board Achievement Tests	708	51	88	699	51	196	700	50	19	690	48	18
Grade Point Average	3.7	.4	141	3.8	.3	276	3.6	.6	49	3.6	.4	40
Proportion of Semesters of As	.4	.3	136	.4	.3	273	.3	.3	50	.3	.3	39
Special Accomplishments	1.2	1.5	143	1.4	1.4	277	1.3	1.4	50	1.2	1.4	40
Total Awards	2.8	2.3	143	2.5	2.0	277	2.1	2.2	50	2.2	1.9	40
National and State Awards	1.1	1.1	143	.8	1.0	277	.7	1.0	50	.6	.8	40
No. of Types of Activities	4.2	2.2	143	5.3	2.0	277	4.6	2.4	50	4.7	2.1	40
No. of Leadership Activitites	1.3	1.3	143	2.0	1.5	277	1.7	1.7	50	2.0	1.6	40
No. of Offices Held	1.5	1.6	143	2.0	1.8	277	1.9	2.0	50	1.5	1.5	40
Self Esteem	17.2	2.5	138	17.2	2.6	271	17.4	2.6	50	16.4	3.6	39
Locus-of-Control	16.0	2.2	137	16.1	2.1	270	15.9	2.2	50	15.9	2.7	39

*Talent Search SAT-M score
**Talent Search SAT-V score

Society membership. There were also no significant differences in the number of National Merit Finalists in each group, although there were higher percentages in Groups 1 and 2. Finally, few students in any group reported being Presidential Scholars, and the differences were not significant. Group 1 was at a disadvantage for this honor, however, since students who did not complete their senior year would be ineligible. Chi square comparisons were used for these analyses.

Students were also asked the number of school, local, state, and national awards they had won in high school, and no statistically significant differences in the total number of awards reported by each group were found by an ANOVA. Group 1 did win significantly more national and state awards than Group 4, however ($p = .05$) (see Table 1). Special accomplishments were also assessed, including inventing something, making a presentation at a conference, editing a paper or yearbook, writing a published article, working on a special project in art, mathematics, or science, or contributing to an important research project. The average number of accomplishments per student in each group is shown in Table 1. No significant group differences were found. Finally, participation in mathematics or science contests or special honorary programs was considered. Chi square comparisons revealed no significant differences between the groups.

We conclude that few differences were found between any of the groups with regard to special awards and accomplishments. The accelerated students, however, including those who spent less time in high school, appear to have done at least as well as the others in these accomplishments, and Group 1 students won more state and national awards. Moreover, the accelerated students did as well as or better than the non-accelerated students on standardized tests and in high school coursework. Thus, no disadvantages of acceleration were found from these analyses.

EXTRACURRICULAR ACTIVITIES

We were also interested in investigating the effects of acceleration on participation in extracurricular activities. Students were asked if they participated in any of 14 types of school and community activities such as academic clubs, service clubs, student government, performing arts, and athletics, as well as anything else not listed. The mean number of types of activities each group participated in is shown in Table 1. Group 2 participated in significantly more types of activities than Group 1 ($p = .05$). Other comparisons were not significant.

The clubs and activities were also combined according to four categories to determine if the accelerated students were more likely to join a certain type of activity than the nonaccelerated students. The clubs were classified as school clubs, athletics, performing arts, and community organizations. Students were classified as to whether they did or did not participate in each type of activity. Chi square comparisons were then made. Group 2 had the most participants in school clubs (97%, $p = 01$), followed by Group 1 (92%) while Groups 3 and 4 had 86% and 88% participation, respectively. In athletics, Groups 2 and 3 had the most participants (66% and 68%, respectively), and Group 1 the least (53%), but the differences were not significant. In the performing arts, Group 4 had the most participants (70%) followed by Group 2 (64%), while Group 1 had the least (52% $p = .056$). Groups 2 and 3 had the most students involved in community organizations (58% in each compared to approximately 45% for the other two groups) ($p = .05$).

Since these analyses did not measure the extent of commitment to each activity, the students were asked the types of activities in which they had assumed a leadership role. The mean number of leadership activities reported by each group is shown in Table 1. Students may, of course, have been involved in more than one activity in a category, and that was not measured. Still, a significant difference was found. Groups 2 and 4 reported the most leadership areas, with Group 2 being significantly different from Group 1 ($p = .001$). In a separate but related question, Group 2 also reported being an officer in an organization more than any other group, although Group 3 was a very close second. A significant difference was found only between Groups 1 and 2 ($p = 05$).

Although there is some variation in the results, an apparently consistent trend suggests that Group 2 is the most involved in extracurricular activities. The students in Group 1 appear to be somewhat at a disadvantage in this area, although there are indications that they do participate in some activities. Perhaps students who enjoy activities do not choose to accelerate by skipping any of their high school years.

COLLEGE SELECTIVITY

We used Astin and Henson's (1977) College Selectivity Index to measure the level of selectivity of the colleges these students attended. The index is based primarily on the average SAT scores of the students attending. Since the mean SAT scores in all four groups were extremely high, many of these students could be expected to attend selective colleges. A fairly wide range of colleges was found in all four groups. When we looked at the percent of students in each group, however, who attended a college rated among the top 50 in the United States, Groups 1 and 2 had considerably more (62% for Group 1, 56% for Group 2, 28% for Group 3, and 33% for Group 4). A chi square was significant ($p = .001$). It is, of course, impossible to know whether the accelerative options helped students gain admission to more selective colleges, or whether students who choose to accelerate also choose to attend more selective colleges because they have been exposed to a more rigorous educational program and are better motivated toward academic excellence. Still, this finding is clearly supportive of the advantages of acceleration.

GOALS AND ASPIRATIONS

We were also interested in examining the goals and aspirations of the students in the four groups. The students were asked the academic degrees they planned to earn. Relatively few students did not plan to earn at least a Bachelor's degree. The differences were more apparent at higher levels. When law, medicine, and PhD degrees were combined, 49% of Group 1 and 46% of Group 2 planned to earn a degree at this level, compared to 20% of Group 3 and 23% of Group 4. The chi square was significant ($p = .001$).

The importance of particular goals was also assessed, with students indicating whether these goals were "very," "somewhat," or "not" important to them. Chi square comparisons revealed no differences among the groups on any of the following goals: being successful in work, having lots of money, having strong friendships, finding steady work, being a leader in the community, being able to give your children better opportunities, living close to relatives, correcting social inequities, having leisure time, or having children. "Getting away from this area of the country" was somewhat more important for Group 4 than the other groups ($p = .01$), and marriage and a happy family life were somewhat less important for Group 1 than the other groups. Students were also asked to anticipate their workstyle plans in terms of combining a career and a family, i.e., whether they would work full-time always, part-time always, full-time until they had children, etc. There were seven possible combinations. No important differences were found as the majority in all groups selected the full-time options.

Thus, few differences were found with regard to lifestyle plans and goals, but Groups 1 and 2 did have higher educational goals than Groups 3 and 4. The greater desire of some of these students to earn higher degrees may have contributed to their greater willingness to accelerate. It is also possible that more challenging and appropriate educational experiences as a result of accelerative options have stimulated higher aspirations.

SOCIAL AND EMOTIONAL CHARACTERISTICS

Since the social and emotional adjustment of accelerated students has been of great concern, items were included on the questionnaire that were designed to measure the subjects' feelings about their own self-worth and their ability to control the direction of their lives. The items used were obtained from the sophomore questionnaire of the National Longitudinal Study sponsored by the National Center for Education Statistics (Conger, Peng & Dunteman, 1976; Peng, Fetters & Kolstad, 1981). To improve reliability, four items were combined to form a self esteem scale, and four items were combined to form a locus-of-control scale. The reliabilities of these scales were assessed using Cronbach's coefficient alpha and were found to be .82 for the self esteem scale and .46 for the locus-of-control scale. Analysis of variance comparing the four groups on these scales revealed no significant differences (see Table 1).

Items derived from the Cattell 16 Personality Factors Questionnaire (Cattell & Butcher, 1968) were included on the questionnaire to assess personality traits. Each item was presented as a scale from 0 to 10, with one extreme of the trait represented as 0 and the other extreme represented as 10. Using ANOVA, no significant differences were found among the groups on any of the items, with one exception. This item ranged from "conservative, stick to established methods" to "radical, willing to experiment." Group 1 had the highest mean score, which indicated that they were the most willing to experiment, and it was significantly different from Group 2. This finding is compatible with the fact that Group 1 was willing to accelerate the most radically of the four groups.

Although the Adjective Check List had been administered only to the group of students identified in 1976, we decided to use those scores in this study because it is standardized and would provide additional validation of our other findings with regard to social and emotional adjustment. On the ACL, the groups were compared on the favorable and unfavorable adjectives checked, the 15 Need Scales, and the Topical Scales of Self Control, Self Confidence, Personal Adjustment, and Ideal Self. There were no significant differences using ANOVA on any of these scales.

On the variables investigated, therefore, no personality differences were evident among the four groups, and no harmful social and emotional effects of acceleration were demonstrated. The only difference found was that Group 1 was less conservative than Group 2, which may partially explain that group's willingness to accelerate.

DISCUSSION

This study investigated the relationships between acceleration and academic achievement, extracurricular activities, goals and aspirations, and social and emotional adjustment for highly able students who have selected accelerative options to varying degrees. The students were identified in SMPY's talent searches as being extremely talented mathematically and/or verbally and were followed up several years later. For this study, the subjects were assigned to one of four groups on the basis of the type of acceleration they had chosen during high school, Group 1 was the most accelerated and participated in some grade skipping; Group 2 took AP or part-time college courses which should have resulted in some college credit, but they did not skip any grades; Group 3 had some subject matter acceleration, special classes, or tutoring, but we had no reason to believe they had received any credit for the experiences; and Group 4 reported no acceleration.

This study did not reveal any harmful effects as a result of acceleration. In all areas of academic achievement, the accelerated students in Groups 1 and 2 did as well as or better than the students in Groups 3 and 4. Even in the area of special awards and accomplishments, the accelerated students did as well, and Group 1 earned more state and national awards in spite of skipping a grade sometime between 8th grade and the end of high school and having less time in which to earn such awards. Moreover, a larger proportion of students in Groups 1 and 2 attended highly selective colleges than in Groups 3 and 4.

In extracurricular activities, Group 1 was at a disadvantage; Group 2 generally seemed to be the most involved in activities. It is possible that students who skip a grade and are therefore younger than their classmates do not feel comfortable joining the older students in activities. A large proportion of the Group I students did participate in some type of school club, however, so this does not appear to be the problem. It is more likely that narrower interests or less free time contributed to these students being involved in fewer activities.

Few differences were found in general lifestyle goals, but important differences were found in educational goals. More students in Groups 1 and 2 planned to earn PhDs or degrees in law or medicine. Possibly the goal of an advanced degree encourages students to accelerate, since they plan to spend more years in school.

Finally, no differences were found among the groups on the variables studied for evidence of social and emotional adjustment. There was no evidence that acceleration produced negative effects in this area. This finding is particularly important, since those who oppose acceleration primarily fear social and emotional maladjustment.

The four groups studied were not exactly comparable in ability, although all were clearly capable of a high level of achievement. The students who subsequently accelerated were somewhat abler mathematically and slightly superior verbally as evidenced by their SAT scores in the talent search. This may be considered a limitation of the study that limits the generalizability of the results.

The benefits of acceleration for students, schools, and society are many. For the student, accelerative strategies offer the opportunity to select an educational program that is challenging and that meets the needs of the individual student. This may not mean grade-skipping; some students may choose to accelerate in only one subject area, for example. The advantage is that acceleration offers many more options for meeting individual needs than any one program can, or it can be used as a supplement to a special program. For schools, acceleration offers a way to challenge highly able students without the expense and effort of designing a special curriculum. For society as a whole, it offers the promise of stimulating gifted youths to achieve more at a younger age and, thus, be more productive members of society for more years.

REFERENCES

Astin, A. W., & Henson, J. W. (1977). New measures of college selectivity. *Research in Higher Education, 6*, 1–9.

Cattell, R. B., & Butcher, H. J. (1968). *The prediction of achievement and creativity.* Indianapolis: Bobbs-Merrill.

Conger, A. J., Peng, S. S., & Dunteman, G. H. (1976). *National longitudinal study of the high school class of 1972: Group profiles on self-esteem, locus of control, and life goals.* Research Triangle Park, NC: Research Triangle Institute.

Daurio, S. P. (1979). Educational enrichment versus acceleration: A review of the literature. In W.C. George, S. J. Cohn, & J. C. Stanley (eds.), *Educating the gifted: Acceleration and enrichment.* Baltimore, MD: Johns Hopkins University Press, 13–63.

Fund for the Advancement of Education. (1979). A summing up. In W.C. George, S.J. Cohn, & J. C. Stanley (Eds.), *Educating the gifted: Acceleration and enrichment.* Baltimore, MD: Johns Hopkins University Press, 138–161. (reprinted from *They went to college early*, Evaluation Report No. 2, Fund for the Advancement of Education, Ford Foundation, New York, April 1957).

Gough, H. G., & Heilbrun, A. B. (1980). *The adjective checklist manual.* Palo Alto, CA: Consulting Psychologists Press, Inc.

Hobson, J. R. (1963). High school performance of underage pupils initially admitted to kindergarten on the basis of physical and psychological examinations. *Educational and Psychological Measurement, 23* (1), 159–170.

Kulik, J. A., & Kulik, C. C. (1984). Effects of accelerated instruction on students. *Review of Educational Research, 54*, 409–425.

Peng, S. S., Fetters, W. B., & Kolstad, A. J. (1981). *High school and beyond*. Washington, DC: National Center for Education Statistics.

Pollins, L. M. (1983). The effects of acceleration on the social and emotional development of gifted students. In C. P. Benbow & J. C. Stanley (Eds.), *Academic precocity: Aspects of its development*. Baltimore, MD: Johns Hopkins University Press.

Pressey, S. L. (1949). *Educational acceleration: Appraisal and basic problems*. Bureau of Educational Research Monographs, No. 31. Columbus: The Ohio State University Press.

Robinson, H. B. (1983). A case for radical acceleration: Programs of the Johns Hopkins University and the University of Washington. In C. P. Benbow & J. C. Stanley (Eds.), *Academic precocity: Aspects of its development*. Baltimore, MD: Johns Hopkins University Press.

Stanley, J. C. (1978). Educational non-acceleration: An international tragedy. *G/C/T*, May-June, Issue No. 3, 2–5, 53–57, 60–64.

Stanley, J. C. (1985a). Young entrants to college: How did they fare? *College and University, 60* (3, Spring), 219–227.

Stanley, J. C. (1985b). How did six highly accelerated gifted students fare in graduate school? *Gifted Child Quarterly, 29* (4, Fall), 180.

Stanley, J. C., & Benbow, C. P. (1982). Educating mathematically precocious youths: Twelve policy recommendations. *Educational Researcher, 11* (5), 4–9.

Stanley, J. C., & Benbow, C. P. (1983a). Intellectually talented students: The key is curricular flexibility. In S. Paris, G. Olson, & H. Stevenson (Eds.), *Learning and motivation in the classroom*. Hillsdale, NJ: Erlbaum, 259–281.

Stanley, J. C., & Benbow, C. P. (1983b). Extremely young college graduates: Evidence of their success. *College and University, 58* (4, Summer), 361–371.

Stanley, J. C. & McGill, A. M. (1986). More about "young entrants to college: How did they fare?" *Gifted Child Quarterly, 30* (2, Spring), 70–73.

7

Educational Decision Making on Acceleration and Grouping

Joyce VanTassel-Baska

College of William and Mary

This article provides an overview of key issues emanating from research and practice on acceleration and grouping. The author focuses on the fundamental importance of these two provisions for the gifted, examines them in the current context of school reform, and recommends a set of decision-making guidelines for practitioners to adopt for each issue. Acceleration guidelines include an emphasis on progressive development of learning based on mastery in content areas, flexibility in entrance and exit requirements for courses, and opportunities for telescoping and grade skipping. Grouping guidelines stress flexibility opportunities for various forms of grouping, and independent learning options.

Editor's Note: From VanTassel-Baska, J. (1992). Educational decision making on acceleration and grouping. *Gifted Child Quarterly*, *36*(2), 68-72. © 1992 National Association for Gifted Children. Reprinted with permission.

In response to social-political demands, education has embarked on a course of school reform that affects organizational and curricular structures for all students. Calls for higher achievement levels, increased capacity of students to think, and greater emphasis on accommodating to cultural and social diversity have led educational personnel to make at least surface changes in how schools are organized. These changes have been most notable in the areas of grouping and classroom strategies.

How does gifted education fit into this scheme? One direction that gifted education has explored in the current climate of school reform is that of blending in with the movement for heterogeneous grouping and cooperative learning. One such example is the thrust toward redefining the role of teachers for the gifted as cooperative teachers in the regular classroom; they often demonstrate lessons and assist the regular classroom teacher in planning for gifted children (VanTassel-Baska, Landrum, & Peterson, in press). This blending strategy may be appeasing in the local context, but the overall impact of such diffused efforts on gifted education may well be detrimental. This strategy may detract from achieving what is basic to a quality gifted program, namely acceleration and ability grouping. These approaches are fundamental and must be attended to in some form in order to ensure that programs are meaningful for this special group of learners. A major thesis of this paper is, therefore, that acceleration and grouping are the lightning rod issues that test the level of acceptance that gifted programs enjoy in a local school district. The greater the commitment to serving gifted students, the greater the acceptance of advancing and grouping them appropriately.

ACCELERATION AND GROUPING: DEFINITIONS AND CONTROVERSY

Educators and parents have a fallacious conception of what acceleration means. Too frequently it is perceived as an intervention visited upon children to speed up their program and drive them to graduate from various levels of schooling earlier. Acceleration should refer to the rapid rate of a child's cognitive development, not the educational intervention provided. What we provide in the name of acceleration is appropriate curriculum and services at a level commensurate with a gifted child's demonstrated readiness and need. Elkind (1988) has noted the importance of changing the term better to reflect the intent of this intervention practice (matching learners to appropriate curriculum), thereby avoiding the common connotation of speeding up a student's rate of progress. Unfortunately, many people deny the fundamental role of acceleration in a program for the gifted. In so doing, they are in effect denying who and what defines the gifted at any stage of development—children who exhibit advanced intellectual development in one or more areas.

Ability grouping, on the other hand, should be defined as the organizational mechanism by which students at proximate ability levels within a school curriculum are put together for instruction. Ability grouping allows for individual and group needs to be addressed in a way that honors individual differences. Without grouping in some form, differentiated curriculum is difficult if not impossible to accomplish. Thus, to reject the practice of ability grouping is tantamount to denying the special instructional needs of gifted children.

Both acceleration and grouping are integral components of a program designed to meet adequately the learning needs of gifted students. Ironically, in the current educational climate acceleration and grouping are being pitted against each other in absurd ways. Grouping of the gifted is under virulent attack, which has led some writers to stress acceleration (Slavin, 1990). It is considered the one acceptable strategy to use with the gifted. Yet we have little reason to believe that less grouping of the gifted will increase the likelihood of more accelerative opportunities (see Jones & Southern, 1992). Less grouping will more likely promote a unitary approach to program intervention that is predominantly classroom-based and dominated by grade-level outcomes. It might also produce, as Slavin (1986) hypothesized, a "Robin Hood" effect for heterogeneous grouping, wherein the gifted can serve others less fortunate in the learning process. The benefits gifted students accrue from such an approach are not clear.

Putting the Research to Use

The review of relevant studies of acceleration and grouping as well as the policy guidelines provided in this paper may be used by local school districts to implement policies regarding these basic provisions for gifted learners. It is suggested that written policy be adopted by local boards of education to ensure consistent procedures of implementation within and across individual school buildings.

LEARNING THEORY ISSUES

What is the rationale for using accelerative and grouping strategies with gifted students? Acceleration and grouping of the gifted fits well with our understanding of learning and developmental theories and research. Csikszentmihalyi (1988) found that high IQ students were able to handle about twice as many challenging tasks as average IQ students. Bloom (1985) observed that high-level talent development is nurtured through exposure to progressively more complex tasks in a prestructured continuum of learning experiences based upon mastery and readiness. This model for talent development was found effective regardless of talent domain. Dweck and Elliot (1983) also demonstrated the relationship between positive achievement motivation and task difficulty at a challenging level. For gifted students to be sufficiently motivated to achieve and ultimately be capable of achieving at very high levels, acceleration or grouping that is flexible, based on individual student need, and carefully organized is a necessary aspect of gifted programming.

However, principles of learning theory that we painstakingly apply to other segments of the school population still are not applied equally to the gifted. Concepts such as learning readiness, continuous progress, and challenge levels for learning are seen as important when designing curriculum for typical students. Yet they are in danger of becoming empty concepts unless they develop meaning for the gifted as well. The gifted cannot be served appropriately until schools are willing to accelerate learning as needed by individuals and groups of gifted children. The gifted also cannot be served well without some form of grouping that provides for appropriate level activities. Whether the design be cross-grade cluster grouping, instructional grouping, or cooperative grouping, the opportunity for socialization of the gifted with other gifted students for at least part of the school day must be provided. This provision is critical for social as well as cognitive development. To do less is to continue to deny relevant educational services for this population.

ACCELERATION: AN OVERVIEW OF RESEARCH AND PRACTICE

Perhaps more has been written about the efficacy of accelerative practices with the gifted than about any other single educational intervention with any population. Reviews of the literature on acceleration have appeared with some regularity over the last 25 years (Benbow, 1991; Daurio, 1979; Gallagher, 1969; Kulik & Kulik, 1984; Reynolds, Birch, & Tuseth, 1962; VanTassel-Baska, 1986). Each review has carefully noted the overall positive impact of acceleration on gifted individuals at various stages in the life span. Successful programs of acceleration, most notably offshoots of the basic talent search model developed by Stanley and others in the 1970s, have demonstrated significant positive impact on the learning of students (Benbow & Stanley, 1983; Kulik & Kulik, 1992; Swiatek & Benbow, 1991a, 1991b). Moreover, a broad-based research agenda has emerged in the field of gifted education, dedicated to understanding the long-term effects of educational acceleration of the gifted (Brody, Assouline, & Stanley, 1990; Brody & Benbow, 1987; Brody & Stanley, 1991; Robinson & Janos, 1986; Swiatek & Benbow, 1991a, 1991b). These recent studies continue to show positive results in cognitive development from acceleration and no negative effects on social emotional development. Brody and Benbow (1987) reported no harmful effects of various forms of acceleration, including grade skipping and advanced course-taking, among SMPY students subsequent to high school graduation. Accelerated students generally earned more overall honors and attended more prestigious colleges. Richardson and Benbow (1990) and Swiatek and Benbow (1991b) subsequently reported no harmful effects of acceleration on social and emotional development or academic achievement after college graduation. Janos et al. (1988) reported no detrimental effects of acceleration on young entrants to college. In another study, Robinson and Janos (1986) found similar adjustment patterns for early entrants in comparison to three equally able nonaccelerated comparison groups, noting only unconventionality as a distinguishing characteristic of the early entrants. In another study of female-only early college entrants, positive personality growth during the accelerated first year of the program was found (Cornell, Callahan, & Loyd, 1991). Finally, Brody et al. (1990) found that among accelerated students the best predictor of college achievement was early and continued Advanced Placement course-taking, suggesting that advanced challenging work on an ongoing basis is a powerful inducement to achievement later.

The theoretical rationale and empirical support would lead one to expect that the world of educational practice would wholeheartedly embrace the concept of acceleration and find diverse ways to employ it effectively in many educational settings. Regrettably, this has not been the case. Instead we have seen a deliberate shunning of this approach by the educational establishment (e.g., Jones & Southern, 1992); Some insight was gained into the dynamics of this situation when the majority of gifted program coordinators themselves were found to be philosophically against the practice (Southern & Jones, 1991). A recent survey of program interventions used with the at-risk gifted (VanTassel-Baska, Patton, & Prillaman, 1991) revealed that acceleration in some form finished fifth behind such approaches as independent study, college coursework, and various enrichment strategies. This relatively low status, coupled with the findings of Jones and Southern (1992), suggest that acceleration is not a routine strategy in gifted programs despite positive research evidence in support of its effectiveness.

GROUPING: AN OVERVIEW
OF RESEARCH AND PRACTICE

Although there is a strong research base for accelerating gifted learners, the evidence favoring grouping of gifted learners is less clear-cut. Interpretations of reviews of research on ability grouping at best see grouping as having modest positive effects on the gifted. Yet so few grouping studies actually focus on the grouping of the gifted that valid conclusions are not easily forthcoming. Even though the reviews of research have limited emphasis on gifted learners (Kulik & Kulik, 1987), the field of gifted education has recently articulated a clear response to the attack on grouping (e.g., Slavin, 1990) through a paper that carefully examines various types of studies on ability grouping (Rogers, 1991). This response clearly supports its use.

Studies suggest that:

1) The achievement of gifted students at both elementary and secondary levels is enhanced by a variety of forms of ability grouping, including instructional

grouping in core academic areas, cross-grade grouping, and special interest grouping (Slavin, 1986). Moreover, the achievement of other groups of learners appears to be unaffected by grouping the gifted in such ways (Kulik & Kulik, 1987, 1992).

2) Grouping by ability produces no significant effect on the self-esteem or general school attitude of any group of students either at elementary or secondary levels. Yet grouping by ability produces a positive attitude toward subject matter for all groups of learners (Kulik & Kulik, 1982, 1984).

3) Ability grouping without curriculum and instructional provisions has no effect on any group of learners (Slavin, 1986). Yet students enrolled full-time in programs for the gifted have shown marked academic gains (Rogers, 1991; Vaughn, Feldhusen, & Asher, 1991). Thus, the benefits of ability grouping appear to be activated through a differentiated instructional plan based on student level of readiness.

4) Cooperative learning models do not enhance the achievement of the gifted unless some form of ability grouping is employed. Mixing low-ability and high-ability students together typically results in no growth for the high-ability group (Slavin, 1986).

5) Low-ability students do not model their behavior on gifted students (Schunk, 1987). Thus, the argument that "mixing" ability groups provides important learning models for less able children cannot be supported.

6) Although the direct effects of grouping may not be discernible, the indirect effects are somewhat convincing. High-ability students are more likely to plan for college and actually attend than other groups (Gamoran & Berends, 1987). Grouping thus demonstrates a positive developmental path for secondary students.

Although ability grouping may have been overused in many school settings, the belief that doing away with it can positively affect either the achievement level or self-concept of any student is highly questionable. To suggest that there is evidence to support the elimination of grouping gifted students is to ignore the existing body of research (see Kulik & Kulik, 1992).

POLICY IMPLICATIONS

The findings revealed by the above review of studies evaluating acceleration and grouping and their rationale have not been ignored by educational and political groups who have a strong stake in educational reform. For example, the 1990 National Governor's Report of the Task Force on Education, while challenging educators to eliminate widespread ability grouping and tracking, specifically states that "eliminating these practices does not require ending special opportunities for students such as the gifted and talented or special education students or Advanced Placement classes" (p. 3). Thus, the current and highly visible educational movement to reduce the practice of ability grouping should not be construed to mean that gifted students should not be grouped in various ways or that programming for gifted and talented learners is inappropriate.

Moreover, educators in responsible positions should not naively believe that anyone would benefit from dismantling grouping practices necessary to provide gifted and talented programs. Educational reform is not about allowing able learners to stagnate in age-grade lock-step classrooms. If schools were willing to adopt flexible models of grouping that allowed student needs rather than administrative fiat or the fashions of the time to dictate practice, the needs of all children might be better met. If schools were as willing to alter instruction based on need as they are willing to move children around administratively, the needs of all children might also be better met. The problem is not ability grouping but rather a lack of flexibility and imagination in the application of educational principles in practice.

Improving the quality of education for all requires that we be sensitive to the needs of all and plan educational experiences accordingly. Equality of opportunity and equality of treatment in education, however, are not the same, nor should they be. In any profession, the needs of the client dictate the nature of the prescription. High-quality services should be available to all, but the nature and organization of those services should vary based on diagnosed need, just as in the medical profession. Education can ill afford to level its services lest the bitter pill of mediocrity be absorbed into the bloodstream of all our students.

ACCELERATION AND
GROUPING: MINORITY STUDENTS

The relationship of acceleration and grouping to minority students needs to be addressed because implicit in the argument against ability grouping is the implication that gifted and talented programming takes away from or negatively affects minority achievement. Gifted students come from all socio-economic, racial, and ethnic groups. African-American writers have eloquently spoken to the need for developing what they called "the talented tenth," the most promising group of students within the culture to carry out leadership roles. Minority achievement programs would do well to heed this advice and focus some of their resources on enhancing the development of high-achieving minority students as gifted education has recently done. The current federal allocation of money for gifted has targeted the identification and programming of underrepresented groups, such as minority students, low-income students, and the handicapped, as a priority need. In fact, developing the potential of gifted students from diverse cultural groups should be a major priority for education in general since these students will become the leaders of the next generation. In this context, it should be noted that national survey data have demonstrated that when socioeconomic status and prior achievement are controlled for, minority students have at least an equal chance of participating in high-track classes at secondary levels (Gamoran, 1990).

The interests of minority students are and can be well served in the context of gifted education. Serving these students effectively, however, requires more attention to individual differences and needs, not less. It also requires more acceleration and grouping, not less.

RESPONSIBLE SCHOOL DECISION MAKING: RECOMMENDATIONS

It should be evident that the central thesis of this paper is that educating our most able learners in appropriate ways is a challenge that this society must take seriously. We can ill afford to foster underachievement, disaffection, and alienation among these students. Even now, international comparisons on achievement, drop-out rates, and delinquency data suggest that a disproportionately high percentage of our most capable learners are not maximizing their abilities.

What decisions should schools be making at this time regarding acceleration and grouping of gifted learners? The following list of recommendations is made in the hope that policies and procedures on acceleration and ability grouping might be adopted by local boards of education sensitive to the nature and needs of the gifted in their communities.

ACCELERATION POLICIES FOR THE GIFTED LEARNER

1. Each learner is entitled to experience learning at a level of challenge, defined as task difficulty level slightly above skill mastery. For gifted learners, this implies the opportunity for continuous progress through the basic curriculum based on demonstrated mastery of prior material. In all planned curriculum experiences for the gifted care must be taken to ensure that students are placed at their instructional level. This level may be determined by diagnostic testing, observation of mastery, or performance-based assessments.

2. Gifted learners should be afforded the opportunity to begin school-based experiences based on readiness and to exit them based on proficiency. Thus, both early entrance and early exit options should be provided. The gifted learner requires a school system to be flexible about when and where learning takes place. Optimally, some students can be best served by a pre-reading program at age 4; other students may be well served by college opportunities at age 16. Individual variables must be honored in an overall flexible system of implementation.

3. Some gifted learners may profit from telescoping 2 years of education into one or by-passing a particular grade level. Provision for such advanced placement should be made based on individual student demonstration of capacity, readiness, and motivation. Placement in actual grade levels should be determined by many factors beyond age. Tailoring learning levels, as well as by-passing them, is another important way to ensure implementation of this policy (Elkind, 1988).

GROUPING POLICIES FOR THE GIFTED LEARNER

1. Grouping of the gifted should be viewed as a fundamental approach to serving them appropriately rather than merely as an organizational arrangement. Grouping gifted students is a basic program provision that should be used in tandem with other provisions, such as curriculum modification, alternative choice of materials, and learning centers.

2. Grouping strategies for the gifted should remain flexible, based on individual needs of both identified and nonidentified learners. Dyads, small instructional groups, cooperative learning groups, and the seminar model all provide important alternatives for teachers to employ depending on the learning task and the readiness of the learner to engage in it.

3. Gifted learners should have the opportunity to interact with others at their instructional level in all relevant core areas of learning in the school curriculum. Usually, this would imply at least instructional grouping in reading and mathematics at the elementary level and special subject area classes and Advanced Placement classes at the secondary level in available course areas. Recommended grouping for science and social studies instruction is also advocated.

4. Gifted learners should be grouped according to special interest areas with other learners who share those interests. Opportunities for small group project work should involve students interested in the same topics or problems. Students then need instruction in the process to be employed in their investigation or a model for constructing their own line of investigation.

5. Gifted learners should have the opportunity for independent learning based on both capacity and interest. Not all work with gifted learners need be carried out in group settings. Their preference for working alone and their capacity to carry out independent work should also be honored and provided for in school settings.

CONCLUSION

This paper has laid out an argument for the use of both acceleration and grouping practices to meet the needs of gifted children. It has also explored school-based policy initiatives necessary to ensure the continuation of gifted programs over the next several years. Although the field of gifted education should continue to participate in ongoing educational reform initiatives, it needs to be clear and vocal about issues that undergird the operational aspects of successful program initiatives. Acceleration and grouping constitute two such areas.

REFERENCES

Benbow, C. P. (1991). Meeting the needs of gifted students through use of acceleration. In M. Wang, M. Reynolds, & H. Walberg (Eds.), *Handbook of special education: Research and practice* (pp. 23–36). New York: Pergamon Press.

Benbow, C. P., & Stanley, J. C. (Eds.). (1983). *Academic precocity: Aspects of its development.* Baltimore, MD: Johns Hopkins University Press.

Bloom, B. (1985). *Developing talent in young people.* New York: Ballantine Books.

Brody, L., Assouline, S., & Stanley, J. (1990). Five years of early entrants: Predicting successful achievement in college. *Gifted Child Quarterly, 34,* 138–142.

Brody, L. E., & Benbow, C. P. (1987). Accelerative strategies: How effective are they for the gifted? *Gifted Child Quarterly 3*(3), 105–110.

Brody, L. E., & Stanley, J. C. (1991). Young college students: Assessing factors that contribute to success. In W. T. Southern & E. D. Jones (Eds.), *Academic acceleration of gifted children* (pp. 102–132). New York: Teachers College Press.

Cornell, D., Callahan, C., & Loyd, B. (1991). Personality growth of female early college entrants: A controlled prospective study. *Gifted Child Quarterly, 35*(3), 135–143.

Csikszentmihalyi, M. (Ed.). (1988). *Optimal experience.* New York: Cambridge University Press.

Daurio, S. P. (1979). Educational enrichment versus acceleration: A review of the literature. In W. C. George, S. J. Cohn, & S. J. Stanley (Eds.), *Educating the gifted, acceleration and enrichment* (pp. 13–53). Baltimore, MD: The Johns Hopkins University Press.

Dweck, C., & Elliot, E. S. (1983). Achievement motivation. In E. M. Hetherington (Ed.), *Handbook of child psychology* (4th ed.) (Vol. 4, pp. 643–691). New York: Wiley.

Elkind, D. (1988). Mental acceleration. *Journal for the Education of the Gifted, 2*(4), 19–31.

Gallagher, J. (1969). Gifted children. In R. L. Ebel (Ed.), *Encyclopedia of education research* (4th ed.) (pp. 537–544). New York: Macmillan.

Gamoran, A. (1990). How tracking affects achievement: Research recommendations. Madison, WI: *Newsletter,* National Center for Effective Secondary Schools, 5(1), 2–6.

Gamoran, A., & Berends, M. (1987). The effects of stratification in secondary schools: Synthesis of survey and ethnographic research. *Review of Educational Research, 57,* 415–435.

Janos, P. M., Robinson, N. M., Carter, C., Chapel, A., Cofley, R., Corland, M., Dally, M., Guilland, M., Heinzig, M., Kehl H., Lu, D., Sherry, D., Stolloff, J., & Wise, A. (1988). A cross-sectional developmental study of the social relations of students who enter college early. *Gifted Child Quarterly, 32*(1), 210–215.

Jones, E., & Southern, T. (1992). Programming, grouping, and acceleration in rural school districts: A survey of attitudes and practices. *Gifted Child Quarterly, 36,* 111–116.

Kulik, C. C., & Kulik, J. A. (1982). Effects of ability grouping on secondary school students: A meta-analysis of evaluation findings. *American Educational Research Journal, 19*(3), 415–428.

Kulik, J. A., & Kulik, C. C. (1987). Effects of ability grouping on student achievement. *Equity and Excellence, 23*(1–2), 22–30.

Kulik, J. A., & Kulik, C. C. (1984). Synthesis of research on effects of accelerated instruction. *Educational Leadership, 42*(2), 84–89.

Kulik, J. A., & Kulik, C. C. (1992). Meta-analytic findings on grouping programs. *Gifted Child Quarterly,* 72–76.

Reynolds, M., Birch, J., & Tuseth, A. (1962). Review of research on early admission. In M. Reynolds (Ed.), *Early school admission for mentally advanced children* (pp. 7–18). Reston, VA: Council for Exceptional Children.

Richardson, T. M., & Benbow, C. P. (1990). Long-term effects of acceleration on the social-emotional adjustment of mathematically precocious youth. *Journal of Educational Psychology, 82,* 464–470.

Robinson, N., & Janos, P. (1986). Psychological adjustment in a college-level program of marked academic acceleration. *Journal of Youth and Adolescence 15*(1), 51–60.

Rogers, K. (1991). *The relationship of grouping practices to the education of the gifted and talented learner.* Storrs, CT: National Research Center on the Gifted and Talented.

Schunk, D. H. (1987). Peer models and children's behavioral change. *Review of Educational Research, 52*(2), 149–174.

Slavin, R. W. (1986). Best-evidence synthesis: An alternative to meta-analytic and traditional reviews. *Educational Researcher, 15*(9), 5–11.

Slavin, R. W. (1990). Ability grouping, cooperative learning, and the gifted. *Journal for the Education of the Gifted, 14,* 3–8.

Southern, W. T., & Jones, E. D. (Eds.). (1991). Academic acceleration of gifted children. New York: Teachers College Press.

Swiatek, M. A., & Benbow, C. P. (1991a). Effects of fast-paced mathematics courses on the development of mathematically precocious students. *Journal for Research in Mathematics Education, 22,* 139–150.

Swiatek, M. A., & Benbow, C. P. (1991b). Ten-year longitudinal follow-up of ability-matched accelerated and unaccelerated gifted students. *Journal of Educational Psychology, 83,* 528–538.

VanTassel-Baska, J. (1986). Acceleration. In J. Maker (Ed.), *Critical issues in gifted education* (pp. 179–196). Rockville, MD: Aspen Publications.

VanTassel-Baska, J., Landrum, M., & Peterson, K. (in press). Cooperative learning for the gifted. *Journal of Behavioral Education.*

VanTassel-Baska, J., Patton, J., & Prillaman, D. (1991). *Gifted youth at-risk.* Reston, VA: Council for Exceptional Children.

Vaughn, V., Feldhusen, J., & Asher, W. (1991). Meta-analysis and review of research on pull-out programs in gifted education. *Gifted Child Quarterly, 35*(2), 92–98.

8

Grouping Gifted Students: Issues and Concerns

John F. Feldhusen and Sidney M. Moon

Purdue University

Gifted and talented students need instruction at a level and pace as well as conceptual complexity commensurate with their advanced levels of ability and achievement. Grouping heterogeneously and providing cooperative learning in heterogeneous groups leads to lowered achievement and motivation as well as poorer attitudes toward school. Academic achievement of American youth is lower than the achievement of youth in many Asian and European countries. If we wish to sustain or increase the academic achievement of American youth they should be grouped for instruction according to ability and achievement levels, but grouping practices should be flexible, and rigid tracking should be avoided.

Do gifted and talented youth learn best under conditions of homogeneous grouping with intellectual peers, cooperative learning in heterogeneous

Editor's Note: From Feldhusen, J. F., & Moon, S. M. (1992). Grouping gifted students: Issues and concerns. *Gifted Child Quarterly, 36*(2), 63-67. © 1992 National Association for Gifted Children. Reprinted with permission.

groups, working alone, or combinations of all the above? Under what instructional grouping conditions do gifted and talented youth develop the necessary motivation and commitment to strive for excellence and high level career goals? These are critical questions facing educators who are developing and administering programs for gifted and talented youth.

Cooperative, learning and heterogeneous grouping are being promoted as panaceas for school problems. People who have worked in schools, however, would find it difficult to envision heterogeneous varsity basketball, football, and baseball teams, or a heterogeneous band comprised of beginning, intermediate, and advanced musicians. Or heterogeneous calculus for all who wish to enroll. Grouping students with similar achievement and talent levels seems to be essential if we wish to help students achieve at levels commensurate with their abilities and sustain or increase their motivation to learn. Motivation suffers when new learning tasks are too easy or too difficult. The level of challenge must be appropriate to students' level of readiness and teachers must concentrate their energies on helping all students master the challenges.

Similarly, cooperative learning seems to be effective in teaching some basic skills, but its value in teaching highly able students is questionable when the cooperative learning groups are heterogeneous (Robinson, 1990). Students of high ability are able to learn more rapidly, to work at advanced levels in the subject matter, and to focus on higher level conceptual content. Thus, grouping them with low or average level achievers cannot help but retard their progress in learning. However, cooperative learning among youth of high ability, focused on high level conceptual material and accelerated to a level and pace appropriate to their precocity, may be a very effective instructional activity.

It is important for educators of the gifted to be knowledgeable about grouping, acceleration, and cooperative learning. The issues are complex; the research evidence needs careful interpretation. If we are to help gifted students maximize their potential, we must grapple with these interrelated concepts.

ISSUES AND PROBLEMS

We are faced with incredible problems of underachievement among gifted youth in America. For example, Darling-Hammond (1990), a professor of Education at the Center for School Reform, Teachers College, who has summarized information about the underachievement of American youth, notes that only 5% of American 17-year-olds can synthesize specialized reading materials, only 6% can solve mathematical problems requiring more than one step, and only 7% can draw conclusions from detailed scientific knowledge. These statistics strongly suggest that many bright students are not reaching their potential.

In addition, bright American students appear to be underachieving when compared to students in other nations. For example, approximately 3% of American students take calculus; four to five times that number do so in other countries (Darling-Hammond, 1990). American gifted students also lag behind those in other countries in the sciences. Out of 13 countries, the most advanced U.S. 12th-graders ranked 9th in physics, 11th in chemistry, and 13th in biology (Darling-Hammond, 1990). In light of these statistics, we can only conclude that gifted high school students in America are not achieving their full potential.

Putting the Research to Use

The research discussed in this article indicates that flexible grouping practices can be beneficial for gifted students. Grouping gifted learners together for instruction can lead to substantial gains in academic performance. Gifted students have unique learning needs that are difficult, if not impossible, to meet in heterogeneous learning environments. They need instruction that is conceptually more complex and abstract than most learners can handle. Gifted students learn better in unstructured environments and benefit from indirect teaching methods. Less able learners, on the other hand, tend to do better with structured learning environments and direct, structured instruction. Sensible grouping practices match student needs with curricular opportunities. For gifted students, sensible grouping practices provide opportunities for interaction with other gifted students in educational environments that are specially designed to meet the unique learning needs of gifted learners.

Numerous reports from the National Assessment of Educational Progress (1988, 1990a, 1990b) also document the low or declining achievement of American youth. Additionally, reports from the International Association for the Evaluation of Educational Achievement (Miller, 1986; Rosier, 1987; Jacobson et al., 1986) present an often dismal picture of the achievement of American youth compared with student achievement in other countries. It is clearly a time for grave concern about the achievement of American youth. Furthermore, as Sederburg and Rudman (1986) have shown in a statewide study in Michigan, there are severe problems of underachievement among youth of high ability as reflected in standardized achievement test scores.

How can educators reverse this situation? How can we help America's gifted and talented youth to achieve their potential? More specifically, what philosophy of grouping and instruction will best help gifted students to develop the motivation and skills necessary for high-level achievement?

The Call for Homogenization

It seems amazing then that, at a time of mass underachievement among American youth, we have serious researchers such as Slavin (1990a) and Oakes

(1990) advocating heterogeneous grouping and opposing ability grouping. Slavin (1990a) says, "I am particularly opposed to any school organization plans in which programs for the gifted create de facto ability grouping" (p. 5). Oakes (1990) says " . . . alternatives [to grouping] should be sought. Such alternatives will require the development of new school organizational schemes that support efforts to provide *equal* [italics added] classroom opportunities" (p. 110).

It is important to recognize that value systems that have little to do with school learning and achievement may be at work in the proposals of some of these scholars, especially Oakes. Oakes (1985) clearly explicates the values that undergird her position on grouping:

> Until a major social reorganization [in America] occurs that results in cultural, political, and economic equity for all groups or until a major reconstruction of schooling takes place in which the educational process encourages individuals to refuse to tolerate an unequal social system, more limited reforms should be attempted to help *equalize* (italics added) the effects of schooling. A reorganization of secondary school grouping patterns appears to be one such necessary reform. (p. 211)
>
> It seems clear that Oakes (1985) is calling for a cultural revolution in America starting with the schools but eventually permeating all aspects of American society. Homogenization of educational experience is advocated primarily as a means to social change. The rush to heterogeneous grouping and cooperative learning is probably heavily influenced by social and political value systems.

Sensible Approaches to Grouping

If we wish to embrace a different set of values based on the best American educational traditions, we must recognize that any time students enter or begin a new unit or topic of instruction they differ widely in their background knowledge, specific aptitudes, learning styles, and motivation to learn in that specific area. Some are ready for fast-paced, high-level, very abstract instruction; for others instruction must be adjusted to fit their particular needs or deficiencies. The aptitudes and achievements of students interact with instructional arrangements and curricula and produce differential learning outcomes, as ATI (aptitude-treatment interaction) research shows (Snow, 1989).

In a summary of ATI research Snow (1989) suggests that it is important to understand the psychological and cognitive differences that more and less able learners bring to the learning situation. More able learners learn better in less structured environments and benefit from indirect, unstructured teaching methods. Less able learners have very different learning needs. They do better with more structured environments and direct, structured instruction. "Direct and complete instruction provides the extensive scaffolding needed to raise the threshold of less able learners" (Snow, 1989, p. 49). However, the very scaffolding that helps raise the threshold of less able learners lowers the threshold of more able ones. If more able learners are forced to learn in an environment designed to meet the needs of less able learners, the more able students tend to become bored and unmotivated (Snow, 1989).

Students also differ in their ability to deal with conceptually complex and abstract curricular material. Gallagher (1966) reviewed research on the new conceptually oriented curricula of the 1960s and concluded that the introduction of conceptually complex material in the sciences and mathematics makes ability grouping almost mandatory. Brighter students are able to grasp such materials far more quickly and completely than their less able peers. In other words, "virtually the only way that a wide range of ability can be tolerated in the classroom is to teach conceptually simple materials" (Gallagher, 1966, p. 16).

Special grouping in the regular classroom and beyond becomes increasingly necessary for students whose achievement levels, aptitudes, learning styles, and motivations are at extremes and whose needs are not met by the regular classroom. The needs increase as students move to higher grade levels and to conceptually more complex and abstract curricula and become more diverse in their achievements. Thus, along with increasing need for grouping comes a need for acceleration of subject matter for highly able and high achieving learners.

Sensible approaches to grouping also require clarity in terminology. In common parlance the terms *tracking* and *grouping* are often used interchangeably. Indeed, much of the current criticism of ability grouping equates grouping and tracking. We believe it would be more helpful to define the two terms carefully in order to make clear the distinctions between rigid and flexible grouping practices.

Tracking ordinarily implies assignment to a special sequence or program of classes with other students of similar general ability for a relatively long period of time. As practiced in many European and Asian schools, students might be assigned to a track as early as the fourth or fifth grade on the basis of test scores. There is usually little or no chance to change tracks thereafter.

Grouping, on the other hand, is, or should be, a flexible process, based mainly on prior achievement levels in particular curricular areas. Thus there might be an advanced group in math, science, or reading. When grouping is used, selection for advanced groups is based on periodic evaluation of student progress in each subject matter area. Movement into and out of special groups is possible at almost any time as youth show new capabilities or fail to perform well in a group assignment.

Good grouping practices are also based in large part on students' own interests and preferences. High level classes in social studies and English, for example, should be open to students who may not make the cut on tests and/or teacher nomination but who are motivated, inclined to work hard, and willing to take chances on a low grade or failure. Counselors should be available to provide guidance to students who are considering enrollment in high-ability classes.

In summary, sensible grouping practices match student needs with curricular opportunities. Some students are capable of moving more rapidly and mastering more complex materials. These students need to be grouped together if they are to achieve their full potential. Sensible grouping practices are flexible and based on periodic reassessment of student progress.

Homogenization attempts to create justice by equal treatment of unequals. We believe this approach is inherently unjust to the most and least able. Justice is achieved not by equality of treatment, but by *equality of opportunity*. With sensible grouping practices, all children are given equal opportunities to participate in advanced and differentiated classes designed to meet the special learning needs of the most able.

RESEARCH EVIDENCE

The research evidence also appears to support the benefits of flexible grouping practices, especially for able and gifted learners. For example, in a series of meta-analytic reviews of the research on ability grouping Kulik and Kulik (1982, 1987, 1990) concluded that ability grouping produces significant academic benefits for students of high ability. Gamoran (1990) also reviewed the literature on grouping, carried out original research on grouping and tracking, and concluded that the achievements of high-ability students decline when they are grouped heterogeneously.

In contrast, Slavin's (1990c) best evidence synthesis of the research on ability grouping at the secondary level concluded that there are no significant benefits. However, the latter review reveals no negative effects either. In fact, even Slavin (1990a) accepts the need for some grouping when he says, " . . . cooperative learning does not require dismantling ability group programs" and "cooperative learning has been used successfully with ability-grouped classes . . ." (p. 7). Elsewhere he suggests within-class ability grouping in mathematics and reading as alternatives to between-class grouping and concludes that " . . . there is no evidence that simply moving away from traditional ability grouping practices will in itself enhance student achievement" (Slavin, 1990c, p. 492). The latter conclusion goes hand in hand with his conclusion that " . . . assignment to the low-ability group is *not* (italics added) detrimental to student learning" (1990c, p. 490).

Slavin (1990b) recognizes the need for grouping for instruction in another context:

> In my ideal world . . . very able students would spend some time in accelerated classes, with the amount of time . . . relatively small in elementary school and increasing gradually through high school. (p. 28–29)

Slavin (1990a) has also supported the need for acceleration of instruction for high-achieving students:

> . . . they [programs for the gifted] are most justifiable when the content of the special program represents true acceleration, or in any case a

markedly different curriculum which would be inappropriate for average or low achievers. (p. 4).

Although Slavin (1990a) believes that enrichment programs do not produce achievement benefits and has voiced his opposition to ". . . enrichment programs such as ones in which gifted children are allowed to do more experiments, independent reports, field trips, and so on" (p. 5), recent research indicates that enrichment programs can result in significant learning for gifted students. For example, a meta-analytic synthesis of research by Vaughn, Feldhusen, and Asher (1991) showed significant gains in achievement and thinking skills for gifted youth enrolled in pull-out enrichment programs, and a retrospective study of the PACE pull-out enrichment program found substantial long-term benefits had accrued to students who participated in the program in elementary school (Moon, 1991; Moon & Feldhusen, in press).

Allen (1991) has analyzed and reviewed the meta-analyses of Slavin (1990c) and Kulik and Kulik (1990) with particular reference to decision making in school settings and the academic achievement of gifted or high-ability students. She concludes that "gifted and high-ability children show positive academic effects from some forms of homogeneous grouping" (p. 64). She goes on to point out that the effects of grouping result from the acceleration and special curriculum that can be provided in such classes. The linkage among grouping, acceleration, and differentiated curriculum is an essential aspect of the instructional service that produces higher achievement among gifted and/or high-ability students.

Rogers (in press) has also conducted meta-analyses of the research literature on grouping and has provided a conceptual framework for dealing with a number of issues in the area of grouping. She proposes five fundamental questions to be addressed: (a) What are the grouping options for the gifted? (b) What are the academic effects of grouping? (c) What are the social and psychological effects? (d) What problems are there in grouping the gifted? (e) What are the costs of not grouping? For the first question she suggests that there are many options ranging from full-time programs to within-class ability grouping. Her answer to question two, based on review of the research literature is that " . . . the academic gains are substantial for a wide variety of grouping options for gifted learners." With regard to social and psychological effects there is no pattern of improvement or decline as a result of grouping. A number of problems are noted in her response to question four, especially the low representation of disadvantaged youth in gifted programs. And finally, for question five, she concludes that substantial declines in achievement and attitude of gifted students can be expected from heterogeneous grouping for instruction.

The achievement of gifted and highly able students suffers when grouping methods are abandoned (Gamoran, 1987; Gamoran, 1990; Gamoran & Berends 1987). Brown and Steinberg (1989) have also documented the adverse effects of negative peer pressure on these students. Instruction in high-ability groups or classes is and should be geared to a higher level of cognitive learning; it is more conceptual in nature. The nature and methods of instruction in high-, middle-, and low-ability classes differ as a result of the pattern of interaction between students and teachers. Students bring to school attitudes and behaviors related to learning and subject matter which profoundly affect their responses to schooling (Gamoran & Nystrand, 1990).

Additional support for grouping can be found in Oakes' (1985) description of the high quality of learning which she and fellow researchers observed in high-track classes:

> Students in high track classes saw themselves as being more involved in their classes . . . had significantly more positive attitudes . . . had higher educational aspirations . . . more on-task behavior. (pp. 130–133)

Conversely, these are some of her descriptions of low-track classes:

> Angry and hostile interactions . . . more arguing, yelling, and fighting . . . hostile and disruptive interchanges . . . a student who tends to be off-task, uninterested, noncompliant, and apathetic. . . ." (pp. 126–132)

These large differences in student behavior and response to instruction certainly *would not* lead one to conclude that heterogeneous grouping would solve the problems of underachievement among low-track students, and these differences do raise the specter of classroom conditions that would lower achievement for middle- and high-track students. Furthermore, the management task for teachers becomes nearly impossible or at least terribly discouraging in a mixed class with all the problems noted by Oakes.

Cooperative Learning

Robinson (1990) presented a comprehensive review of the research and practice literature regarding cooperative learning as it relates to gifted and talented students. She noted that most of that research has been focused on low-level, basic skills learning, that the achievements of gifted and talented students in cooperative learning are rarely examined, and that results for higher level learning such as problem solving are contradictory. She also points out that using bright students to teach others can be exploitative, resulting in neglect of the learning needs of talented students, and that many cooperative learning researchers and practitioners mistakenly view intellectually gifted students as social misfits who need socializing.

The fad now is to blame schools and teachers for all the differences between tracks and to advocate heterogeneous grouping and cooperative learning as sure-fire cures. However, there is no longitudinal research to show us what happens to gifted students as a result of heterogeneous grouping nor is there any positive evidence concerning the effects of cooperative learning on the gifted. For now we agree with Kulik and Kulik (1990), who conclude:

Programs of separate instruction for high aptitude and gifted students are usually effective; they are fair to both gifted and talented students and to other students in our schools; and they are necessary if we wish to cultivate our nation's resources of intellectual talent. (p. 191)

CONCLUSION

Schools should not be adopting new grouping or cooperative learning practices without considering their impact on gifted and high-ability students. Appropriate grouping, acceleration of instruction to the students' level of readiness, teachers who can create truly challenging classroom instructional activities and help students rise to the challenges, and association with peers of equal ability in a warmly supportive educational climate free of negative peer pressures—these are the ingredients of excellent instruction for our most able students.

REFERENCES

Allen, S. D. (1991). Ability-grouping research reviews: What do they say about grouping and the gifted? *Educational Leadership, 48*(6), 60–65.

Brown, B. B., & Steinberg, L. (1989). How bright students save face among peers. *Newsletter, National Center for Effective Secondary Schools, 4*(2), 2–8.

Darling-Hammond, L. (1990). Achieving our goals: Superficial or structural reforms. *Phi Delta Kappan, 72*(4), 286–295.

Gallagher, J. J. (1966). [Research summary]. Report to Illinois Superintendent of Public Instruction.

Gamoran, A. (1987). The stratification of high school learning opportunities. *Sociology of Education, 60,* 135–155.

Gamoran, A. (1990). How tracking affects achievement, research and recommendations. *Newsletter, National Center for Effective Secondary Schools, 5*(1), 2–6.

Gamoran, A., & Berends, M. (1987). The effects of stratification in secondary schools: Synthesis of survey and ethnographic research. *Review of Educational Research, 57*(4), 415–435.

Gamoran, A., & Nystrand, M.(1990). Tracking, instruction, and achievement. Paper presented at the World Congress of Sociology, Madrid, Spain.

Jacobson, W. J., Takemura, S., Doran, R. L., Humrich, E., Kojima, S., & Miyake, M. (1986). *Analyses and comparisons of science curricula in Japan and the United States.* New York: Second IEA Science Study—U.S., Teachers College, Columbia University.

Kulik, C. C., & Kulik, J. A. (1982). Effects of ability grouping on secondary school students: A meta-analysis of evaluation findings. *American Educational Research Journal, 19,* 415–428.

Kulik, J. A., & Kulik, C. C. (1987). Effects of ability grouping on student achievement. *Equity and Excellence, 23,* 22–30.

Kulik, J. A., & Kulik, C. C. (1990). Ability grouping and gifted students. In N. Colangelo and G. A. Davis (Eds.), *Handbook of gifted education* (pp. 178–196). Boston: Allyn and Bacon.

Miller, J. (1986). *An analysis of science curricula in the United States.* New York: Second IEA Science Study—U.S., Teachers College, Columbia University.

Moon, S. M. (1991). The PACE program: *A high school follow-up study.* Unpublished doctoral dissertation, Purdue University, West Lafayette, IN.

Moon, S. M., & Feldhusen, J. F. (in press). A follow-up study of an enrichment program for gifted youth based on the Purdue Three-Stage Model. In K. Arnold & R. Subotnik (Eds.), *Beyond Terman: Longitudinal studies in contemporary gifted education.* Norwood, NJ: Ablex.

National Assessment of Educational Progress. (1988). *The mathematics report card, are we measuring up?* Princeton, NJ: Educational Testing Service.

National Assessment of Educational Progress. (1990a). *The reading report card, 1971–1988.* Princeton, NJ: Educational Testing Service.

National Assessment of Educational Progress. (1990b). *The writing report card, 1984–1988.* Princeton, NJ: Educational Testing Service.

Oakes, J. (1985). *Keeping track, how schools structure inequality.* New Haven, CT: Yale University Press.

Oakes, J. (1990). *Multiplying inequalities, the effects of race, social class, and tracking on opportunities to learn mathematics and science.* Santa Monica, CA: Rand Corp.

Robinson, A. (1990). Cooperation or exploitation? The argument against cooperative learning for talented students. *Journal for the Education of the Gifted, 14*(1), 9–27.

Rogers, K. B. (in press). Grouping the gifted and talented: Questions and answers. *Roeper Review.*

Rosier, M. (1987). The Second International Science Study. *Comparative Education Review, 31*(1), 106–128.

Sederburg, W. A., & Rudman, H. C. (1986). Educational reform and declining test scores. *Michigan School Board Journal, 30,* 8–10, 24.

Slavin, R. E. (1990a). Ability grouping, cooperative learning, and the gifted. *Journal for the Education of the Gifted, 14*(1), 3–8.

Slavin, R. E. (1990b). Response to Robinson: Cooperative learning and the gifted: Who benefits? *Journal for the Education of the Gifted, 14*(1), 28–30.

Slavin, R. E. (1990c). Achievement effects of ability grouping in secondary schools: A best evidence synthesis. *Review of Educational Research, 60*(3), 471–499.

Snow, R. E. (1989). Aptitude treatment interaction as a framework for research on individual differences in learning. In P. L. Ackerman, R. J. Sternberg, & R. Glaser (Eds.) *Learning and individual differences* (pp. 13–591). New York: W. H. Freeman.

Vaughn, V. L., Feldhusen, J. F., & Asher, J. W. (1991). Meta-analyses and review of research on pull-out programs in gifted education. *Gifted Child Quarterly, 35*(2), 92–105.

9

Cooperative Learning and Ability Grouping: An Issue of Choice

Carol J. Mills and William G. Durden

The Johns Hopkins University

Cooperative learning has been enthusiastically embraced by schools as a way of addressing many of the ills faced in education. Cooperative learning has been pitted against ability grouping since many of the *strongest supporters of cooperative learning are also the most vocal* critics of ability grouping. The purpose of this article is to clarify some of the issues surrounding, and research supporting, the applications of both cooperative learning and ability grouping. A more balanced, critical approach to the use of a variety of educational practices to meet the varied needs of students is advocated.

Faced with a growing concern about the "fairness" of ability grouping, some parents and schools believe they have no choice but to abolish the practice. This

Editor's Note: From Mills, C. J., & Durden, W. G. (1992). Cooperative learning and ability grouping: An issue of choice. *Gifted Child Quarterly*, 36(1), 11-16. © 1992 National Association for Gifted Children. Reprinted with permission.

movement has been encouraged and fueled by the popular press. For example, the message comes across loud and clear in the lead-in from a news article on ability grouping entitled "Sorting Classmates" which appeared in *The Baltimore Sun* last year: ". . . the time-honored assumptions behind this practice have come under heavy attack. Leading the charge is a growing number of principals, superintendents, and researchers, who say that grouping by ability—and the so-called tracking that often results from it—almost certainly harms many children and probably doesn't do much to help others" (Lally, 1990). The same article quotes Robert Slavin, principal research scientist at The Johns Hopkins University Center for Research on Elementary and Middle Schools: "It's distasteful in a democracy to make these kinds of distinctions about young kids." Finally, the reporter states that Slavin believes "grouping can lead to horrifying consequences."

As so often happens in educational circles, when one practice is called into question or is no longer "politically correct," another emerges as the solution. This year's solution appears to be cooperative learning. The popularity of cooperative learning is riding a crest. Whole schools have labeled themselves "cooperative learning schools" and teachers are flocking to workshops to learn about this "new" practice.

The acceptance of cooperative learning appears to be pervasive and largely uncritical. Even Robert Slavin, an outspoken opponent of ability grouping and proponent of cooperative learning, expressed some concern that "cooperative learning has been suggested as the solution for an astonishing array of educational problems" (Slavin, 1991a, p. 71).

The most disturbing aspect of the current ascendancy of cooperative learning is the accompanying demise of ability grouping. Although the two practices are not mutually exclusive, they have been linked together in educators' minds because the strongest supporters of cooperative learning also tend to be the most vocal critics of ability grouping.

In a recent issue of the *Communicator*, the State Superintendent for Public Instruction of California, Bill Honig, felt compelled to clarify the position of his department on this issue. He wrote, "It has come to my attention that some schools and districts are eliminating advanced classes based on a belief that the California Department of Education is encouraging or requiring heterogeneous grouping of students at all times and for all instructional activities. This is not the case" (Clark, 1990).

Because students have so much to lose if effective instructional options are eliminated, it is imperative to encourage a rational and balanced discussion of this very emotional and public debate. Although the outcome of this controversy has direct implications for a wide variety of students, in this article we will address our comments most directly to the education of academically talented students. Our goal is not to prove the superiority of either cooperative learning or ability grouping as an instructional practice, but rather to clarify some of the issues surrounding the applications of each. As educators, we believe that we should be focusing our energies and attention on ensuring the quality and appropriateness of curriculum and instruction for all learners.

Putting the Research to Use

The current controversy surrounding ability grouping and the ever-increasing popularity of cooperative learning is one that can have long-lasting effects on structure and programming in schools throughout the country. Although the results of these changes will affect all students, the first and most obvious outcome is the abandonment of ability grouping practices and special classes for the highly able. Teachers, parents, administrators, and researchers are urged to take a close and critical look at all of the research currently available on both ability grouping and cooperative learning. The present review of the research suggests that both practices can result in educational benefits for students when implemented within certain parameters. A reasonable and productive response would be to acknowledge the diverse needs of students and embrace a variety of practices, including acceleration and ability grouping in combination with cooperative learning.

ABILITY GROUPING AND COOPERATIVE LEARNING: THE RESEARCH

Both ability grouping and cooperative learning in their various forms have strong research bases to support their effectiveness. There are, however, a number of limitations of the research that should be noted, along with some qualifications about implementation.

Ability Grouping

Ability grouping has been an instructional practice in schools for over 70 years (Miller & Otto, 1930). Although the term has many meanings, in general, ability grouping refers to the grouping of students for instruction by ability or achievement with the purpose of reducing group heterogeneity. Most of the articles discussing the pros and cons of the practice categorize its many forms along two lines: between- and within-class grouping. Between-class grouping would include:

Ability-grouped class assignment (assigning students to one self-contained classroom on the basis of ability or achievement)

Ability grouping for selected subjects (heterogeneous grouping for home-room classes for part or most of the day, with regrouping according to achievement level for one or more subjects; e.g., reading and/or mathematics)

Joplin Plan (a special form of regrouping for reading across grade lines [Floyd, 1954])

Nongraded plans (a variety of grouping plans, usually involving flexible grouping by performance level rather than age, continuous progress instruction, and flexible pacing for individual students through an instructional sequence [Goodlad & Anderson, 1963])

Special classes (classes for students with learning problems and academically talented students)

Within-class ability grouping would include:

Mastery Learning (a form of flexible within-class grouping [Block & Anderson, 1975])

Regrouping by subject (student assignment by achievement or ability level to a small group for instruction in reading or mathematics; similar to between-class grouping for individual subject instruction)

Individualized instruction (each student follows an individual instructional plan, usually allowing for flexible pacing and continuous progress)

When examining the literature on the effects of ability grouping, it is necessary to separate the findings and subsequent discussion according to the type of grouping involved.

Little disagreement exists regarding the positive achievement benefits of regrouping for specific subject areas, whether the regrouping is done between- or within-classes. For example, Slavin (1987b, 1988a) states that research findings support the benefits of grouping when it is done subject-by-subject and the instructional level and pace are adapted to student performance levels. In particular, he points to the effectiveness of the Joplin Plan, in which students are grouped across grade levels for reading, and similar nongraded plans (Hart, 1962) in both reading and mathematics. Previously, Pavan (1973) also reviewed the positive benefits of nongraded plans. A number of studies have shown that individualized instruction (when properly managed) also results in significant positive achievement effects for students (Slavin, 1987c; Slavin, Leavey, & Madden, 1984). Along these same lines, a paper by Slavin and Karweit (1984) clearly concludes that, in general, within-class ability grouping benefits students.

Although Kulik and Kulik (1987) separate the within-class grouping studies designed for mixed-ability students and those specifically designed for academically talented students, they find that achievement effects are uniformly positive. The most substantial gains, however, were found for the academically talented students.

The most controversial of all grouping plans is comprehensive ability grouping with assignment to classes on the basis of general ability or IQ. Some critics also object to special classes for academically talented students, claiming that such classes conflict with America's "democratic ideals" (Oakes, 1985; Slavin, 1987b, 1991b). They do not, however, provide any evidence to show the superiority of heterogeneously grouped, cooperative learning classes over special classes for these students. In fact, in Slavin's most frequently quoted review of ability grouping and student achievement (1987b), he specifically excludes studies of special classes for the gifted.

In several reviews of the research on ability grouping, Kulik and Kulik (1984, 1987, 1989, 1990) report that there are definite academic benefits when grouping is accompanied by curricular and instructional modifications based on student differences. In fact, they find that "academic benefits are striking and large in programs of acceleration for gifted students" (Kulik & Kulik, 1990, p. 191). Slavin (1990a) also admits that grouping students into special classes for the purpose of instructional acceleration benefits the students involved.

In spite of the evidence supporting the effectiveness of ability grouping, claims that there is no support for the practice continue to be made and believed. This belief is fueled by descriptive reviews such as that by Oakes (1985) in which no distinction is made between ability grouping and tracking.

Relying entirely on personal impressions, Oakes concludes that there are no benefits for students in the top "tracks," and students in lower tracks lose academic ground, self-esteem, and ambition. In fact, evidence exists to the contrary. Kulik and Kulik (1982) and Kulik (1985) present evidence that ability grouping can have *positive* effects on student attitudes and self-concept. In general, research indicates that students model their behavior on that of others who are of similar ability and who are coping well in school (France-Kaatrude & Smith, 1985; Schunk, 1987).

Since contradictory and confusing claims regarding the effectiveness of ability grouping (in any form) are often cited by opponents of ability grouping, the reader should be aware of the limitations and deficiencies of the research upon which these claims are made. Although many of these limitations have been addressed in recent reviews (Allan, 1991; Clark, 1990; Fiedler-Brand, Lange, & Winebrenner, 1990; Gamoran, 1987; Hiebert, 1987; Kulik, 1991; Robinson, 1990), the reader may find the following summary useful:

1. Studies showing no achievement benefits for ability grouping do not include classes where students are ability grouped to allow for curriculum acceleration and advanced instruction. For example, as was pointed out above, Slavin in his "best evidence" synthesis (1987b) specifically excluded such classes on the basis that they involve changes in curriculum, goals, and instructional strategies. We would argue that these are the very reasons why such classes should have been included; ability grouping allows such changes to be implemented.

2. The assessment instruments used in these studies to determine achievement gains are limited in their ability to measure the performance of students who routinely score in the top percentiles of standardized tests. For students of

high ability, it is necessary to use "above-level" tests (tests designed for older children) to assess reliably and validly the full extent of their learning (Keating, 1975).

3. One of the most important limitations, however, is that the studies cited make comparisons between heterogeneous and homogeneous groupings within "traditional" classrooms without an accompanying change in curriculum content level or pacing.

This last point is an important one to consider. When students are subjected to the same lock-step, grade-restricted curriculum and teacher-controlled pace of instruction, grouping practices alone cannot be expected to produce differences in achievement. It is not surprising, therefore, that little if any effect is found for ability grouping when both the "treatment" variable (curriculum) and the criterion measure (on-level achievement tests) introduce a ceiling on learning and performance for the highest ability students.

As Gamoran (1987) pointed out in a critique of Slavin's (1987b) review of ability grouping research, none of the studies reviewed distinquish between *organizational structure* (how students are arranged between or within classes) and *instruction* (or the processes occurring within classes or groups). "Grouping does not produce achievement," Gamoran concluded. "Instruction does." This is an important point (and limitation of this line of research) that is often overlooked in the controversy.

In the final analysis, when grouping is done in such a way that heterogeneity is truly reduced (e.g., grouping by achievement or ability in a specific academic area such as reading or mathematics) and instruction is indeed changed to accommodate student needs, the research consistently shows achievement gains (Slavin, 1987b; Kulik & Kulik, 1984, 1990). In fact, this holds for students of all ability and achievement levels, "at-risk" students (Slavin & Madden, 1989) as well as economically disadvantaged and minority students (Lynch & Mills, 1990).

COOPERATIVE LEARNING

In a recent guest editorial in *Educational Leadership*, Slavin (1990c) declares cooperative learning an extraordinary success, referring to its "excellent research base, many viable and successful forms, and hundreds of thousands of enthusiastic adherents." His editorial concludes optimistically, "Cooperative learning is here to stay."

In the most general sense, cooperative learning simply means students working together on a school-related task. There are, however, many different forms of the practice, each designed to achieve specific purposes (Graves & Graves, 1990; Joyce, 1991). Slavin and his colleagues focus mainly on the specific academic content areas and report achievement gains in cooperative learning classrooms (Slavin, 1988b). It is clear, however, that they are also concerned with the social and personal implications of grouping. Johnson and Johnson (1990), on the other hand, address the benefits of cooperation itself.

Some proponents of cooperative learning point out that certain key elements are needed to produce achievement gains. For example, Slavin makes a point of saying that the critical features needed to produce achievement benefits are "group goals" and "individual accountability" (Slavin, 1991a). Although most proponents of cooperative learning advocate forming groups that contain children with widely varying abilities, heterogeneous grouping has never been identified as one of the "necessary" or "key elements." This is an important point since the controversy and debate over ability grouping (to reduce variance) clearly pits the practice against cooperative learning (Slavin, 1991b). Yet, in another recent article, Slavin (1990a) states that "use of cooperative learning does not require dismantling ability group programs" (p. 7). And, as Joyce (1991) points out, "grouping to maximize variance is a matter of choice rather than necessity" (p. 74).

Without taking away from the research base upon which the success of cooperative learning is founded, educators may want to temper their enthusiasm and restore some perspective to the universal application of this approach, especially as it relates to programming for highly able students.

Although researchers are usually careful to point out that the claims made for the superiority of cooperative learning are based on comparisons with *traditional* classrooms, this point is often overlooked. For example, in Slavin's latest synthesis of the studies examining the effectiveness of cooperative learning (1991a), he states quite clearly that these studies are all based on comparisons with "traditionally taught control groups." The claim, therefore, that cooperative learning is the most effective means of serving the needs of all students, even the "gifted," cannot be made since it is not based on a direct comparison between cooperative learning and all other instructional practices. Although some cooperative learning arrangements may be an improvement over traditional approaches, there may be other equally beneficial or, in some cases, more effective educational options. Flexibly paced instruction (Daniel & Cox, 1988), continuous-progress programs (Slavin & Madden, 1989), and ability-grouped classes for subject-matter acceleration all have been shown to be effective instructional methods.

In particular, there is a great deal of research documenting the achievement benefits of curriculum acceleration for academically talented students (Daurio, 1979; Fox, 1979; Kulik & Kulik, 1984, 1990; Lynch, 1990; Petersen, Brounstein, & Kimble, 1988; Sisk, 1988). There is, however, no equivalent research base documenting the superiority of a cooperative learning classroom over an ability-grouped classroom with curriculum acceleration.

It is also important to note that in much of the cooperative learning research the terminology used to identify the populations being studied is often confusing and poorly defined. For example, the term "high ability students" is used interchangeably with "high achievers." Both terms are often used to refer to the top third of a mixed ability class.

Although researchers like Slavin point out that they are not referring to the "gifted" or "extremely able" students (students scoring in the top few percentiles on standardized tests) when they make claims about the superiority of cooperative learning classes over all other options, educators often base decisions about what is best for this population on their writings.

Although cooperative learning does appear to have some potential for improving classroom instruction, those who elect to adopt it as an option for their classroom should be aware of the limitations of the practice. Not all forms of cooperative learning have been shown to have positive benefits, even when compared to "traditional" instructional practices (Ross, 1988; Slavin, 1988a, 1991a). As Sapon-Shevin and Schniedewind (1990) warn, ". . . simply because a lesson is implemented cooperatively does not assure its value. Using cooperative techniques to have students cover the same boring, inconsequential, or biased material or to have them 'get through' worksheets with more efficiency doesn't demonstrate the approach's full potential for changing what goes on in schools" (p, 64). And yet this is exactly what is happening in many cooperative learning classrooms across the country when teachers must find a group project for students with widely varying abilities and skill levels.

Like any educational practice, both ability grouping and cooperative learning are vulnerable to abuse (Clark, 1990; Gamoran, 1987; Robinson, 1990; Slavin, 1990b). The effectiveness of a particular strategy depends largely on how it is implemented in an individual school, class, or system. Expectations should be high for all students; underexpectation is an intolerable practice. The organization of the system should be flexible enough to allow for a variety of instructional options to meet the needs of individual students. If grouping is used, regrouping on the basis of student performance should be the norm. The quality of instruction should be uniform across all ability and achievement levels. Finally, a standard, intellectually engaging curriculum should be required of all students with support programs (both in-and out-of-school) to make sure that they are able to complete successfully the requirements of the program. On the other hand, opportunities for an accelerated pace of learning through the curriculum, as well as opportunities for students to "enrich" their learning beyond this commonly shared standard, should be available to all students.

In the final analysis, the surest road to inappropriate use of any practice is to mandate that it be used to solve all problems and meet all needs. Used appropriately and optionally, either in combination or alone, cooperative learning and ability grouping are both useful educational practices.

What Can We Conclude?

After a close examination of the research, one can conclude that grouping, in and of itself, does not affect achievement. Simply putting students of different or similar abilities together does not ensure that more or less learning will take place. Rather, it is the appropriateness of the content and instruction that accompanies the grouping that determines the educational outcomes for students.

The benefits of grouping of any kind emerge only through the implementation of a differentiated instructional plan based on the individual student's level of readiness. Although this can theoretically be accomplished in cooperative learning groups with students of widely differing abilities, it is most efficiently and effectively done through some form of grouping by ability and/or knowledge levels. This is especially the case when curriculum acceleration is necessary to meet the needs of a student with exceptional ability in a specific content area. One of the most obvious advantages of ability grouping is that it allows highly able students to move ahead in their studies at a faster pace than would be possible otherwise.

"Educators should be realistic about individual differences. Teaching students what they already know or are as yet incapable of knowing wastes effort . . . ." (Walberg, 1989, p. 5). When students with exceptional ability in a specific content area are grouped with students of similar ability and then provided with opportunities for appropriate curricular acceleration, they demonstrate substantial achievement gains (Brody & Benbow, 1987; Kulik & Kulik, 1984, 1990; Lynch, 1990; Moore & Wood, 1988; Stanley, 1973, 1976). In one of his latest articles, even Slavin clearly states that for the highest ability students some form of acceleration is necessary (1990a).

Slavin, however, would severely limit the number of students participating in accelerated programs and would prefer to meet their needs in the cooperative learning situation in the regular classroom through programs like "Team Assisted Individualization" (TAI) and "Cooperative Integrated Reading and Composition" (CIRC). But this is unrealistic. If these highly able students are truly allowed to move ahead in their learning, the gap between them and others in the class will widen to the point where heterogeneously grouped cooperative learning situations will no longer be educationally beneficial for any of the students involved. Students who are several grade levels apart in their learning of a subject are rarely able to contribute equally or feel engaged in a group endeavor.

The message is clear. Differentiated instruction, accelerated pacing, and advanced level material that goes beyond arbitrary grade level cut-offs are essential. If held to the pace and level of instruction typical for their grade level—even with the advantages of cooperative learning techniques—highly able students (those who are in the very top percentiles in comparison to national norms) will not realize their full potential (Feldhusen, 1989; Willis, 1990).

The point is that abandonment of all forms of (homogeneous) ability grouping and the wholesale, uncritical acceptance of cooperative learning (in any form) is at the very least premature, and most likely unwarranted. Many of the appropriate comparisons have not been made and the research is often confusing at best. Depending on who is doing the looking, the same set of research findings can be interpreted in very different ways and diametrically opposed conclusions can be reached. And, unfortunately, the conclusions are often based on ideology rather than research. Witness this statement by Slavin: ". . . separating students by ability goes against the grain of our democratic, egalitarian ideals. . ." (1987b, p. 325)

INDIVIDUAL DIFFERENCES AND THE VALUE OF CHOICE

The debate over which is better—cooperative learning or ability grouping—is diverting our attention away from the acknowledgment of individual differences, the necessity of making educational choices according to students' needs, and the important topic of *what* is to be taught. Although the desire to find one simple solution to all of our educational problems is understandable, it is unrealistic given the complexity of the issues and the diversity of student needs.

Students differ in many ways and their educational needs are quite different. Our only hope of meeting these individual needs is to consider a variety of educational practices carefully and critically, implement them responsibly, and then evaluate their effectiveness for our particular situation. For teachers to give up this responsibility and privilege is to diminish their standing as professionals.

Cooperative learning is a viable and reasonable educational practice that should be considered, along with a variety of other possibilities. There are some logical and quantifiable benefits attached to its use, and it is intuitively appealing to many. We do not believe, however, that it *alone* can best meet the needs of highly able students, or of any other students. And, it is not inherently more "American" or morally/ethically valuable than other practices. Other options, including ability grouping in a variety of forms, acceleration, and special classes should be a part of any educational system that purports to serve the needs of all students. Slavin (1990a) is correct when he states: "We must move toward the use of instructional programs which accommodate the diverse needs of all learners so that all, including the 'gifted,' can achieve their full potential" (p. 7). Fully embracing such a position requires that individual learning and cooperative learning, as well as other valid strategies, co-exist. Since ability grouping and cooperative learning can be used effectively in combination or alone, there is no reason for a school to feel compelled to choose one over the other. Educators should be given the professional freedom to choose which method to apply and when to apply it, for choice has long been an American educational tradition.

Instead of making decisions on the basis of what is most expedient, or what is most "politically correct," we believe that educators should look at what is best for each student—high as well as low ability, high achieving as well as low achieving, regardless of racial or ethnic background. In this way we may have a chance of achieving the ideal of an "optimal match" (Robinson & Robinson, 1982) between each student's educational needs and the system based on demonstrated ability, achievement, and interest. Such an ideal is consistent with the original design of American education in which students were encouraged to proceed "from textbook to textbook at their own pace," and where flexibility, compromise, individual strengths, and community spirit were equally respected (Cremin, 1970).

REFERENCES

Allan, S. D. (1991). Ability-grouping research reviews: What do they say about grouping and the gifted? *Educational Leadership, 48*(6), 60–74.

Block, J. H., & Anderson, L. W. (1975). *Mastery learning in classroom instruction.* New York: Macmillan.

Brody, L. E., & Benbow, C. P. (1987). Accelerative strategies: How effective are they for the gifted? *Gifted Child Quarterly, 3*, 105–110.

Clark, B. (1990). An update on ability grouping and its importance for gifted learners. *Communicator, 20*(5), 1, 20–21.

Cremin, L. A. (1970). *American education: The colonial experience 1607–1783*, New York: Harper Torchbooks.

Daniel, N., & Cox, J. (1988). *Flexible pacing for able learners*, Reston, VA: The Council for Exceptional Children.

Daurio, S. P. (1979). Educational enrichment vs. acceleration: A review of the literature. In W. C. George, S. J. Cohn, & J. C. Stanley (Eds.), *Educating the gifted: Acceleration and enrichment* (pp. 13–63). Baltimore, MD: Johns Hopkins University Press.

Feldhusen, J. (1989). Synthesis of research on gifted youth. *Educational Leadership, 54*(6), 6–12.

Fiedler-Brand, E., Lange, R., & Winebrenner, S. (1990). Tracking, ability grouping, and the gifted: Myths and realities. Glenview, IL: lllinois Association for Gifted Children.

Floyd, C. (1954). Meeting children's reading needs in the middle grades: A preliminary report. *Elementary School Journal, 55*, 99–103.

Fox, L. (1979). Programs for the gifted and talented: An overview. In A. Passow (Ed.), *The gifted and talented: Their education and development.* (pp. 104–126). Chicago: University of Chicago Press.

France-Kaatrude, A., & Smith, W. P. (1985). Social comparison, task motivation, and the development of self-evaluative standards in children. *Developmental Psychology, 21*, 1080–1089.

Gamoran, A. (1987). Organization, instruction, and the effects of ability grouping: Comment on Slavin's "Best-Evidence Synthesis." *Review of Educational Research, 57*(3), 341–345.

Goodlad, J. I., & Anderson, R. H. (1963). *The nongraded elementary school* (rev. ed.). New York: Harcourt, Brace, & World.

Graves, N., & Graves, T. (1990). *Cooperative learning: A resource guide.* Santa Cruz, CA: The International Association for the Study of Cooperation in Education.

Hart, R. H. (1962). The nongraded primary school and arithmetic. *The Arithmetic Teacher, 9*, 130–133.

Hiebert, E. H. (1987). The context of instruction and student learning: An examination of Slavin's assumptions. *Review of Educational Research, 57*(3), 337–340.

Johnson, D. W., & Johnson, R. T. (1990). *Cooperation and competition: Theory and research.* Edina, MN: Interaction Book Company.

Joyce, B. R. (1991). Common misconceptions about cooperative learning and gifted students. *Educational Leadership, 48*(6), 72–74.

Keating, D.P. (1975). Testing those in the top percentiles. *Exceptional Children, 41*(6), 435–436.

Kulik, C.-L. C. (1985, August). Effects of inter-class ability grouping on achievement and self-esteem. Paper presented at the 93rd annual convention of the American Psychological Association, Los Angeles, CA.

Kulik, J. A. (1991). Findings on grouping are often distorted: Response to Allan. *Educational Leadership, 48*(6), 67.

Kulik, J. A., & Kulik, C.-L. C. (1982). Effects of ability grouping on secondary school students: A meta-analysis of evaluation findings. *American Educational Research Journal, 19*, 415–428.

Kulik J. A., & Kulik, C.-L. C. (1984). Effects of accelerated instruction on students. *Review of Educational Research, 54*, 409–425.

Kulik, J. A., & Kulik, C.-L. C. (1987). Effects of ability grouping on student achievement. *Equity and Excellence, 23*, 22–30.

Kulik, J. A., & Kulik, C.-L. C. (1990). Ability grouping and gifted students. In N. Colangelo & G. A. Davis (Eds.) *Handbook of Gifted Education*, Boston, MA: Allyn & Bacon.

Lally, K. (1990, May 13). Sorting schoolmates. *The Sun*, pp. 1A, 10A.

Lynch, S. (1990). Fast-paced science for the academically talented: Issues of age and competence. *Science Education, 74*(6), 585–596.

Lynch, S., & Mills, C. (1990). The skills reinforcement program (SRP): An academic program for high potential minority youth. *Journal for the Education of the Gifted, 13*(4), 363–379.

Miller, W. S., & Otto, H. J. (1930). Analysis of experimental studies in homogeneous grouping. *Journal of Educational Research, 21*, 95–102.

Moore, N. D., & Wood, S. S. (1988). Mathematics with a gifted difference. *Roeper Review, 10*(4), 231–234.

Oakes, J. (1985). *Keeping track*. New Haven CT: Yale University Press.

Pavan, B. N. (1973). Good news: Research on the nongraded elementary school. *Elementary School Journal, 73*, 333–342.

Peterson, N., Brounstein, P., & Kimble, J. (1988). Evaluation of college-level coursework for gifted adolescents: An investigation of epistemological stance, knowledge gain and generalization. *Journal for the Education of the Gifted, 12*, 46–61.

Robinson, A. (1990). Cooperation or exploitation? The argument against cooperative learning for talented students. *Journal for the Education of the Gifted, 14*(1), 9–27.

Robinson, N. M., & Robinson, H. B. (1982). The optimal match: Devising the best compromise for the highly gifted student. In D. Feldman, (Ed.), *New directions for child development: Developmental approaches to giftedness and creativity*, pp. 79–94. San Francisco: Jossey Bass.

Ross, J. (1988). Improving social-environmental studies problem solving through cooperative learning. *American Educational Research Journal, 25*(4), 573–591.

Sapon-Shevin, M., & Schniedewind, N. (1990). Selling cooperative learning without selling it short. *Educational Leadership, 47*(4), 63–65.

Schunk, D. H. (1987). Peer models and children's behavioral change. *Review of Educational Research, 57*(2), 149–174.

Sisk, D. (1988). The bored and disinterested gifted child: Going through school lockstep. *Journal for the Education of the Gifted, 11*(4), 5–19.

Slavin, R. (1987a). Grouping for instruction in the elementary school. *Educational Leadership, 22,* 109–127.

Slavin, R. (1987b). Ability grouping and student achievement in elementary schools: A best evidence synthesis. *Review of Educational Research, 57*(3), 293–336.

Slavin, R. (1987c, November). Cooperative learning and individualized instruction. *Arithmetic Teacher,* pp. 14–16.

Slavin, R. (1988a). Synthesis of research on grouping in elementary and secondary schools. *Educational Leadership, 46*(1), 67–77.

Slavin, R. (1988b). *Cooperative learning: Theory, research, and practice.* Englewood Cliffs, NJ: Prentice-Hall.

Slavin, R. (1990a). Ability grouping, cooperative learning and the gifted. *Journal for the Education of the Gifted, 14*(1), 3–8.

Slavin, R. (1990b). Achievement effects of ability grouping in secondary schools: A best-evidence synthesis. *Review of Educational Research, 60,* 471–499.

Slavin, R. (1990c). Here to stay—or gone tomorrow? [Editorial]. *Educational Leadership, 47*(4), 3.

Slavin, R. (1991a). Synthesis of research on cooperative learning. *Educational Leadership, 48*(5), 71–82.

Slavin, R. (1991b). Are cooperative learning and "untracking" harmful to the gifted? *Educational Leadership, 48*(6), 68–71.

Slavin, R., & Karweit, N. (1984, April). Within-class ability grouping and student achievement. Paper presented at the annual meeting of the American Educational Research Association, New Orleans, LA.

Slavin, R., Leavey, M., & Madden, N. (1984). Combining cooperative learning and individualized instruction: Effects on student mathematics achievement, attitudes, and behaviors. *Elementary School Journal, 84*(4), 409–422.

Slavin, R., & Madden, N. (1989). What works for students at risk: A research synthesis. *Educational Leadership, 46*(5), 4–13.

Stanley, J. C. (1973). Accelerating the educational progress of intellectually gifted youths. *Educational Psychologist, 10,* 133–146.

Stanley, J. C. (1976). The case for extreme educational acceleration of intellectually brilliant youth. *Gifted Child Quarterly, 20,* 66–76.

Walberg, H. (1989). [Issue]. *ASCD Update, 5.*

Willis, S. (1990). Cooperative learning fallout? *ASCD Update 32*(8), 6–8.

10

Meta-analytic Findings on Grouping Programs

James A. Kulik and Chen-Lin C. Kulik

The University of Michigan

Meta-analytic reviews have focused on five distinct instructional programs that separate students by ability: multilevel classes, cross-grade programs, within-class grouping, enriched classes for the gifted and talented, and accelerated classes. The reviews show that effects are a function of program type. Multilevel classes, which entail only minor adjustment of course content for ability groups, usually have little or no effect on student achievement. Programs that entail more substantial adjustment of curriculum to ability, such as cross-grade and within-class programs, produce clear positive effects. Programs of enrichment and acceleration, which usually involve the greatest amount of curricular adjustment, have the largest effects on student learning. These results do not support recent claims that no one benefits from grouping or that students in the lower groups are harmed academically and emotionally by grouping.

Editor's Note: From Kulik, J. A., & Kulik, C. C. (1992). Meta-analytic findings on grouping programs. *Gifted Child Quarterly*, *36*(2), 73-77. © 1992 National Association for Gifted Children. Reprinted with permission.

Research on ability grouping has a long history. It goes back at least 75 years to 1916 when a researcher in Urbana, Illinois, studied the effects of special class placement on a group of high-aptitude 5th and 6th graders (Whipple, 1919). In the years since, researchers have carried out hundreds of additional studies of grouping, and reviewers have written dozens of reviews on the topic. Few educational practices have been scrutinized by researchers and reviewers for a longer period of time.

Despite all the effort, however, few clear-cut conclusions have emerged. Some reviewers have concluded that research supports the practice of grouping. Others have concluded the opposite. And some reviewers have simply reported that clear-cut conclusions are impossible when research findings are so variable and conflicting. Basic questions therefore continue to trouble educators. Does anyone benefit from grouping? Who benefits most? Is anyone harmed? How? Why?

It seems to us that there are at least two good reasons for asking once again what the research says about such matters. First, social scientists have developed objective, scientific methods for research reviewing during the past decade (e.g., Glass, McGaw, & Smith, 1981). These methods were not available during the heyday of grouping research, and most older reviews therefore relied on impressionistic and subjective methods for summarizing and interpreting research literature. With the new scientific methods now available, we are finally in a good position to determine what the research actually says.

There is another reason for turning our attention once again to research on ability grouping. Ability grouping has come under strong attack recently. Oakes (1985), a leader in the attack, has charged that ability grouping is discriminatory, unfair, and ineffective. In her view, no children gain from placement in homogeneous classes, and children in slower groups are harmed both intellectually and psychologically by grouping. Educators need to know whether the research actually supports such charges.

Our purpose therefore is to reexamine the findings on grouping using state-of-the-art methods for summarizing and interpreting the literature. We will examine findings on five distinct programs that separate students by ability:

1. *Multilevel classes*. Students in the same grade are divided into groups—often high, middle, and low groups—on the basis of ability, and the groups are instructed in separate classrooms either for a full day or for a single subject.

2. *Cross-grade grouping*. Children from several grades are formed into groups on the basis of their level of achievement in a subject, and the groups are then taught the subject in separate classrooms without regard to the children's regular grade placement.

3. *Within-class grouping*. A teacher forms ability groups within a single classroom and provides each group with instruction appropriate to its level of aptitude.

Putting the Research to Use

Advocates of *de-tracking* are today calling on schools to eliminate all forms of ability grouping. Meta-analytic results suggest that this proposed reform would damage American education. Teachers, counselors, administrators, and parents should be aware that student achievement would suffer from the wholesale elimination of school programs that group students by aptitude.

The harm would be relatively small from the simple elimination of multilevel classes, in which high, middle, and low groups cover the same curriculum. If schools replaced all their multilevel classes with mixed-ability ones, the achievement level of higher aptitude students would fall slightly, but the achievement level of other students would remain the same. If schools eliminated grouping programs with differentiated curricula, the damage to student achievement would be greater, and it would be felt broadly. Both higher and lower aptitude students would suffer academically from elimination of such programs. The damage enriched and accelerated classes for their brightest learners. The achievement level of such students would fall dramatically if they were required to move at the common pace. No one can be certain that there would be a way to repair the harm that would be done.

4. *Enriched classes for the gifted and talented.* Students who are high in aptitude receive richer, more varied educational experiences than would be available to them in the regular curriculum for their age level.

5. *Accelerated classes for the gifted and talented.* Students who are high in academic aptitude receive instruction that allows them to proceed more rapidly through their schooling or to finish schooling at an earlier age than other students.

Our conclusion is that effects of grouping are a function of program type. Multilevel classes, which usually entail only minor adjustment of course content for ability groups, typically have little or no effect on student achievement. Programs that entail more substantial curricular adjustment, such as cross-grade and within-class programs, produce clear positive effects. Programs of enrichment and acceleration, which involve the greatest degree of curricular adjustment, have the largest effects on student learning. These results do not support recent claims that no one benefits from grouping or that students in the lower groups are harmed academically and emotionally by grouping.

META-ANALYTIC METHODS

The review method used in this article is called *meta-analysis*. The method was first described in 1976 by Gene V. Glass in his presidential address to the American Educational Research Association. Meta-analysis is simply the analysis of analyses or, more formally, the application of quantitative statistics to the collected results of a large number of independent studies for the purpose of integrating the findings. To carry out a meta-analysis, a reviewer usually (a) finds as many studies as possible of an issue through an objective search of the literature; (b) codes the characteristics of these studies; (c) expresses the results of each study on a common metric; and (d) uses statistical methods to describe relationships between study characteristics and outcomes.

For each study included in a meta-analysis, the treatment effect is expressed in standard deviation units, or as an *effect size*. In principle, the computation of effect sizes is simple. A reviewer simply divides the gain or loss for an experimental group by an estimate of the population standard deviation on the outcome measure. An *effect size* is positive when there is a gain from the treatment and negative when there is a loss. An effect size is large when its absolute value is around 0.8, medium when around 0.5, and small when around 0.2.

We first used meta-analytic methods in 1982 to integrate research findings on ability grouping in secondary schools (Kulik & Kulik, 1982). We later extended our reviews to cover grouping in elementary schools (C. Kulik & Kulik, 1984), programs of accelerated instruction (J. Kulik & Kulik, 1984), and within-class and cross-grade grouping programs (Kulik & Kulik, 1987). Our most recent reports have provided an overview of this earlier work (e.g., Kulik & Kulik, 1991). Slavin (1987, 1990) applied his own variant of meta-analysis, called best-evidence synthesis, to both elementary school and secondary school findings on grouping.

META-ANALYTIC RESULTS

The results reported in this article come from a recent updated statistical analysis that takes into account earlier meta-analytic work by both us and Slavin. The pool of studies used in the analysis is very similar to the combined pool of studies used in the two earlier sets of meta-analyses. It is not identical, however. We reread all the studies used in earlier analyses and reviewed Slavin's critique of various studies, and on this basis we eliminated from this new analysis a few studies included in earlier analyses. We also reviewed coding of all studies, and we revised our earlier coding when it seemed appropriate to do so. Our goal was to base conclusions in this report on the best interpretation of the best and most complete set of studies that we could assemble. A full report on our updated analysis of grouping findings is available from the National Research Center on the Gifted and Talented (Kulik, 1991).

Multilevel Classes

In 1919 Detroit became the first large city to introduce a formal multilevel plan of ability grouping (Courtis, 1925). The Detroit plan called for intelligence testing of all school children at the start of Grade 1 and then placement of children into X, Y, and Z groups on the basis of test results. The top 20% went to the X classes, the middle 60% to Y classes, and the bottom 20% to Z classes. Standard materials and methods were used in all classes, and no real adjustment of curriculum and methods was made for the ability groups.

Although many school systems followed the Detroit model and instituted three-tier grouping in subsequent years, their plans sometimes differed from the Detroit plan in significant ways. Few schools relied so exclusively on intelligence tests for initial placement in groups, and few separated students at such an early age. In addition, in many programs, especially those in high schools, the separation was not for a full day but was restricted instead to a single subject. Like the Detroit plan, however, most programs were set up simply to make things easier for teachers by reducing pupil variation in their classes. Few programs used multilevel classes as a way of providing differentiated curricula to the ability groups.

A total of 56 studies examined effects on students of placement in multilevel classes. A total of 51 of the 56 studies measured effects on achievement tests. Nearly 60% of the studies found higher examination scores in the multilevel classes; about 40% found higher examination scores in the mixed-ability classes. The difference in scores from homogeneous and mixed-ability classes was trivial or small, however, in virtually every one of the 51 studies. The average effect size in all programs was 0.03. This effect is only slightly less than the one (0.06) that we found in our earlier meta-analyses, and it is consistent with the effect of zero found by Slavin for multilevel grouping programs (Kulik & Kulik, 1991; Slavin, 1987, 1990). The effect is not large enough to be considered statistically different from zero.

A total of 36 of the 51 studies examined results separately by ability level. Effects varied slightly with aptitude. The average effect size was 0.10 for higher aptitude, −0.02 for middle aptitude, and −0.01 for lower aptitude students. The average effect size of 0.10 for higher aptitude students was significantly greater than zero, and it was significantly higher than the average effect sizes for middle and lower aptitude students.

Effects showed little relation to study features. Results were very similar, for example, in true experiments and quasi-experimental studies, in studies reported in journals and dissertations, in studies evaluating full-day grouping programs and studies evaluating single-subject grouping, and so forth.

Thirteen of the 56 studies described effects of grouping on student self-esteem. The average overall effect of grouping in the 13 studies was to decrease self-esteem scores by 0.03 standard deviations, a very small and statistically non-significant amount. Eleven of the 13 studies also reported results separately by ability level. The average effect size was 0.19 for lower aptitude students, −0.09 for middle aptitude students, and −0.15 for higher aptitude students. Instruction in homogeneous classes thus tended to raise the self-esteem scores of lower aptitude students and to reduce the self-esteem of higher aptitude students.

Cross-Grade Grouping

The best known plan for cross-grade grouping is the Joplin plan. This grouping approach was devised by Cecil Floyd, who was then assistant superintendent of schools in Joplin, Missouri, and it was first used in the Joplin schools in 1953. The plan called for cross-grade grouping of fourth, fifth, and sixth graders for reading instruction. During the hour reserved for reading, children in these grades would break up into groups that went to reading classes on anything from the second- to the ninth-grade level. In these classes, the children would work with other fourth, fifth, and sixth graders who were reading at the same level. After this period was over, the children returned to their age-graded homerooms for a 25-minute period of reading for enjoyment. Almost all formal evaluations of cross-grade grouping involve the Joplin plan for reading instruction in elementary schools.

Cross-grade grouping is like multilevel grouping in that students of different ability levels are taught in separate classrooms. But in cross-grade plans, there are typically more levels. In a typical Joplin program, for example, a fifth grader might be assigned to any one of nine different reading groups. In addition, cross-grade grouping is single-subject grouping, and so group placement is usually tied closely to a specific skill. Perhaps the most important difference between cross-grade and multilevel grouping, however, is in the amount of curricular adjustment in the two approaches. In cross-grade programs, students in different ability groups work with different materials and different methods. In most multilevel programs, little or no effort is made to adjust curriculum to group ability level.

Fourteen studies investigated effects of such cross-grade programs. Eleven of the studies found that students achieved more when taught in these cross-grade programs; two studies found that performance was better when students were taught in conventional mixed-ability classes; and one study found no difference in results of the two approaches. The average effect size in the 14 studies was 0.30, a small effect but one that is significantly greater than zero.

Two of the studies reported results separately by ability level. The average effect was 0.12 for the high-ability students; −0.01 for the middle-ability students; and 0.29 for the low-ability students. Because of the small number of studies of cross-grade grouping in the literature, it was not possible to examine further the relationship between study characteristics and study outcomes. None of the studies reported on effects of cross-grade grouping on self-esteem.

Within-Class Grouping

Elementary school teachers often group the children in a class into subgroups for specific activities and purposes. They use such subgroups especially often for reading and arithmetic lessons, and they sometimes form subgroups for science and social science projects as well. The teacher usually presents a lesson to one of the subgroups while the remaining groups engage in other activities.

Two facts about within-class grouping plans make them especially interesting. First, most within-class grouping plans call for differentiated instruction for the groups. For the practice of within-class grouping to make sense, the teacher must present different material to each group. It would be inefficient for a teacher to divide a class into thirds on the basis of ability and then to make the same presentation separately to each of the three groups. Thus, within-class programs are like cross-grade programs in that they involve differentiated curriculum. Second, within-class programs do not involve assignment of groups to separate classrooms. Within-class programs differ from both multilevel and cross-grade programs in this respect.

Eleven studies described results from within-class grouping programs. Nine of these studies reported a higher overall achievement level with within-class grouping; only two studies reported a higher overall achievement level with mixed-ability instruction. The average overall effect of grouping in the 11 studies was to raise examination scores by 0.25 standard deviations, a significant but small effect.

Six of the 11 studies reported results separately by ability group. Effects were small to moderate for students at all ability levels. The average effect size was 0.30 for the higher ability students; 0.18 for the middle ability students; and 0.16 for the low-ability students. Too few studies were available for analysis of the relationship between study features and effect sizes.

Enriched Classes for the Gifted and Talented

Some grouping programs are designed especially to meet the needs of gifted and talented students. Learners in these programs are ordinarily a distinctive group with unusually high academic aptitude. Teachers in such programs usually believe that their students have special needs, and they usually have a strong commitment to meeting these needs. The result is typically a highly challenging educational program with distinctive materials and methods adapted to student ability.

We found a total of 25 studies of special programs for the gifted and talented. Twenty-two of the 25 studies found that talented students achieved more when they were taught in special programs. The average effect in the 25 studies was 0.41. This effect is moderate in size and significantly greater than an effect size of zero. We were unable to find any study feature that was significantly related to variation in effect size. The small number of studies available for analysis might account in part for this failure to find significant relationships.

Five of the 25 studies of special programs for the gifted and talented investigated effects on self-concept. In 4 of the 5 studies, self-concepts were more favorable when the gifted and talented were taught in separate groups. The size of the effect was small or trivial, however, in all of the studies. The average effect size in all 5 studies was 0.10.

Accelerated Classes for the Gifted and Talented

Acceleration of the gifted can take a variety of forms. Some programs entail radical acceleration of individual students; some involve more moderate advancement of groups of students. We were able to find 23 controlled studies of accelerated instruction in the literature. The 23 studies did not examine effects of radical acceleration but instead evaluated more modest forms of rapid advancement. These included compressing a curriculum for talented students (e.g., 4 years in 3) and extending the calendar to speed up the progress of such students (e.g., completing the work of 4 years in 3 school years with five summer sessions).

The 23 studies used two different study designs that reflected fundamentally different research purposes. In one group of studies, the groups being compared were initially equivalent in age and aptitude, but because one group was accelerated and the other was not, the two groups differed in grade level when educational outcomes were measured. In a second group of studies, accelerated students were compared with older, highly talented nonaccelerates in the grades into which the accelerates had moved.

These two types of studies produced distinctly different results. Each of the 11 studies with same-age control groups showed greater achievement in the accelerated class; the average effect size in these studies was 0.87. Studies with older comparison groups were as likely to produce positive as negative differences between groups. The average effect size in the 12 studies with older comparison groups was -0.02.

Only a small number of studies investigated other outcomes of acceleration, and findings were not entirely consistent from study to study. On the average, however, acceleration appeared to have little or no effect on students' attitude toward school, participation in school activities, popularity, or adjustment. Acceleration had a strong effect on vocational plans in two studies but trivial effects on vocational plans in four other studies. The effect on vocational plans apparently varied as a function of program type.

DISCUSSION AND CONCLUSION

Oakes (1985) concluded that no one gains academically from ability grouping and that lower aptitude children lose a good deal of academic ground when taught in homogeneous groups. Our analyses do not support this conclusion. They point instead to some clear and consistent academic benefits from grouping programs. The academic benefits are clearest for those in the higher ability groups, but students in the lower groups are not harmed academically by grouping and they gain academic ground in some grouping programs.

For all types of students, however, the size of academic gains is a function of program type. Multilevel classes generally have little or no effect on student achievement levels; within-class and cross-grade programs generally produce small positive effects; enriched and accelerated classes produce moderate-to-large positive effects. Several different factors might account for the difference in program results. We believe, however, that the key factor is the degree to which course content is adjusted to group ability in the programs.

Reports on multilevel classes seldom describe planned curricular adjustment to group ability. For some of the older studies of multilevel classes, in fact, teachers were told to keep content constant across ability groups. Even in more recent studies of multilevel classes, adjustment of content to ability group is usually informal and at the discretion of individual teachers. In contrast, reports on cross-grade and within-class programs usually describe planned adjustment of content to group ability. In cross-grade programs, students move up or down grades for reading instruction to ensure a match between their ability and their reading instruction. In within-class programs, teachers divide students into ability groups so that they can work on different materials with children of differing ability levels.

Enriched and accelerated classes are by definition classes in which material is adjusted to the needs of special groups. In enriched classes, the emphasis is on giving students a richer and more varied educational experience than they would receive in regular classes. In accelerated classes, the emphasis is on providing instruction that allows children to proceed more rapidly through schooling or to finish at an earlier age. Gains on tests are larger for children in accelerated classes, but gains in enriched classes also seem impressive when one considers the special emphases in the classes. In some enriched classes, children spend as much as half their time on cultural material (e.g., foreign languages, music, art) not covered on standard achievement tests.

It is also important to note that ability grouping does not have devastating effects on student self-esteem, as Oakes (1985) has charged. Effects of grouping on self-esteem are near-zero overall. They appear to be slightly positive for lower ability students and slightly negative for higher aptitude ones. Talented students may become slightly less satisfied with themselves when taught with their intellectual peers; slower students may gain slightly in self-confidence when they are taught with other slower learners.

Our conclusions are therefore very different from those reached by Oakes. Whereas Oakes concludes that grouping programs are unnecessary, ineffective, and unfair, we conclude that the opposite is true. We believe that American schools would be harmed by the elimination of programs that tailor instruction to the aptitude, achievement, and interests of groups with special educational needs.

REFERENCES

Courtis, S. A. (1925). Ability-grouping in Detroit schools. In G. M. Whipple (Ed.), *The ability grouping of pupils,* 35th Yearbook of the National Society for the Study of Education (Part I, pp. 44–47). Bloomington, IL: Public School Publishing.

Glass, G. V. (1976). Primary, secondary, and meta-analysis of research. *Educational Researcher, 5,* 3–8.

Glass, G. V., McGaw, B., & Smith, M. L. (1981). *Meta-analysis in social research.* Beverly Hills, CA: Sage.

Kulik, C.-L. C., & Kulik, J. A. (1982). Effects of ability grouping on secondary school students: A meta-analysis of evaluation findings. *American Educational Research Journal, 19,* 415–428.

Kulik, C.-L., & Kulik, J. A. (1984, August). *Effects of ability grouping on elementary school pupils: A meta-analysis.* Paper presented at the annual meeting of the American Psychological Association, Toronto. (ERIC Document Reproduction Service No. Ed 255–329)

Kulik, J. A. (1991). *Ability grouping.* Research-based decision-making series. Storrs, CT: National Research Center on the Gifted and Talented, University of Connecticut.

Kulik, J. A., & Kulik, C.-L. C. (1984). Effects of accelerated instruction on students. *Review of Educational Research, 54,* 409–426.

Kulik, J. A., & Kulik, C.-L. C. (1987). Effects of ability grouping on student achievement. *Equity and Excellence, 23,* 22–30.

Kulik, J. A., & Kulik, C.-L. C. (1991). Ability grouping and gifted students. In N. Colangelo & G. Davis (Eds.), *Handbook of gifted education* (pp. 178–196). Boston, MA: Allyn & Bacon.

Oakes, J. (1985). *Keeping track: How schools structure inequality.* New Haven, CT: Yale University Press.

Slavin, R. E. (1987). Ability grouping and student achievement in elementary schools: Best evidence synthesis. *Review of Educational Research, 57,* 293–336.

Slavin, R. E. (1990). Achievement effects of ability grouping in secondary schools: A best-evidence synthesis. *Review of Educational Research, 60,* 471–499.

Whipple, G. M. (1919). *Classes for gifted children.* Bloomington, IL: Public School Publishing.

11

An Investigation of the Effects of Total School Flexible Cluster Grouping on Identification, Achievement, and Classroom Practices

Marcia Gentry

Minnesota State University—Mankato

Steven V. Owen

University of Texas Medical Branch

This paper presents the findings of a longitudinal, causal comparative investigation of an elementary school cluster grouping program. Both quantitative and qualitative methodologies were used. Although the cluster grouping program was originally designed to provide differentiation of

Editor's Note: From Gentry, M., & Owen, S. V. (1999). An investigation of the effects of total school flexible cluster grouping on identification, achievement, and classroom practices. *Gifted Child Quarterly, 43*(4), 224-243. © 1999 National Association for Gifted Children. Reprinted with permission.

content and instruction for gifted students, positive effects were also found on the achievement of all students in the school. During the three program years, students involved in the school using cluster grouping were more likely to be identified as high achieving or above average. Fewer students were identified as low achieving. A significant increase in achievement test scores of all students was found when these students were compared to similar students from a comparison school district. Qualitative analyses yielded three core categories—the use of grouping, the impact of teachers, and the general school environment—that helped to provide an understanding of the quantitative findings.

BACKGROUND

Cluster grouping is a widely recommended and often used strategy for meeting the needs of high achieving students in the regular elementary classroom. Its use has gained popularity in recent years because of the move toward inclusive education, budget cuts, and heterogeneous grouping policies that have eliminated programs for gifted students (Purcell, 1994). However, little research exists on the effects of using cluster grouping on the achievement of gifted students, and none exists that has examined its effects on students of other achievement levels (Gentry, 1996; Hoover, Sayler, & Feldhusen, 1993).

Gentry (1996) noted many variations in definitions and applications of cluster grouping and identified three common themes in the existing literature on this topic. First, a group of students (varying in number from 3 to more than 10) identified as gifted, high achieving, or high-ability is placed into a classroom with students of other achievement levels. Second, the reason for cluster grouping is to differentiate curriculum. Third, the teacher of the high ability cluster should have background, training, and experience in working with gifted students.

Putting the Research to Use

This research describes the implementation of a total school application of cluster grouping over time with two entire graduation classes of students. It provides a rich example of the effects that a gifted program can have on an entire school when that program is integrated with the general education program and considers the needs of all students and teachers. It reinforces the notion that grouping, when done flexibly and with appropriately adapted curriculum and instruction, can help students of all achievement levels grow academically while assisting teachers in their efforts to better meet the individual needs of their students. Based on the findings of the study, the implications for practice include: (1) professional development in gifted education should not be restricted to just those teachers responsible for students identified as gifted because the use of gifted education "know how" has the potential to improve general education practices; (2) placing a cluster of high achievers in one classroom can increase the chance that their needs will be met while offering the opportunity for talent to emerge in the other classrooms; and (3) unlike suggestions by many reformers, the elimination of ability grouping may not be beneficial to students and teachers.

Current research indicates that there are several major benefits of cluster grouping: Gifted students regularly interact with their intellectual peers *and* age peers (Delcourt & Evans, 1994; Rogers, 1991; Slavin, 1987a); cluster grouping provides full-time services for gifted students without additional cost (Hoover et al., 1993; LaRose, 1986; Winebrenner & Devlin, 1994); curricular differentiation is more efficient and likely to occur when a group of high-achieving students is placed with a teacher who has expertise, training, and a desire to differentiate curriculum than when these students are distributed among many teachers (Bryant, 1987; Kennedy, 1995; Kulik, 1992; Rogers, 1991); removing the highest achievers from most classrooms allows other achievers to emerge (Kennedy, 1989; Winebrenner, 1992); and, finally, cluster grouping reduces the range of achievement levels that must be addressed within the classrooms of all teachers (Coleman, 1995; Delcourt & Evans 1994; Rogers, 1993). Conversely, the literature reveals several concerns about the use of cluster grouping, and these concerns parallel those raised regarding the use of ability grouping in general. These include the effect that removing the brightest students from classrooms has on the students and teachers in these classrooms (Hoover et al., 1993; Oakes, 1985; Slavin 1987a), the methods for selecting teachers for the high-achieving cluster classroom (Oakes, 1985; Slavin, 1987b), and whether cluster grouping provides appropriate differentiation for the high-achieving students (Delcourt & Evans 1994; McInerney, 1983; Rogers, 1991; Westberg, Archambault, Dobyns, & Salvin, 1993).

Recent studies that examined cluster grouping include survey research conducted by Hoover et al. (1993) and two studies by Delcourt and her colleagues (Delcourt, Loyd, Cornell, & Goldberg, 1994). Hoover et al. reported that classroom teachers believed that cluster grouping benefited both gifted and nongifted students. However, these researchers also concluded that "despite clear potential benefits of cluster grouping, there have been no empirical studies of the prevalence of cluster grouping nor of its effects, perceived or actual, on gifted children" (p. 13). Delcourt et al. examined four programming arrangements for gifted students, including special schools, separate classes, pull-out programs, and within-class programs, and their effects on achievement and affective outcomes. Of the 11 districts included in the study, one used cluster grouping, which was classified as a within-class program. However, across all programs, gifted students from within-class programs received the lowest scores in all areas of achievement when compared to their gifted peers in the other programming options. Delcourt et al. concluded that "since within-class programs are a popular model in gifted education, their curricular and instructional provisions for the gifted must be carefully maintained lest they disintegrate into a no program format" (p. 77). Yet, in a follow-up study (Delcourt & Evans, 1994) that examined exemplary programs in gifted education, a school using cluster grouping was selected as the best example of a within-class program. Key variables that distinguished these exemplary programs were leadership, atmosphere and environment, communication, curriculum and instruction, and attention to student needs. In addition, the exemplary programs were found to influence student achievement and motivation through exposure to challenge and choices. The extent to which these themes are evident within a cluster grouping program may help explain both its success and its impact on student achievement.

Rogers (1991) recognized that the research base on cluster grouping is limited and cautioned that the cluster teacher must be trained and motivated to work with gifted and talented students and that the curriculum must be appropriately differentiated. In a meta-analysis of the research on ability grouping, Kulik (1992) found that youngsters of all achievement groups benefited from ability grouping programs when the curriculum was appropriately adjusted to the aptitude levels of the groups. As a result, he recommended that schools use various forms of flexible ability grouping.

Although many experts advocate the use of cluster grouping (Balzer & Siewert, 1990; Brown, Archambault, Zhang, & Westberg, 1994; Coleman, 1995; Davis & Rimm, 1985; Hoover et al., 1993; Juntune, 1981; Kaplan, 1974; Kulik & Kulik, 1991; LaRose, 1986; Renzulli, 1994; Rogers, 1991; Winebrenner, 1992), surprisingly little evidence exists regarding its effectiveness. Clearly, research that can provide evidence about the effects of cluster grouping on students is needed.

RESEARCH QUESTIONS

This study examined the use of cluster grouping during a four-year period in a small, rural school district in the Midwest. The following research questions guided the study:

1. Is cluster grouping related to teacher perceptions of student achievement as measured by teacher identification categories?

2. How do students in the cluster grouping school compare with students from a similar school who are not involved in cluster grouping after adjustment for initial differences with regard to achievement?

3. What factors exist within the classrooms and the school using cluster grouping that may influence student achievement?

BACKGROUND OF THE TREATMENT PROGRAM

Schools, classrooms, teachers, and students are complex, interactive entities, making their study challenging at best, and the results from such study ambiguous. Yet, programs must be studied in their full context to provide insight into their workings and their possible effects. It is from in-depth examination of real programs in real schools that the opportunity to learn about schools presents itself. It is for these reasons that this study examined the existing use of cluster grouping in a small, rural school district, purposefully selected because of its innovative use of cluster grouping with students of all achievement levels in all classrooms.

Cluster grouping in the treatment district began in grade 3 and continued through grade 5, with a flexible identification process beginning at the end of second grade that included information from teachers, parents, and achievement tests. Teachers were involved with the identification and placement of students into the classrooms, which was done using grade level conferencing. Each year in May, second-, third-, and fourth-grade teachers

1. rated their students' academic performance as *high-achieving, above-average, average, low-average,* or *low* (students' academic performance as observed by the teacher and the Scales for Rating the Behavioral Characteristics for Superior Students (Renzulli, Smith, Callahan, White, & Hartman, 1977) functioned as a basis for these ratings);

2. indicated those students who received special education or Chapter 1 services; and

3. noted students who had behavior problems or who should be separated.

Teacher ratings were compared with achievement scores on the Iowa Tests of Basic Skills (Hieronymus, Hoover, & Lindquist, 1984), and discrepancies were discussed. By using both teacher ratings and achievement scores, it was possible for a student who tested poorly or for a student whose classroom performance did not reflect his or her ability to be identified as *high-achieving* or *above-average* without the use of *cutoff* scores. This system of checks and balances is similar to that suggested by Renzulli and Reis (1985) in the Revolving Door Identification Model. Although there were no cutoff scores for identification, the process was done consistently by the same teachers on a yearly basis.

There were five classrooms per grade level in which students were placed yearly on the basis of their identification categories. One classroom had the cluster of *high-achieving* students, with the remainder of the class comprised of *average, low-average,* and *low-achieving* students. The other four classrooms each had students who achieved at *above-average, average, low-average,* and *low* levels. Additionally, two of these classrooms had clusters of special needs students who received Chapter 1 or special education assistance. In each of these two rooms, an aide or a teacher-consultant worked with the classroom teacher for the majority of the day. By arranging classes in this manner, each heterogeneous classroom had a group of *above-average* achieving students, but one class had the specific cluster of *high-achieving* students. In this way, the use of resource personnel was maximized. Behavioral problems—from all achievement levels—were evenly distributed among the five classrooms.

When the cluster grouping program was adopted, all teachers were provided with a general overview of gifted education and talent development based on the Schoolwide Enrichment Model (Renzulli & Reis, 1985) and were involved in two half-day in-service training sessions regarding the above described approach to cluster grouping. Annual in-services in gifted education (e.g., curriculum compacting, curricular and instructional differentiation, and thinking skills) and opportunities to attend regional, state, and national conferences on gifted education were made available to all teachers. The teachers responsible for teaching the *high-achieving* cluster volunteered and were selected by the staff and administration. Each of these teachers took classes in gifted education and attended several workshops to improve their methods for working with high-achieving students. It should also be noted that, as in any school, cluster grouping was not the only type of grouping or treatment that occurred. In fact, in this school, there were a variety of grouping arrangements that took place, including regrouping between classes for math and reading. Also, because of the increased number of students who were identified as high-achieving, a class of these students existed by fifth grade. The complexity of the grouping arrangements made it impossible to analyze the relative effects of each arrangement on student achievement. For further discussion of the treatment program, including its philosophy and practices, refer to Gentry (1996).

METHODS AND PROCEDURES

Research Design

The research design was causal-comparative and longitudinal, employing both quantitative and qualitative methodologies. The first two research questions were addressed using descriptive and inferential statistics, and the third research question was addressed with qualitative methods. The combination of quantitative and qualitative methods allowed a more thorough description of how cluster grouping was implemented within the complex context of a real school. Although it was not possible to isolate the effects of a single variable— cluster grouping—this study provided a realistic picture of how cluster grouping worked in concert with other variables found within schools. Causal-comparative

Table 1   Demographic Factors Upon Which Treatment and Comparison Schools Were Matched

Factor	Treatment	Comparison School
Geographic Region	Rural Midwest	Rural Midwest
Ethnic Composition	White, < 1% minority	White, < 1% minority
Student Population*	1,499	1,202
Socioeconomic Status*	Low	Low
School Configuration	1 elementary school	1 elementary school
	K-5	K-6
	5 classes/grade level	4 classes/grade level
Pupil to teacher ratio*	20:1	21:1
Per pupil revenue*	$3,704	$4,071
Rank in state for spending on basic needs programs* (out of 524 districts)	503rd	491st

Note.*Source: 1992-93 Bulletin 1014 (Michigan Department of Education, 1994)

research is done after the fact using existing data, and it does not seek to attribute causality; rather it seeks to establish relationships and trends from which future research can be conducted.

Sample

Purposive sampling was used in this study. The treatment sample included all students from two graduation class years who attended the school from grades 2 through 5 (Class of 2000: $n = 97$; Class of 2001: $n = 100$). The comparison school was selected based on its demographic similarity to the treatment school (see Table 1) and because its students had not been involved in cluster grouping or gifted programming (Class of 2000: $n = 68$; Class of 2001: $n = 69$). Any students for whom achievement data were unavailable for grades 2, 3, 4, and 5 were eliminated from the analyses. The Classes of 2000 and 2001 were selected because longitudinal data could be obtained from both the treatment site and comparison site to compare the students' academic achievement.

The sample also included teachers and administrators from the treatment site who were involved in the program. Follow-up interviews were conducted with 14 of 15 grade 3–5 teachers and with three of five administrators who were originally involved with the program and were involved for the entire time during which the program took place.

Instrumentation

To examine student achievement effects, the present study used existing achievement data from both the treatment and comparison schools. Normal curve equivalent (NCE) scores were collected for each student (grades 2–5) in the areas of total math and total reading from standardized achievement measures used by the schools. The treatment school used the Iowa Tests of Basic Skills (ITBS), Form G (Hieronymus, Hoover, & Lindquist, 1984), while the comparison school used the California Achievement Test (CAT), Form E (1984) to measure yearly student achievement. Because of the ex post facto nature of this study, available instrumentation was used. Airasian (1989) stated that the CAT "compares very favorably to other achievement batteries of its genre such as . . . the *Iowa Tests of Basic Skills*" (p. 128). Thus, although the content of these two standardized tests was not identical, the NCE scores provided an achievement standing relative to the respective test's norm in a group and allowed comparison in achievement to be made on the basis of normed scores.

To address Research Question 3, a semi-structured interview protocol was developed based on themes identified by Delcourt and Evans (1994) (leadership, atmosphere and environment, communication, curriculum and instruction, attention to student needs) and factors identified by Westberg et al. (1993) (questioning and thinking, providing challenges and choices, reading and written assignments, curriculum modifications, enrichment centers). Interviews were taped and transcribed.

Analyses

BMDP statistical software (Dixon, 1992) was used to screen and analyze the data (one outlier was eliminated from the Class of 2001: Mahalonobis D-squared distance value $p < .0003$). Descriptive statistics were used to address Research Question 1 and inferential statistics—including multivariate repeated measures ANCOVAs and planned contrasts—were used to address Research Question 2. Although discriminant function analyses is a preferred follow-up for MANOVA and MANCOVA, it cannot be used with repeated measures; therefore, univariate ANOVA and ANCOVA were used to examine the multivariate main effects. Grade 2 NCE scores in math and reading were used to adjust the groups for initial differences. Separate analyses were run for each graduation year (Class of 2000, Class of 2001). Assumptions for the analyses for each research question were examined (namely normal distribution, homogeneity of variance, and sphericity), and no violations were found.

To address Research Question 3, data from interviews with teachers and administrators ($n = 17$) and documents were gathered, and qualitative procedures were employed (Spradley, 1980). Together with the quantitative findings, the interview transcriptions enabled triangulation of data, a technique that provides checks for both reliability and validity of data through the comparison of multiple sources and data collection methods (Mitchell, 1986). Interview transcriptions and document reviews were coded and analyzed for patterns and themes (Strauss & Corbin, 1990). Trustworthiness was enhanced by using a "devil's advocate," triangulating the data, and checking and questioning the data.

RESULTS AND IMPLICATIONS

Identification Findings and Implications for Research Question 1: Is Cluster Grouping Related to Teacher Perceptions of Student Achievement as Measured by Teacher Identification Categories?

Descriptive statistics provided insight into the identification of students in the treatment school during the three program years. Overall for both data sets (Class of 2000 and Class of 2001), more students were identified as *high achieving* each successive year, while fewer students were identified as *low achieving*. By fifth grade, each of these classes had one entire classroom of students identified as *high achieving*, yet all other classrooms still contained groups of students identified as *above average*. Figure 1 depicts the changes in the number of students identified as *high achieving* for both data sets during the three program years, and Figure 2 depicts changes in the frequencies of students identified as *low achieving* during the three program years.

Changes in students' identification categories during the three program years were classified as *increased, decreased, no change*, or *varied*, and these changes were tabulated. *Increased* was defined as moving up, for example, from *average* to *above average*, and *decreased* was defined as moving down, for example, from *high achieving* to *above average* during the course of three years. No change was used to describe those students whose identification category remained constant for each of the three program years. Students whose identification category changed, but did not increase or decrease as described above, were counted as *varied*. A large percentage of students' identification categories in both classes increased (Class of 2000: 47%; Class of 2001: 34%), or saw no change (Class of 2000: 40%; Class of 2001: 45%), whereas only a small number of students' identification categories decreased (Class of 2000: 3%; Class of 2001: 9%). Students in this program were regarded by their teachers as higher achievers as they progressed from third to fifth grade in the program, a result that led to the analyses of achievement scores.

Qualitative follow-up to these findings yielded interesting results that might explain the trend of identifying more students achieving at higher levels during the course of the three program years. Many teachers ($n = 13$; 93%) and all administrators ($n = 3$) believed that the increase in the number of students identified at higher levels was directly related to the grouping practices used in this school. For example, as Teacher 4C explained:

> Maybe cluster grouping has a lot to do with it. The cluster grouping may give the lower achieving students more self-confidence, because I think they become more involved in class when the high [achieving] kids are removed. And you know that those high kids are competitive and tend to dominate class sometimes. Also, the average student or high-average student really blossomed, too, which may be due to cluster grouping.

Figure 1   Changes in High Achievement Identification From Grade 3 to Grade 5
for Students in the Class of 2000 and the Class of 2001

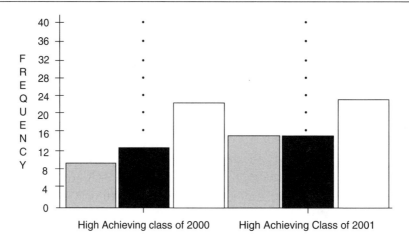

Figure 2   Changes in Low Achievement Identification From Grade 3 to Grade 5
for Students in the Class of 2000 and the Class of 2001

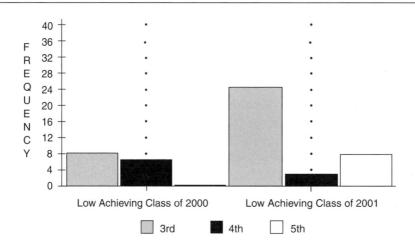

From the perspective of Teacher 3E:

We've talked about why we find more higher achieving students for
several years. Part of it, I feel, is that when you pull those really high
kids out—those who always have their hand up first and jump in with
the answers—when you get rid of those students by putting them
together in a cluster classroom—the other kids have a chance to shine.
They take risks more often and see themselves as being leaders of the
group. They are no longer frightened to offer answers.

As Teacher 3A discussed:

> I think the low and average children really benefited, because we only spent as much time on things as they needed to and then we moved on. Even if they moved at a slower pace, they were feeling successful. I feel even the low students had good self-esteem because they were constantly successful. I think that's why we also had fewer low students. There's a fine line between high average and high achieving, and I think a child who is in a classroom where there are not other children taking front stage has that opportunity and starts to shine. Their confidence builds, and I think that turns a high-average child into a high-achieving child.

The teachers in this study believed that removing the highest achievers from four of the five classrooms gave other students the opportunity to grow and achieve at higher levels than they might have if the highest achieving students had remained in the classroom. This result is consistent with the findings of Kennedy (1989), who found that when the gifted students were absent from the regular classrooms, new talent emerged from other students.

Additionally, other teachers ($n = 8$; 64%) and administrators ($n = 2$; 67%) suggested that the increase in achievement was due to efforts by the teachers to facilitate achievement among all of their students. These efforts included maintaining high expectations, creating a positive learning environment, and using a variety of strategies to challenge individual students. As Teacher 5A explained:

> One thing that caused more students to be identified was our expectations. I think that when kids are expected to achieve at a higher level, they try to do that. And I think that high expectations help students to try, and this effort boosts their scores. I think when students are exposed to higher level thinking skills and challenging work, it helps them achieve. When they are with other kids who are working at high levels, I think that helps them. I know I found that with the cluster grouping.

Teacher 5C described her thoughts:

> The high students were all with [Teacher 5A], and we expected more [from the students] we had. By removing some of the higher kids, it may have influenced the others to work harder . . . and maybe teachers expected more because we didn't have the higher students and treated it as a regular classroom and expected the average students to rise to the occasion.

Summary of Findings for Research Question 1

A combination of grouping and teacher practices may have been responsible for the changes in identification of students in this study. As achievement of students increased within the classrooms, they were more likely to be identified as higher achieving. The cluster grouping program may have provided these students with more opportunity to achieve by removing the highest achievers from four of the five classrooms in each grade level. Teachers believed in the program and in their students' abilities. The teachers indicated that the grouping and placement used in the cluster program helped them to better meet individual needs, and, with the highest achieving students removed from their classrooms, other students gained in achievement and confidence. These findings, which are contrary to popular views in the reform movement that grouping somehow damages the low-achieving students (George, 1993; Oakes, 1985; Slavin, 1987a; Wheelock, 1992), should be considered together with analyses of ability grouping (e.g., Kulik & Kulik, 1992; Rogers, 1991) when decisions are made regarding how children will be placed in elementary classrooms. Cluster grouping may offer students opportunities for academic growth as well as recognition by their teachers, and its use should be seriously considered by elementary, schools.

Achievement Findings and Implications for Research Question 2: How Do Students in the Treatment School Compare with Students from the Comparison School with Regard to Achievement?

To investigate the trends in identification, standardized student achievement was compared with the achievement of students from the comparison school. Repeated-measures MANOVA was used with school as the independent variable and grade 3, 4, and 5 NCE math and reading scores as dependent variables. Second-grade math and reading scores were used as covariates, because purposive sampling made randomization impossible. The covariates were significant for both the Class of 2000, $F(4, 300) = 81$, $p < .05$, and the Class of 2001, $F(4, 326) = 79.92$, $p < .05$, but not highly correlated with the independent variables, with canonical correlations of .16 for both data sets (accounting for only 2.6% of the variance that might otherwise explain the dependent variables).

After adjustment by the covariates, there were significant differences in the main and interaction effects for the Class of 2000. The main effect of school, $F(2, 150) = 16.98$, $p < .001$, and the interaction of school and time, $F(4, 610) = 8.01$, $p < .001$, were significant. Because a large sample can more easily yield statistical significance, effect sizes for these results were examined. The effect sizes (R^2) were calculated as 1 minus Wilks' Lambda (Tabachnick & Fidell, 1989). For the significant main effect of school, the effect size was $R^2 = .18$, and the interaction had an effect size of $R^2 = .10$, both practically significant with medium and small effects, respectively (Cohen, 1988). Therefore, after adjustment for initial differences in achievement scores between the schools, the school that the students attended accounted for 18% of the variation in achievement scores measured by the combined supervariable of math and reading. The interaction of school and time accounted for 10% of this variation.

For the Class of 2001, after adjusting for initial differences, significant differences were found in main effects of school, $F(2, 162) = 10.14$, $p < .001$; and time, $F(4,662) = 6.65$, $p < .001$; and in the interaction of school by time, $F(4, 662) = 4.32$, $p < .002$. Effect sizes for these significant differences were $R^2 = .11$, $R^2 = .08$, and $R^2 = .05$, respectively, all small, but practically significant (Cohen, 1988). The school that the students attended accounted for 11% of the variation in achievement scores measured by the combined supervariable of math and reading; the repeated occasions of testing accounted for 8% of this variation; and the interaction of school and time accounted for 5% of the variation, after adjustments by the covariates.

Explaining the Omnibus Test: Between School Contrasts

The first set of contrasts used BMDP program 2V ANCOVA procedures to compare the achievement of students in reading and math by grade level between schools. In each contrast, the reading or math score was the dependent variable, school was the independent variable, and the grade 2 reading or math score was the covariate.

Table 2 includes the results of these contrasts for the Class of 2000, and Table 3 portrays results of the same analyses for the Class of 2001. As indicated in Table 2, after adjustment for initial differences, on average, students in the Class of 2000 comparison school scored significantly higher ($M_c = 53.84$) than students in the treatment school ($M_t = 47.94$) in grade 3 reading scores, with a small effect size of $R^2 = .055$. Yet, by grade 5, students in the treatment school were averaging significantly higher scores ($M_t = 53.25$) than students in the comparison school ($M_c = 48.16$), with a small effect size of ($R^2 = .042$) (Cohen, 1988).

Also indicated in Table 2, with regard to mathematics scores of the students from the Class of 2000, significant differences were found between the schools at grade 3, grade 4, and grade 5 after adjusting for initial differences. The treatment school students averaged higher adjusted scores than the comparison school students on each occasion (grade 3: $M_t = 55.98$; $M_c = 49.79$; grade 4: $M_t = 55.60$; $M_c = 50.87$; grade 5: $M_t = 58.01$; $M_c = 48.25$), with the largest difference between the scores occurring at grade 5. The effect sizes for differences at grades 3 ($R^2 = .039$) and 4 ($R^2 = .032$) were practically significant, yet small, and the effect size for the grade 5 differences was medium $R^2 = .099$ (Cohen, 1988).

As depicted in Table 3, after adjusting for initial differences, comparison school students from the Class of 2001 averaged significantly higher scores than treatment school students in reading achievement when in grade 3 ($M_c = 52.62$; $M_t = 46.79$), but there were no significant differences in reading achievement in either grade 4 or grade 5. The medium effect size, $R^2 = .066$, was practically significant and accounted for 6.6% of the variation in adjusted reading scores. By grade 5, the treatment students had increased the mean adjusted score in reading achievement ($M_t = 49.27$) to a level that eliminated statistical differences between the groups.

As indicated in Table 3, with regard to the mathematics scores of the students from the Class of 2001, significant differences in achievement were found for grades 4 and 5 after adjusting for initial differences. In each case, the students in the treatment school scored higher than the students in the comparison school (grade 4: $M_t = 57.12$, $M_c = 51.49$; grade 5: $M_t = 55.54$, $M_c = 47.92$). The difference at grade 4 had a small, but significant effect size of $R^2 = .044$, and the grade 5 difference had a medium and practically significant effect size of $R^2 = .076$.

Explaining the Omnibus Test: Within Schools Contrasts

The second set of planned contrasts compared student achievement in reading and math by the repeated measure of time. Within each school, scores were contrasted between grades 3 and 4; grades 4 and 5; and grades 3 and 5 to determine when significant changes occurred. For each contrast, the independent variable was time and the dependent variable was math or reading score. These scores were contrasted for each data set using BMDP program 2V ANOVA procedures. Because these contrasts were performed within the individual school data sets, no covariates were used.

For the treatment school Class of 2000, significant differences were found in mean reading achievement scores between grades 3 ($M = 46.11$) and 4 ($M = 49.00$), $F(1,85) = 4.59$, $p < .05$, and grades 3 ($M = 46.11$) and 5 ($M = 51.23$), $F(1,85) = 12.87$, p < .05. The difference in reading scores between grade 3 and grade 5 had practical significance and a large effect size of $R^2 = .13$, or 13% of the variance between the grades (Cohen, 1988). However, no differences existed in math achievement for these students.

The comparison school Class of 2000 contrasts included significant differences in mean reading achievement between grades 4 ($M = 53.59$) and 5 ($M = 50.69$), $F(1,66) = 5.14$, $p < .05$, and grades 3 ($M = 56.22$) and 5 ($M = 50.69$), $F(1,66) = 20.49$, $p < .05$, with student scores decreasing. The decrease between grade 3 and grade 5 had large practical significance ($R^2 = .23$), which explained 23% of the variation in scores between these grades. As with the treatment school, no differences were found in math achievement between any grade levels.

Treatment students from the Class of 2001 showed significant increases in average reading achievement between grades 3 ($M = 46.11$) and 4 ($M = 50.21$), $F(1,97) = 10.30$, $p < .05$, a practically significant increase with a medium effect size of $R^2 = .095$. No significant differences in math achievement were found between any of the grades.

Planned contrasts for the comparison school students from the Class of 2001 indicated no differences in reading achievement with respect to time, but all contrasts of math achievement were found to be statistically significant with decreases in mean scores between grades 3 ($M = 57.84$), 4 ($M = 53.42$), and 5 ($M = 50.10$). This steady decrease between grades 3 and 5, $F(1,67) = 18.58$, $p < .05$, had a large effect size of $R^2 = .214$.

Table 2   Class of 2000 Planned Contrasts: Means, Standard Deviations, Adjusted Means, and F-values for Reading and Math Achievement Measures in Grade 2, 3, 4 and 5

Achievement measure	Treatment School		Comparison School			
	Mean (SD)	Adjusted mean	Mean (SD)	Adjusted mean	F value	E.S.
(Covariate)						
Reading Grade 2	49.42 (23.83)		56.71 (28.84)			
Reading Grade 3	46.12 (17.15)	47.94	56.22 (18.49)	53.84	8.89*	$R^2 = .055$
Reading Grade 4	49.13 (17.27)	50.98	53.59 (18.62)	51.13	.01	
Reading Grade 5	51.30 (18.05)	53.25	50.69 (17.90)	48.16	6.75*	$R^2 = .042$
(Covariate)						
Math Grade 2	53.98 (21.24)		59.00 (19.96)			
Math Grade 3	54.58 (21.32	55.98	51.62 (17.12)	49.79	6.41*	$R^2 = .039$
Math Grade 4	54.44 (16.47)	55.60	52.40 (17.31)	50.87	5.12*	$R^2 = .032$
Math Grade 5	56.48 (22.96)	58.01	50.35 (18.81)	48.25	16.73**	$R^2 = .099$

Note. $n = 155$; $*p < .05$; $**p < .001$

Summary of Findings for Research Question 2

Even though students in the treatment schools began with lower reading scores than did students in the comparison school, after three years in a flexible cluster grouping program, the treatment school students outperformed or equaled their comparison school counterparts. Additionally, the growth in reading achievement had both practical and statistical significance for the treatment school students. Qualitative findings revealed that treatment school students from both the Class of 2000 and the Class of 2001 were regrouped between classes for reading instruction on the basis of performance in reading during each year of the program (grades 3–5). Administrators from the comparison school indicated that heterogeneous and whole-group instruction were used for teaching reading in their elementary classrooms, and they were not involved in achievement grouping. These findings may indicate that the effects of the cluster grouping combined with regrouping for reading instruction had a positive impact on the reading achievement of treatment school students in the three years.

Table 3   Class of 2001 Planned Contrasts: Means, Standard Deviations, Adjusted Means, and F-values for Reading and Math Achievement Measures in Grade 2, 3, 4 and 5

Achievement measure	Treatment School Mean (SD)	Adjusted mean	Comparison School Mean (SD)	Adjusted mean	F value	E.S.
(Covariate)						
Reading Grade 2	50.67 (21.91)		53.22 (15.03)			
Reading Grade 3	46.11 (19.38)	46.79	53.60 (14.56)	52.62	11.71**	$R^2 = .066$
Reading Grade 4	50.21 (17.00)	50.90	51.62 (15.20)	50.64	.01	
Reading Grade 5	48.59 (18.57)	49.27	52.78 (15.14)	51.80	1.78	
(Covariate)						
Math Grade 2	52.04 (18.33)		57.78 (16.45)			
Math Grade 3	56.04 (19.68)	57.70	57.84 (18.45)	55.43	.96	
Math Grade 4	55.79 (17.75)	57.12	53.42 (13.49)	51.49	7.72*	$R^2 = .044$
Math Grade 5	54.03 (17.93)	55.54	50.10 (16.20)	47.92	13.56**	$R^2 = .076$

Note. $n = 155$. *$p < .05$. **$p < .001$

With regard to math achievement for both data sets, students in the treatment school scored significantly higher than the comparison school students in mathematics during the three program years, with the largest differences in grade 5 after adjusting scores for initial differences. However, unlike reading achievement, treatment school students did not show significant changes in math achievement, possibly because the math scores were already high (as indicated by mean NCE scores above 50 for students from each data set). For the three program years, the average NCE math score for the Class of 2000 was 53.75, and for the Class of 2001 it was 55.28. Students were regrouped for math instruction between classes by achievement levels. As with reading, the collection of high teacher expectations, the use of grouping, and the use of challenging instructional strategies may have been responsible for the high achievement in mathematics of the students from the treatment school.

As indicated in the qualitative part of this analysis, many teachers ($n = 11$; 79%) and all administrators ($n = 3$) thought that the restriction of the range of achievement in classrooms, as well as the between-class grouping by achievement levels in reading and math, helped teachers meet the individual needs of students in their classrooms. Qualitative findings also indicated the use of a variety of instructional strategies around the themes of challenge, choice, and interests. High teacher expectations and the use of grouping may also have influenced student achievement in the treatment school. Again, contrary to the popular anti-grouping sentiment, these findings reinforce the idea that the use of flexible grouping coupled with appropriate instruction may positively influence student achievement. The implication for elementary schools is that flexible achievement grouping used in conjunction with challenging curriculum should be considered when designing educational programs. As Teacher 3C explained:

> By using achievement grouping, we are able to challenge the high achievers and meet the needs of the low achievers without having the low achievers or the high achievers feel like they had been singled out. We are able to adjust our curriculum and instruction to meet the individual needs of the students at their levels.

Qualitative Findings for Research Question 3: What Factors Exist in the Classrooms and the School Using Cluster Grouping That May Have Influenced Student Achievement?

The findings discussed in this section emerged as core categories after open, axial, and selective coding had been applied to the data as recommended by Strauss and Corbin (1990). This coding yielded three core categories: *the use of grouping, the apparent impact of the teachers, and the general school environment.* Response frequencies greater than or equal to six (over half of the teachers not responsible for the high-achieving cluster students) were considered to represent a general consensus and are reported as a theme within a core category. With regard to the administrators, two of three responses indicated a theme.

The Use of Grouping

Because cluster grouping implies ability grouping, both the program documents and the teacher interviews focused on the use of various forms of grouping in the program between grades 3 and 5. Grouping occurred within classrooms and between classrooms and, in both cases, was flexible. Like the identification procedures that were used to place students into classrooms, grouping was employed in a variety of ways, and students were not locked into specific groups for the duration of the day. Additionally, many teachers ($n = 13$; 93%) reported that they thought the cluster grouping was directly related to the increase in the number of *high-achieving* students identified during the three program years. Others ($n = 11$; 79%) reported that they believed the cluster grouping program helped them better meet the needs of the individual students within their classrooms.

Between-class groups. It became evident after the first few interviews that even though cluster grouping was used for placing students in classrooms, students were regrouped by achievement for reading and math instruction in grades 3, 4, and 5. This meant that, within each grade level, the teachers regrouped the students for reading and math instruction by achievement levels, and different teachers instructed students who were not necessarily the students from their regular class. This regrouping applied to the Class of 2000 for reading in grades 3–5 and for math in grades 4 and 5. The Class of 2001 was regrouped for instruction for reading and math in grades 3–5. Teachers at each grade level chose to do this to better meet the needs of students. One teacher would take the low-achieving students, another would take the advanced students, and the remaining three teachers would have students who were achieving near average in reading and math. The teacher who had the *high-achieving* cluster did not necessarily teach these students for reading and math. Therefore, other teachers had the opportunity to work with the most advanced students. The teachers explained that more students than those in the *high achieving* cluster could be in the *high reading* or *high math* sections, and that these sections did not necessarily include the same students. As Teacher 3A explained:

> We had so many high math students who weren't in the high cluster, we thought, to really meet the needs of the grade level, we would have a cluster group strictly for math. We also had the high cluster reading group to meet the needs of other children who may not have been identified or who had strengths that weren't evident across the board. We were able to target more children for high reading by regrouping within the grade level for reading.

Teacher 3B, who taught the low math class, explained:

> I teach the low math group, which includes the learning disabled students and those identified for Chapter 1 assistance. With these students, I am able to teach in different ways and go at a slower pace, but they think that they are great at math because the better students are not in the room to make them feel slow. We do a lot of hands-on things like base-10 blocks, patterning, and touch math, because many of them can't get it in the traditional ways. We do a lot of problem solving, mental math . . . I challenge them at grade level . . . I don't dumb down the curriculum, I just teach it differently so they can be successful, too.

This teacher also taught the advanced reading section where she used a literature-based curriculum, and students worked beyond grade level, had their curriculum compacted, and were involved in many different writing activities. When teaching the low-achieving students who had been regrouped for math, she had the assistance of a teacher consultant and a Chapter 1 aide.

In addition to using between-class grouping by achievement for math and reading, the three *high-achieving* cluster teachers indicated that they used between-grade grouping when it was needed to meet the needs of individual students. For example, Teacher 5A explained:

> Some students went to sixth grade to take math in the middle school, because they were even beyond where I was with the high math group. After math in the middle school, they would return for the rest of the day in fifth grade.

Within-class groups. The types of within-class grouping that were reported included interest grouping ($n = 8$), cooperative grouping ($n = 7$), and flexible grouping ($n = 6$). Six teachers explained that they used flexible grouping and, depending on the lesson, students often chose their groups or partners. Teacher 4D described her use of grouping in the following way:

> I do all those things, cooperative learning, interest groups, peer teaching, whole group instruction. We're driven . . . to do what works for children and use a variety of methods. So, anything that we feel we can use in our classrooms to facilitate whatever the needs are, we do that.

Teacher 3A described,

> I used all forms of grouping, including cooperative learning, flexible groups, and interest groups. Sometimes I chose the groups, sometimes it was by interest, and sometimes groups were chosen independently by the students.

Flexible groups. Flexibility emerged as a key component of both the within-class grouping and the between-class grouping. Seven teachers explained that the grouping between classes was always flexible, and that if a student needed to be in another section, the cooperation and flexibility existed within each grade level to move students around as needed. With the exception of the four teachers who said that their primary mode of instruction was whole-group instruction, it was evident from the many comments that the use of grouping within the classrooms varied and was flexible in nature. For example, Teacher 4C explained:

> The types of groups that I use in my class depend on the activity; sometimes I use cooperative learning, or peer tutoring, other times I use interest grouping, or I group students by ability. The main thing with my use of grouping is that it is flexible.

Even though students were identified in various achievement levels for placement into classrooms, it became evident that these identification categories were not fixed, nor were they used consistently to group students for instruction. Rather, students were grouped and regrouped in many flexible ways designed by the teachers to help them be successful.

Cluster grouping and meeting the needs of individual students. Eleven teachers (79%) indicated that cluster-grouping placement strategies made it easier for them to meet the needs of individual students in their classrooms. The superintendent and the assistant principal agreed. Eight teachers (57%) said that cluster grouping allowed them more time to work with lower achieving students at a level appropriate for these students, whereas all three of the teachers who worked with the high achievers indicated that they were able to do much more to challenge and promote growth in these students than had previously been possible. In the 1990 program evaluation report submitted to the Board of Education, four teachers explained how cluster grouping had helped them better address individual student needs in their classrooms.

The teachers who taught the high-achieving clusters said that it was beneficial to the high achievers to be clustered together because they challenged each other and didn't always get to be the best. Teacher 4A explained, "They [high-achieving students] challenge and motivate each other, and with just one or two kids, I don't think that would happen."

Nine teachers (64%) indicated that the restricted range of achievement levels created by cluster-grouping placements made meeting individual needs easier for them.

> Yes. That's one thing teaching for the first 10 years, I always felt guilty, like I always felt I wasn't giving enough time to the low kids, and I also felt like I wasn't challenging the high kids enough. Because I think the gap is narrower so I can zero in on their needs. (Teacher 3B)
>
> The kids were more deliberately placed, so we didn't have as broad of a range and didn't have to deal with the extremes. I also had an aide and a teacher consultant, which helped to meet the needs of the students who were struggling. (Teacher 4B)

The majority of the teachers agreed that cluster grouping helped them meet the needs of individual students in their classrooms. The restricted range of achievement levels created more time for the teachers to work with students in their classrooms. They also reported that cluster grouping was beneficial to students because it allowed students of like achievement levels to work together and challenge each other.

The Apparent Impact of Teachers

Positive classroom environments. Teachers and administrators reported positive classroom environments and said that school was a place where students wanted to be. This finding was confirmed by school climate surveys, completed in 1990 and 1991 as part of school improvement planning, in which students in the upper elementary school indicated that they were, on average, happy with their classrooms and felt that school was friendly and safe. Parent satisfaction surveys were high each year, as reported in the annual reports to the

Board of Education and to the State Department of Education. During the semistructured interviews, teachers were asked to describe the atmosphere of their classrooms.

> Excited. The kids don't want to miss school, even when they're sick. I never have a motivation problem, because they like what they are doing and are challenged and feeling successful. (Teacher 3A)
>
> I think it's safe for them to be who they are, to be different, and to disagree with me. If they offer suggestions on my teaching, I listen to them. I think they understand that I really care, but that there are high expectations for learning. (Teacher 5A)

Both teachers and administrators discussed how the teaching strategies and the curriculum modifications were used to benefit the students. Many teachers ($n = 12$) discussed adjusting assignments, helping students to feel successful, and making their classrooms places that students wanted to be. A theme of concern and caring was continuously discussed by teachers.

High, yet realistic teacher expectations. All of the teachers reported that their expectations for students were high, and two said that they expected more than one year's growth from their students. Two other teachers stated that their expectations were the same as when the high-achieving students had been in their classrooms. Fifth-grade teachers discussed preparing their students for success at the middle school. The general tone of the interviews indicated that the teachers believed in the need to challenge, but at the same time, help the students experience success. Three teachers said they had been accused of having standards that were "too high." None of the teachers said that removing the high-achieving students from their classrooms had, in any way, influenced their expectations. Comments from teachers regarding their expectations included:

> I always keep my expectations of the high achievers high and work and make sure I really push the kids to do more than they want to do. I give work back to them, tell them they have good ideas, and encourage them to expand [their ideas], because they are capable of more. (Teacher 3A)
>
> I truly expected all students to achieve . . . regardless of where they are or who they are. I want to meet the needs of students and feel my standards or expectations are high. (Teacher 5E)
>
> I don't believe because a child has an LD or EMI label means that they are low. I think that's a problem with education—just because a child is identified with a disability or something, some people tend to think, Well, they're low. I expect a lot from them—I don't think they are dumb. I think they can do just as many things as gifted kids, maybe not to the full extent, but in some things they can go beyond. If it's their interest, they can excel just as much as anybody else can. (Teacher 3B)

As the quantitative analyses of the identification categories and achievement data indicated, students seemed to be successful in these classrooms.

Strategies for challenging students and meeting students' needs in the cluster-grouped classroom. Most teachers indicated that they were concerned with meeting the needs of individual students. The strategies these teachers used to challenge and meet the needs of students in their cluster-grouped classrooms are summarized in Table 4. The related themes of challenge, choice, and student interest emerged through all these strategies. Strategies are presented according to which of these themes or combination of themes they belong.

As indicated in Table 4, the majority of these strategies were reported to have been used by the teachers who taught the classrooms with the high-achieving cluster students. However, many strategies were used in other classrooms with students of all achievement levels. For example, curriculum compacting was used by all teachers who had the high-achieving students, but also by five other teachers. Four teachers with regular classrooms had implemented the choice of independent study with their students, and seven teachers regularly provided enrichment experiences beyond the curriculum to their students. Teachers in many classrooms reported using thinking, questioning, and problem-solving strategies, and over half of the teachers reported that they gave students choices in group assignment and curriculum assignments. A variety of methods were used to incorporate student interests including the use of enrichment/interest centers ($n = 10$); curriculum compacting ($n = 8$); and independent study in an area of student choice and interest ($n = 7$). As Teacher 4A described:

> Because their ideas are implemented, their ideas become part of what we do. Students are pretty empowered in the classroom. For example, a couple of years ago, we had two girls really interested in special education. They did some research and worked once a week with the hearing impaired teacher and her students, and then they came back to class and taught us sign language and shared what they learned.

As indicated by the teachers of the high-achieving cluster students, there was a balance of acceleration and enrichment through appropriate challenges and choices.

> In the homeroom with the high cluster, I found with English and science we were able to move much faster and at a higher level. We didn't need to do spelling every day like other classrooms. I was able to use that time for independent studies and special projects with children. I really liked it because I thought I was challenging the students, and it was productive. I pretest and give them other choices instead. I also move at a faster pace, at a higher level, with higher expectations. (Teacher 3A)
> I use fifth grade math and spelling. I use all kinds of enrichment things—mind benders, we pull in Engin-Uity, inventions, Invent

America stuff, they get involved in poetry writing, Science Olympiad, Math Olympiad. (Teacher 4A)

Academically talented [students] were allowed to move up to the sixth grade or in some way [work] independently. We did various types of activities. They would have choices . . . they could put on a drama to present their material, they could write a book, they use poetry, they could sing a song. . . . Then, we had different enrichment programs throughout the school that kids could apply for and attend. If they liked to write, they could go to a residence in writing; sometimes, we had a mentor in drama or art with them, and they were allowed to pursue those things. I would pretest; if they knew it, then we would cover only the things that they hadn't mastered. With independent studies, they had choices to select things they were interested in, but they were required to meet a certain standard, a certain way of writing; they had to produce a product, had to share with an audience . . . that sort of thing. I tried to have writing assignments across the curriculum, plus their independent study was like a thesis-type paper. (Teacher 5A)

The General School Environment

Strong administrative leadership and support. Teachers supplied evidence of strong administrative leadership. Only one teacher said the administration had not been supportive, two others expressed that support had been mixed, and 11 indicated that there had been firm support on the part of the administration.

Professional development opportunities. Professional development was ongoing, and most teachers indicated that it was an important part of their success as teachers and with the cluster grouping program. Before choosing to implement the cluster grouping program, all staff attended a one-day workshop on the concept of duster grouping, and seven teachers went on site visitations to a school that was successfully using cluster grouping. National, state, regional, and local professional development opportunities in gifted education were made available to staff, with all participating in at least the local opportunities (e.g., curriculum compacting; differentiating and individualizing curriculum and instruction; LD gifted and underachievers; meeting the needs of gifted math and science students). In all, a total of 64% of the teachers attended national, state, or regional professional development conferences or workshops in gifted education. Additionally, six teachers mentioned how helpful it was to have the teachers who teach the *high-achieving* cluster in the building as resources. As Teacher 3B explained:

I've learned so much from [Teacher 3A], and I adapt many of the strategies that she uses with her high achievers and use them with my LD and low achievers. I don't think that gifted education is just for gifted students.

Table 4   Strategies for Challenging and Meeting Students' Needs in the
Regular Cluster Grouped Classroom: Frequency of Use by Grade
Level Responses

Strategy	Grade 3 Responses (n = 5)	Grade 4 Responses (n = 4)	Grade 5 Responses (n = 5)
CHALLENGE			
Integrating High Order Thinking Skills	5*	3*	3*
Developing Critical Thinking Skills	2	3*	3*
Using Creative Thinking Skills	2*	2*	2*
Integrating Problem Solving	3*	2*	3*
Assigning Projects	3*	1*	1*
Using Acceleration	1*	2*	1*
Adjusting Assignments	4	3*	3
CHALLENGE & INTEREST			
Spending Time with High Achievers	1*	1*	1*
Developing Curricular Extensions	5*	4	3*
CHOICE & INTEREST			
Providing Choice of Partners or Groups	2*	2*	4*
Providing Choice to Work Alone or Together	3*	2*	3*
CHALLENGE, CHOICE, & INTEREST			
Using Open-Ended Questioning	5*	4*	3*
Offering Independent Study	2*	2*	3*
Using Challenge Questions	2*	2*	1
Implementing Curriculum Compacting	4*	1*	3*
Providing Enrichment Experiences	5*	2*	3*
Providing Choice of Problems or Assignments	2*	2	3*

Note. *Indicates that one of the respondents included the teacher of the high achieving cluster.

Belief in colleagues and collaboration. The administration and teachers demonstrated strong support of and confidence in the teachers. There was a general atmosphere in this school of quality and of caring by teachers who seemed to do their best to work with students. Fifty-five percent of the teachers who were not responsible for the *high-achieving* students indicated that they used strategies in their classrooms that they thought were typically "gifted education" strategies. All of the third-grade teachers, for example, indicated that they were glad that Teacher 3A had the cluster of high achievers because she had to put so much extra effort into meeting these students' needs, and she was talented in working with those children. The teachers had confidence in each other, worked together, and were regarded as competent by the administration.

Program benefits to all students and teachers. The program was viewed as successful because the teachers and administrators believe it was beneficial both to the teachers and to the students. The teachers liked the program, and many believed it helped them better meet the needs of the students in their classrooms. Teacher 3B explained how she came to view the program:

> One thing—I remember how skeptical I was at the beginning because I'm not a risk-taker. I thought the same thing a few other people thought—oh, you take those top kids out and I'm not going to have any spark. And that was so far from being true. I see lots of sparks in my room. . . . and having my daughter in [the program] . . . there's such a difference in her attitude and her love for school is back . . . before being placed in the high-achieving cluster, she wasn't being challenged in school, now to see her doing research projects as an eight-year-old . . . she's doing projects so beyond what I ever thought and she is so excited about school.

The administrators who were interviewed expressed their belief that the cluster-grouping program had helped the teachers do their jobs. As the superintendent explained:

> Well, I think we've got some real benefits. I had a great deal of skepticism when we first started because I thought, Well, are we looking at an elitist program where we're taking the cream of the crop and separating them even though they may be within a classroom with other students that's going to "dummy down" the other classes. In fact, it's had just the opposite effect. We have been able to have leadership rise in other classes where we don't have the very bright students who have been in those classes. So, it's had a real bonus effect for more general education students, from what I can see . . . and at the same time accomplishing more challenges for the gifted kids. Additionally, I think that the cluster grouping program actually makes the teachers' jobs easier.

Summary of Findings for Research Question 3

Qualitative findings provided further insight into the treatment school and classrooms. The teachers in this study created positive classroom environments in which high expectations were held for all of their students. They used a variety of strategies, including various forms of grouping, to challenge and meet student needs. The program was supported by strong administrative leadership, and teachers had continuing professional development and growth opportunities in which most teachers chose to become involved. Both teachers and administrators worked collaboratively and indicated confidence in their colleagues' abilities. These findings were similar to those found in the exemplary programs for gifted investigated by Delcourt and Evans (1994), who cited the following characteristics of these programs: strong leadership, supportive atmosphere and environment, and flexible curriculum and instruction matched to student needs.

DISCUSSION

The quantitative findings (increased reading achievement, higher math achievement, and increased numbers of students identified as *high-achieving* in the treatment school) combined with the qualitative findings indicate that cluster grouping, when combined with high teacher expectations, the use of strategies to challenge and meet individual needs, and positive classroom environments, may have a positive impact on all students in a school. All teachers and administrators ($n = 17$) involved in the program believed that cluster grouping was beneficial to both students and teachers, because it helped students be successful by structuring classes in a manner that helped teachers better address individual needs. These findings support research-based suggestions by Kulik and Kulik (1992) and Rogers (1991), who suggested that grouping by ability, when used in conjunction with appropriate differentiated instruction, can be beneficial to student achievement.

Contrary to findings by Oakes (1985, 1995), the teachers in this study who did not have the cluster of high-achieving students were not regarded as the poor teachers, and they did not lower their expectations for their students. In fact, they reported that the opposite occurred, and they expected the same or more from their students as highlighted by the following teacher comments.

> I guess I have the same high standards for the average and low-achieving student as I do for any other student. (Teacher 4C)

> I think it's our expectations. I think l just thought that they could all do it and expected them to do it. (Teacher 5D)

As noted by Tomlinson and Callahan (1992), Renzulli (1994), Reis, Gentry, and Park (1995), and the U. S. Department of Education (1993), the use of gifted education "know-how" has the potential to improve general education practices. The cluster-grouping program investigated in this study was designed to simultaneously address the needs of high-achieving students *and* the needs of other students. As a result of this connection with the general education program, professional development opportunities in gifted education were made available to all staff, and dialogue between teachers of the high-achieving cluster students and the rest of the staff was encouraged. As a result, all teachers received professional development in gifted education strategies and reported using these strategies in their classrooms with all of their students.

Unlike the classrooms described by Archambault et al. (1993) and observed by Goodlad (1984) and Westberg et al. (1993), the classrooms in this school were characterized by a variety of challenging activities and varied instructional strategies. Renzulli (1994) noted that the practice in many schools of diagnosing and remediating weaknesses should be replaced with a talent development approach to enrichment learning and teaching that recognizes student interests, strengths, and talents as a basis for their education. In this study, integration of the cluster-grouping program with the general education program seemed to impact all teachers and students in the school. The treatment school teachers applied many strategies from gifted education to their daily teaching, something that might not have happened had professional development in gifted education been reserved only for the teachers of the high-achieving students. The implication is that all staff and, consequently, all students can benefit from in-service in gifted education strategies. Therefore, schools should be careful not to limit their professional development in gifted education to just those teachers who work with identified gifted students. By offering more teachers opportunities to learn and to apply gifted education know-how, perhaps student achievement can be raised in schools.

The findings of this study should interest school districts that are struggling with how to meet the needs of gifted students in the regular classroom. Although current reform trends suggest that heterogeneous grouping is preferred (George, 1993; Hopfenberg & Levin, 1993; Oakes, 1985; Slavin, 1987a; Wheelock, 1992) when developing elementary classroom configurations, the findings of this study suggest that the deliberate placement of a narrower range of achievement groups in teachers' classrooms, including the placement of a group of *high-achieving* students together in one room, is beneficial to both students and teachers. It stands to reason that if the *high-achieving* students are placed with a teacher who has the background and willingness to adjust curriculum and instruction to meet these students' special needs, their needs are more likely to be met than if they are randomly placed into all teachers' classrooms for the sake of heterogeneous grouping. Further, as was done in the program in this study, if the placement of students in the other teachers' classrooms is done thoughtfully, and includes a group of students who are above average, then districts might see growth in identification and achievement similar to that observed in this study. The implication for districts is that a well-developed cluster-grouping program, such as the one in this study, can offer gifted education services to *high-achieving* students while helping teachers better meet the needs of all students.

Elementary classroom teachers might find the results of this study interesting as they struggle to meet the individual needs of students. Of special interest are the reports by teachers in this study that removing the highest achievers from four of five classrooms per grade level did not affect the way teachers viewed the students in their classrooms. There was no report of "losing the spark" by teachers who were not responsible for the *high-achieving* students. On the contrary, these teachers reported that having the *high-achieving* students removed from their classrooms helped them better meet the needs of individual students, while encouraging new talent to emerge. As Teacher 5B suggested:

> I really believe that those high-achieving kids are not models for the other kids. The other kids know where they are . . . so they don't model themselves after those kids. When [the high achievers are] taken out and able to move at their own rate, then these other kids who are good and

could be better begin to surface and begin to shine and not sit back and let those extremely high achievers take control of the classroom.

Other teachers may want to consider the views of the teachers involved in this study when deciding whether to try a cluster-grouping approach to programming and classroom placements.

The varied uses of grouping found in this study have implications for teachers who have questions regarding its appropriate uses. The teachers in this study used achievement grouping in math and reading, reporting that this made it easier for them to challenge the student at appropriate levels. They also used other forms of flexible grouping. The implications are that flexible achievement grouping has the potential to produce academic gains for all students.

Although the weaknesses of causal comparative research are well documented (Gall, Borg, & Gall, 1996), a study such as this is valuable in other ways. First, it enabled the investigation of a practice that was implemented and carried out in an actual school setting. Second, it investigated a school-initiated innovation, as opposed to an innovation demanded by external sources, such as federal funding or special mandates. Because the innovation was school-based, local control and ownership were invested in the program. Although there are problems associated with the use of intact groups, the use of intact groups provided a distinct advantage in this research. The intact groups examined were stable over time and facilitated longitudinal comparisons of students between and within groups during the course of a three-year program. Finally, this study examined an often-recommended practice for which little research exists, and the findings can serve as the basis for further, more carefully controlled experimental or quasi-experimental research. A discussion of limitations follows.

Limitations

Internal validity of the study was limited by instrumentation, history, differential selection, the use of intact groups, and multiple treatments (Gall, Borg, & Gall, 1996). Regarding instrumentation, existing measures of achievement had to be used, and these measures were on two different tests. The use of NCE scores, the similarity of the ITBS and the CAT, the large number of students involved in the study, and the use of ANCOVA enabled the use of these two instruments to compare student achievement over time. The use of two data sets and repeated measures helped to control for the threat of history and increase confidence that results were not simply due to chance. However, results must be interpreted with caution because other events (of which the researchers were unaware) that occurred during the time the program took place may also have influenced results. The similarity of the comparison school and the use of a covariate helped to control for the threat of differential selection.

Huck and Cormier (1996) warned that a covariate must be used with caution when there are intact groups. However, the covariate was not highly correlated with the independent variable, and the use of nationally normed instruments on which students scored near the national mean helped to increase confidence in the use of the covariate. Additionally, whenever intact groups are used, there is the problem of intraclass correlation (ICC), meaning that the subjects' scores on dependent variables are often correlated simply because they are in the groups (Barcikowski, 1981; Scariano & Davenport, 1987), which violates the assumption that data are independent and inflates the alpha level. One method for addressing the problem of ICC is to make the classroom the unit of analysis. This was impossible here for several reasons. First, students were examined over a three-year period, and their classroom placements changed. Second, flexible grouping also changed the groups that students worked in throughout the day. Finally, no information regarding classroom placements was available for the comparison school. To control for the inflated probability of Type I error, alpha levels were examined within the context of this problem. Multivariate ANCOVA analyses produced significance at $p < .0001$, and the contrasts produced significance ranges from $p < .05$ to $p < .001$, indicating that findings were likely significant despite the increased probability of Type I error. As Cohen (1994) suggested, examining practical significance estimated by effect sizes is more meaningful than reporting statistical significance. Effect sizes were reported throughout this study. These alpha levels and effect sizes increase confidence in the results when considering the problems associated with non-independence of scores.

The effect of multiple treatments must be acknowledged. This study was not intended to isolate one variable, study that variable, and attribute causality to that variable. Rather, the intent was to acknowledge the complexity of a real program that existed in a real school. There was more going on than just "cluster grouping," as there would be in any school. It was not intended, nor was it possible, to isolate the effects of cluster grouping from the effects of several other variables, including regrouping by achievement for math and reading, the clustering of special needs students as well as high-achieving students, and the entire class of high-achieving cluster students that existed by fifth grade. However, viewed in total, the findings are powerful, and much can be learned about classroom practices, identification, and student achievement by examining the ways in which cluster grouping was integrated with and applied to an elementary school program, its curriculum, and instruction. Cluster grouping was the basis from which the school programs developed, but it was not the sole program existing in this school. Therefore, it would not be appropriate in this study of cluster grouping to make a claim that simply placing students in a cluster group will increase achievement among students without the flexible grouping within and between classes, the staff development and ownership, high teacher expectations, differentiation of curriculum and instruction for all levels of students, and a reduction of range of achievement levels that the teachers had to teach.

The qualitative portion might have been strengthened by including interviews from parents and students; however, given that this study occurred after the students were in the program, and they had since progressed to middle school, it was decided that such interviews might not provide valid recollections of the elementary school experiences. In further study of cluster grouping that occurs during the program, it would be advisable to include perspectives from both students and parents.

CONCLUSION

The key to the findings of this study is that the use of cluster grouping facilitated many other positive changes in this school—as perceived by the teachers—such as rich staff development opportunities, ownership in a program that they developed, high teacher expectations, and a reduced range of achievement levels in their classrooms that helped facilitate teachers' desire to better meet the individual needs of all students. The use of grouping is a rich and complex issue, and far too many researchers have attempted to isolate and oversimplify its use. The intention of this study was to understand the working dynamics of cluster grouping in a school that saw consistent increases in achievement and identification of their elementary students. To this end, it seems clear that cluster grouping played a role in this school's success.

NOTE

1. The definitions of the terms high-achieving, high-ability, and gifted vary in the literature. The students in this study were identified as high-achieving.

REFERENCES

Airasian, P. W. (1989). Review of the *California Achievement Tests, Forms E and F*. In J. C. Conoley & J. J. Kramer (Eds.), *The Tenth Mental Measurements Yearbook* (pp. 126–128). Lincoln, NE: Buros Institute of Mental Measurement.

Archambault, F. X., Westberg, K., Brown, S. B., Hallmark, B. W., Emmons, C. L, & Zhang, W. (1993). *Regular classroom practices with gifted students: Results of a national survey of classroom teachers*. Storrs, CT: The National Research Center on the Gifted and Talented.

Balzer, C., & Siewert, B. (Eds.). (1990). *Program and service models: Suggested programs and services for identified talented and gifted students, K-12*. (Technical assistance paper 3, Revised.). Salem, OR: Oregon Department of Education.

Barcikowski, R. S. (1981). Statistical power with group mean as the unit of analysis. *Journal of Educational Statistics, 6*, 267–285.

Brown, S. B., Archambault, F. X., Zhang, W., Westberg, K. (1994, April). *The impact of gifted students on the classroom practices of teachers*. Paper presented at the annual conference of the American Educational Research Association, New Orleans, LA.

Bryant, M. A. (1987). Meeting the needs of gifted first grade children in a heterogeneous classroom. *Roeper Review, 9*, 214–216.

California Achievement Test, Form E. (1984). Monterey, CA: CTB/McGraw-Hill.

Cohen, J. (1988). *Statistical power analysis for the behavioral sciences* (2nd ed.). Hillsdale, NJ: Lawrence Erlbaum.

Cohen, J. (1994). The earth is round. *American Psychologist, 49*, 997–1003.

Coleman, M. R. (1995). The importance of cluster grouping. *Gifted Child Today, 18*(1), 38–40.

Davis, G. A., & Rimm, S. W. (1985). *Education of the gifted and talented.* Englewood Cliffs, NJ: Prentice-Hall.

Delcourt, M. A. B., & Evans, K. (1994). *Qualitative extension of the learning outcomes study.* Storrs, CT: The National Research Center on the Gifted and Talented.

Delcourt, M. A. B., Loyd, B. H., Cornell, D. G., & Goldberg, M.D. (1994). *Evaluation of the effects of programming arrangements on student learning outcomes.* Storrs, CT: The National Research Center on the Gifted and Talented.

Dixon, W. J. (Ed.). (1992). *BMDP statistical software manual* (Vols. 1–2). Berkeley, CA: University of California Press.

Gall, M. D., Borg, W. R., & Gall, J. P. (1996). *Educational research: An introduction* (6th ed.). White Plains, NY: Longman.

Gentry, M. L. (1996). *Cluster grouping: An investigation of student achievement, identification, and classroom practices.* Unpublished doctoral dissertation, University of Connecticut, Storrs, CT.

George, P. (1993). Tracking and ability grouping in the middle school: Ten tentative truths. *Middle School Journal, 24*(4), 17–24.

Goodlad, J. I. (1984). *A place called school.* New York: McGraw-Hill.

Hieronymus, A. N., Hoover, H. D., & Lindquist, E. F. (1984). *Iowa tests of basic skills (Form G).* Chicago: Riverside Publishing.

Hoover, S., Sayler, M., & Feldhusen, J. F. (1993). Cluster grouping of elementary students at the elementary level. *Roeper Review, 16*, 13–15.

Hopfenberg, W. S., & Levin, H. A. (1993). *The accelerated schools resource guide.* San Francisco: Jossey-Bass.

Huck, S. W., & Cormier, W. H. (1996). *Reading statistics and research.* New York: Harper-Collins.

Juntune, J. (1981). *Successful programs for the gifted and talented.* Hot Springs, AR: National Association for the Gifted and Talented.

Kaplan, S. N. (1974). *Providing programs for the gifted and talented.* Ventura, CA: Office of the Ventura County Superintendent of Schools.

Kennedy, D. M. (1989). *Classroom interactions of gifted and non-gifted fifth graders.* Unpublished doctoral dissertation, Purdue University, West Lafayette, IN.

Kennedy, D. M. (1995). Teaching gifted in regular classrooms: Plain talk about creating a gifted-friendly classroom. *Roeper Review, 17*, 232–234.

Kulik, J. A. (1992). *An analysis of the research on ability grouping: Historical and contemporary perspectives.* Storrs, CT: The National Research Center on the Gifted and Talented.

Kulik, J. A., & Kulik, C.-L. C. (1991). Ability grouping and gifted students. In N. Colangelo & G. A. Davis (Eds.), *Handbook of gifted education* (pp. 178–196). Boston, MA: Allyn & Bacon.

Kulik, J. A., & Kulik, C.-L. C. (1992). Meta-analytic findings on grouping programs. *Gifted Child Quarterly, 36*, 73–77.

LaRose, B. (1986). The lighthouse program: A longitudinal research project. *Journal for the Education of the Gifted, 9*, 224–232.

McInerney, C. F. (1983). *Cluster grouping for the gifted, the bottom line: Research-based classroom strategies.* A series for teachers. St. Paul, MN: LINE.

Michigan Department of Education. (1994, August). *1992–93 Bulletin 1014: Michigan K-12 school districts ranked by selected financial data.* Lansing, MI: Author.

Mitchell, E. S. (1986). Multiple triangulation: A methodology for nursing science. *Advances in Nursing Science, 8*(3), 18–26.

Oakes, J. (1985). *Keeping track: How schools structure inequality.* New Haven, CT: Yale University Press.

Oakes, J. (1995). More than meets the eye: Links between tracking and the culture of schools. In H. Pool & J. A. Page (Eds.), *Beyond tracking: Finding success in inclusive schools* (pp. 59–70). Bloomington, IN: Phi Delta Kappa Educational Foundation.

Purcell, J. (1994). *The status of programs for high ability students.* Storrs, CT: The National Research Center on the Gifted and Talented.

Reis, S. M., Gentry, M. L., & Park, S. (1995). *Extending the pedagogy of gifted education to all students: The enrichment cluster study.* Storrs, CT: The National Research Center on the Gifted and Talented.

Renzulli, J. S. (1994). *Schools for talent development: A comprehensive plan for total school improvement.* Mansfield Center, CT: Creative Learning Press.

Renzulli, J. S., & Reis, S. M. (1985). *The schoolwide enrichment model: A comprehensive plan for educational excellence.* Mansfield Center, CT: Creative Learning Press.

Renzulli, J. S., Smith, L. H., Callahan, C., White, A., & Hartman, R. (1977). *Scales for rating the behavioral characteristics of superior students.* Mansfield Center, CT: Creative Learning Press.

Rogers, K. B. (1991). *The relationship of grouping practices to the education of the gifted and talented learner.* Storrs, CT: The National Research Center on the Gifted and Talented.

Rogers, K. B. (1993). Grouping the gifted and talented: Questions and answers. *Roeper Review, 16,* 8–12.

Scariano, S., & Davenport, J. (1987). The effects of violations of the independence assumption in the one way ANOVA. *American Statistician, 41,* 123–129.

Slavin, R. E. (1987a). Ability grouping: A best-evidence synthesis. *Review of Educational Research, 57,* 293–336.

Slavin, R. E. (1987b). Grouping for instruction. *Equity and Excellence, 23*(1–2), 31–36.

Spradley, J. P. (1980). *Participant observation.* New York: Holt, Rinehart & Winston.

Strauss, A. L., & Corbin, J. (1990). *Basics of qualitative research: Grounded theory procedures and techniques.* Newbury Park, CA: Sage Publications.

Tabachnick, B. G., & Fidell, L. S. (1989). *Using multivariate statistics.* New York: HarperCollins.

Tomlinson, C. A., & Callahan, C. M. (1992). Contributions of gifted education to general education in a time of change. *Gifted Child Quarterly, 36,* 183–189.

U.S. Department of Education, Office of Educational Research and Improvement. (1993). *National excellence: A case for developing America's talent.* Washington, DC: U.S. Government Printing Office.

Westberg, K. L., Archambault, F. X., Dobyns, S. M., & Salvin, T. J. (1993). *An observational study of instructional and curricular practices used with gifted and talented students in regular classrooms* (Research Monograph 93104). Storrs, CT: The National Research Center on the Gifted and Talented.

Wheelock, A. (1992). *Crossing the tracks: How untracking can save America's schools.* New York: New Press.

Winebrenner, S. (1992). *Teaching gifted kids in the regular classroom.* Minneapolis, MN: Free Spirit Publishing.

Winebrenner, S., & Devlin, B. (1994). *Cluster grouping fact sheet: How to provide full-time services for gifted students on existing budgets.* Lombard, IL: Phantom Press.

12

Programming, Grouping, and Acceleration in Rural School Districts: A Survey of Attitudes and Practices

Eric D. Jones and W. Thomas Southern

Bowling Green State University

The development of gifted education programs is influenced by the characteristics of communities, values of residents, constraints that work against change, and forces that impel change. The levels and types of programming offered to gifted students in rural and urban school districts were compared in this study. Rural and urban districts were also compared to their uses of ability grouping in regular education programs and academic acceleration. The results of the study revealed that rural school districts are less apt to use ability grouping or academic acceleration to

Editor's Note: From Jones, E. D., & Southern, W. T. (1992). Programming, grouping, and acceleration in rural school districts: A survey of attitudes and practices. *Gifted Child Quarterly*, 36(2), 112-117. © 1992 National Association for Gifted Children. Reprinted with permission.

provide a developed range of options for gifted and talented students. Sporadic extracurricular activities tend to play more important roles in rural programs. Factors that influence the nature and quality of education of gifted and talented in rural areas are discussed.

It is frequently difficult for rural school districts to provide programs that offer the same services and experiences that larger urban and metropolitan districts may be able to afford. Compared to districts in urban and metropolitan communities, rural districts tend to be more burdened by requirements to transport students, more poorly financed, more socially and politically conservative, and more lacking in relevant community resources (e.g., well-equipped libraries, universities and colleges).

The relatively smaller size of rural districts broadly influences the program. Some options may be more available and some more feasible for rural districts to operate than others. Furthermore, educators, parents, and students in rural districts may find some options more acceptable than others. Given the wide range of possible program options, and the different levels of local economic and political support for programs in gifted education, it is reasonable to consider that the differences between rural and urban school districts will influence programs for gifted and talented students.

The existing literature on programming for gifted and talented students in rural districts has documented that community values, geographic isolation, and small and low density populations may be expected to affect the nature of programming for gifted and talented students. Rural communities tend to share more closely conservative social and political values (Kleinsasser, 1988). Conservatism and shared values are not necessarily negative factors. They are sources of community pride and stability. In rural communities schools play important and central roles in the communities that are frequently rivaled only by the local churches (Spicker, Southern, & Davis, 1987). In rural communities, schools are clearly seen as both products of and conduits for community values. The strong community values for school programs in rural areas are evidenced by higher per capita contributions to schooling in rural areas than in urban communities (Pendarvis, Howley, & Howley, 1990). Proposals to change school programs are apt to be seen as potential threats to community values and stability (Cummings, Briggs, & Mercy, 1977). Parents with well-established roots in rural communities would be particularly concerned about the introduction of gifted education programs (Nachtigal, 1982). Implicit in most gifted education programming is the notion that the participants will pursue advanced and quite possibly specialized educational careers. Rural communities frequently offer, or are seen as offering, few career opportunities for individuals with advanced academic attainments. Thus, citizens of rural communities may be concerned that gifted education programs would set a group of students apart as elite and siphon off some of the most capable young persons from the community's future. The general satisfaction that rural communities have with their schools, combined with some ambivalence about the value of special programming for gifted students, may reduce the likelihood that differential programs for gifted students will be developed in rural areas (Spicker et al., 1987).

Putting the Research to Use

The availability of programs for the gifted across the United States varies widely. Rural areas appear to have fewer programs and more limited options where programs do exist. This study provides an indication that the attitudes and priorities of coordinators of gifted programs and regular classroom teachers are not different in small towns and cities from those in rural areas. This finding implies that rural areas have fewer programs because they lack resources and because initiation of programs for the gifted is more recent in these areas. One way to address these difficulties involves a concerted effort to use new technology to bring resources to gifted students. A second is for rural districts to collaborate in providing services, pooling resources, and faculty.

One variable that did appear to contribute to more positive attitudes toward various options for gifted and talented children was the amount of training teachers and coordinators had received. In rural areas, access to training is sometimes difficult, but it appears from these results that it is essential. It might be wise for rural districts and colleges and universities who serve rural areas to explore innovative ways to provide training for rural educators.

Despite the general urbanization of the United States, there are many rural communities. In some cases their geographic isolation is extreme. In order to obtain services for gifted and talented students, rural school districts frequently must depend on consortiums with other districts. Even with consortium arrangements, the range of feasible services may still be relatively narrow compared to urban districts. Pitts (1988) observed that high transportation costs and extremely long bus routes make grouping gifted students and some other special services impractical. In areas with low population density, it is difficult to marshal resources needed for gifted education programs. Rural districts lack easy access to such resources as museums, well-stocked libraries, research facilities, universities and colleges, large manufacturing concerns, or diverse professional communities. Thus, rural schools are frequently hard pressed to direct students with broad interests and unusual talents to the appropriate community resources and mentors. Limitations on the availability of such basic resources also influence the characteristics of local programs for gifted students.

Economic conditions in rural communities also militate against the development of new educational programs. Typically tax bases are adequate to finance general education programs but inadequate to support alternatives for gifted and talented students (Howley & Howley, 1988). Salaries are generally lower in rural districts. Although many talented teachers certainly can be found in rural schools, the odds are not good that rural school districts can adequately compete with better financed urban schools to attract highly talented teachers. Teachers in rural districts frequently remain because of ties to family and community that override attractions to more lucrative jobs in urban areas (Spicker et al., 1987).

When teachers in rural districts try to meet the extra needs of their most able students, they are apt to find their best efforts strained by the routine demands of their responsibilities to general education programs. Unlike their peers in urban districts, teachers in rural areas are more apt to lack colleagues to consult with, to share materials with, and to provide insight into the educational concerns that can make providing educational services for the gifted difficult. Rural teachers have more general content area demands. They are often required to prepare instruction for several different content areas each day. Heavy workloads and demands that teachers operate in relative isolation and as generalists complicate their efforts to serve gifted students.

There are a range of possible obstacles to providing gifted education programs in rural areas. It would be surprising if rural districts offered the same number of services and the same options that would be found in urban schools. For example, the dominant model for programming in gifted education has been the resource room (Gallagher, 1985), but it remains to be seen whether it is widely adopted in rural areas. Some acceleration options may be feasible in rural districts (see Southern & Jones, 1991), but popular sentiment for many accelerative options is currently not enthusiastic (Southern, Jones, & Fiscus, 1989a, 1989b). Another option, ability grouping, is commonly used in general education programs. It is advocated by the gifted education community as a medium for addressing individual differences (Robinson, 1990; Slavin, 1990). There are, however, no data on the frequencies with which these different options, or others, are actually used in rural schools.

The purposes of this study were to compare the levels and types of programming offered to gifted students in rural and urban school districts and to obtain explanation from educators for their preferences for different options. Particular attention was given to the comparison of the uses of acceleration and ability grouping in rural districts and urban districts.

METHODS

Study One

Subjects and Settings

Twenty districts serving rural communities and 20 districts serving urban communities were selected at random from the districts in northwest and southern Ohio for participation in the study. One coordinator from each district was contacted and asked to participate in a phone survey on gifted education and ability grouping in that school district. Coordinators from three urban districts could not be contacted for interviews after several calls. Thus, the sample was composed of 37 coordinators from the 40 gifted education programs. Seventeen districts served urban and 20 served rural communities. The coordinators were informed that their responses would be confidential and that the survey would last approximately 15–20 minutes.

The districts in the survey were grouped as either rural or urban. That dichotomous grouping may have been somewhat simplistic, but it was justifiable. The combination of northwest and southern Ohio contains one large urban area, several smaller urban communities, and a host of small rural communities. The National Rural Development Institute (1986) defines rural areas as those with a population density of less than 150 per square mile or counties where 60% or more of the population lives in communities of less than 5000. Each of the small cities surveyed had populations above 5000 or were located in close proximity to larger urban areas. All small cities and the large urban area provided their own gifted education programs; communities classified as rural obtained their services in cooperative arrangements with other small communities through county boards of education. Thus, districts were scored as being rural if they (a) served a community with a population smaller than 5000, (b) were not in close proximity to an urban area, and (c) were identified by the district representative as rural. All districts serving communities with populations over 5000 were classified as urban.[1]

Instrumentation

The phone survey contained 35 items. It addressed perceptions of (a) the district's status as rural or urban, (b) the types of ability grouping used at the elementary and secondary levels, (c) the options for gifted students in the district, and (d) perceived effects of ability grouping on the various aspects of academic growth and personal adjustment for both high- and low-achieving students. Low-achieving students were defined as students with remedial or special education needs.

Study Two

Study Two is based on data gathered earlier by Southern et al. (1989b) in a survey of educators' beliefs about academic acceleration. Although individual respondents frequently could not be identified, school districts could be. Thus it was possible to review the data to determine whether or not the teachers in rural districts differed from teachers in urban districts in their beliefs about the effects of academic acceleration. The following is a synopsis of the methods used in the earlier Southern et al. (1989b) study.

Subjects and Setting

One hundred and seventy-one teachers from 78 school districts responded to a survey of the attitudes of practitioners toward academic acceleration in the fall of 1988. In the original survey the questionnaire was coded so that the communities could be identified. The Ohio Educational Directory (State Board of Education, 1989) was used to classify districts. Responses from county districts were coded as rural. Urban districts were those classified as city districts or exempted villages.

Instrumentation

The questionnaire included (a) an introductory statement that defined acceleration as either early entrance or grade skipping of academically precocious students, (b) demographic items, and (c) a 22-item Likert scale on which the respondents rated the extent to which they agreed with the statements about the effects of academic acceleration. The stems of the statements were derived from reviews of frequently cited literature in gifted education and school-readiness. Questions about the effects of early entrance and grade skipping were divided into four areas: academic achievement, social development, emotional adjustment, and the development of leadership. An analysis of the instrument indicated that attitudinal differences could be almost completely explained by the respondents' concern for social/emotional development (Southern et al., 1989b). The 22-item Likert instrument obtained a high estimate of internal consistency (Cronbach alpha, .94).

Data Analysis

One hundred and twenty-four teachers from 56 rural districts and 47 urban districts responded to the questionnaire. Two types of demographic information from the survey were analyzed: levels of training teachers had attained in gifted education and teacher beliefs about the effects of academic acceleration.

RESULTS

Study One

The frequencies at which rural and urban school districts had (a) ability grouping, (b) special programming for gifted and talented students, and (c) policy provisions for acceleration options for gifted students are provided in Table 1. The data show that most rural and urban districts reported providing special programs for their gifted and talented students at both the elementary and secondary levels. There was no difference, at the $p < .05$ level of significance, between the proportions of rural and urban districts that offered special options for gifted students. There was, however, a tendency—albeit not a statistically significant one—for rural programs to be less likely to offer options for gifted students at the elementary level.

Table 1   Frequencies for the Uses of Ability Grouping, Special Programming for Gifted Students, and Acceleration Options by Rural and Urban School Districts

| | District | | | | | |
| | Urban N = 17 | | Rural N = 20 | | | |
Option	n	%	n	%	chi-square	p
Programs for gifted						
elementary level	17	100	17	85	2.8	.10
secondary level	16	94	16	80	1.6	.21
Grouping						
elementary level	13	76	10	50	3.1	.21
secondary level	15	88	13	65	9.0	.01*
Acceleration options						
early entrance	13	76	10	50	2.8	.25
grade skipping	13	76	10	50	4.0	.14
other accelerative options	13	76	6	30	8.7	.01*

Data in Table 1 also reveal that most urban districts use ability grouping in their regular education programs at both the elementary and secondary levels. Fewer rural districts use grouping at either level. The difference between the proportions of rural and urban districts that use ability grouping was not significant at the elementary level. At the secondary level, however, a significantly greater proportion of urban districts than rural districts reported using grouping. Of the 13 districts that did not have ability grouping in their elementary programs, 9 were rural districts. Seven coordinators from rural districts reported that their districts did not have ability grouping at the secondary level.

The reasons that coordinators gave for using ability grouping could be readily coded as being generally (a) program/teacher oriented (e.g., "teacher planning is easier," "it's easier for teachers because having the same kinds of students requires less preparation," "scheduling is easier," "individualizing is too difficult"), (b) student-oriented issues (e.g. "to meet academic and social needs of individual students," "instruction is less repetitive for higher ability students," "students are best with their academic peers"), or (c) driven by tradition (e.g., "people are comfortable with ability grouping," "it is traditional," "past history"). There was no apparent difference between rural and urban districts in the reasons given for the uses of ability grouping. When asked whether it was necessary to have ability grouping arrangements in the elementary grades to help meet the needs of gifted students, only one coordinator thought it was unnecessary. At the secondary level all coordinators, regardless of whether or not ability grouping was used in their districts, considered that ability grouping was a necessary step in providing for the needs of the most able students in the class.

Coordinators from rural and urban districts seemed to share the belief that grouping was necessary. On the Likert measure, a rating of 1 indicated that grouping was not necessary. A rating of 5 indicated that it was very necessary. For elementary schools, 100% (17) of the coordinators from urban districts and 80% (16) from the rural districts gave ratings of 4 or 5. For secondary schools, 100% (17) of the coordinators from urban districts and 95% (19) from rural schools selected ratings of 4 or 5.

Eighty-two percent (14) of the coordinators from urban districts and 75% (15) of their colleagues from rural districts clearly indicated, however, that they believed grouping was not sufficient for meeting the academic needs of gifted and talented students. There was not a significant difference between the proportions of rural and urban coordinators who held that belief (chi square = 2.1; $p = .35$).

Three fourths of the urban schools and one half of the rural districts provided early entrance and grade skipping as options for the academic acceleration of gifted students. The difference between those proportions was not statistically significant. A significant difference was observed between the proportions of rural and urban districts that provided other accelerative options for gifted students. Less than one third of the rural districts, compared to more than three fourths of the urban districts, offered such options as Advanced Placement, subject matter acceleration, or dual university/high school enrollment.

Table 2 presents descriptive statistics of coordinators' perceptions of the effects of ability groups on different domains of development of high- and low-achieving students. On the 5-point scale, low ratings indicate that ability grouping was considered to present considerable risk, and high ratings indicate that ability grouping was considered to be beneficial to development. Analyses of variance of presumed benefits of ability grouping revealed that coordinators' ratings did not differ according to whether or not they were from rural or urban districts. The analysis did, however, show that ability grouping was consistently considered to have greater benefits for high-achieving students than for low-achieving students in all areas of development that were surveyed (see Table 2).

The proportions of rural and urban districts using various options for gifted programming in the elementary grades are presented in Table 3. Significantly greater proportions of urban programs offered cross-age grouping options. Whole or part day pull-out enrichment programs were also common options for both rural and urban districts. A comparison of the frequencies with which rural and urban districts provided additional options for gifted elementary school students revealed a difference that approached statistical significance. The additional activities could be classified as enrichment (e.g., Odyssey of the Mind, Geography Bowl, field trips, independent research, enrichment seminars). They are easily classified as extracurricular and/or intermittent enrichment activities.

In rural districts the types of gifted program options that were available at the secondary level were less prevalent and less varied than in urban districts. Coordinators from urban districts indicated that the academic needs of gifted high school students were being addressed with a variety of accelerative

Table 2   Descriptive Statistics for Coordinators' Perceptions of the Effects of Ability Grouping on Different Domains of Development for High- and Low-Achieving Students

| | Students | | | | |
| | High-Achieving | | Low-Achieving | | |
Areas of Development	mean	SD	Mean	SD	F(1.72)
academic	4.65	.48	3.48	1.15	32.37
creativity	4.21	.15	3.14	1.16	20.33
social development	3.73	1.05	2.89	1.17	10.52
emotional development	3.92	.98	3.22	1.16	7.92
athletics	3.78	.92	3.16	.83	9.32
leadership	4.05	.97	3.19	1.31	10.43

Higher scores indicate greater expected benefit in that area of development from ability grouping. For all F values, $p < .01$.

Table 3   Frequencies and Proportions for Elementary School Gifted Education Program Options Offered by Rural and Urban School Districts

| | District | | | | | |
| | Urban N = 17 | | Rural N = 20 | | | |
Option	n	%	n	%	chi-square	p
cross-age grouping	7	41%	2	10%	4.9	.05*
pul-out	15	88.2%	13	65%	2.7	.10
self-contained classes	0		0			
other	12	70.6%	8	40%	3.5	.06

options (e.g., Advanced Placement, concurrent college/high school enrollment, academic challenge, academic honors courses, subject matter acceleration); only three coordinators from rural districts enumerated such accelerative options among the alternatives available to gifted secondary students in their districts. No other rural coordinators listed any other accelerative options. Similar to the elementary level, possibilities for gifted secondary school students in rural districts tended to be extracurricular and/or intermittent enrichment activities (e.g., Governor's Summer Institute, Quiz Bowl, mentorships, Odyssey of the Mind).

Study Two

A reanalysis of responses from teachers in the Southern et al. (1989b) study revealed that of the 171 teachers surveyed, 47 (27.48%) were from urban districts

Table 4   Descriptive Statistics for Training in Gifted Education of Teachers in
Rural and Urban Districts and Their Sentiments Toward Acceleration

Training	Rural			Urban		
	n	*x*	*SD*	*n*	*x*	*SD*
Yes	31	58.5	11.1	22	55.1	13.0
No	93	63.3	12.7	25	62.0	12.7

Note: Lower scores indicate more positive attitudes toward acceleration (cf. Southern et al., 1989b).

and 124 (72.52%) were from rural districts. A two-factor ANOVA (training x location) of the total score on the 22-item Likert questionnaire revealed that teachers who had training in gifted education scored significantly more positive sentiments toward acceleration than teachers who did not have the training ($F(1,169) = 6.98$, $p = .01$). See Table 4 for descriptive statistics. Significance was not observed for either the main effect for location or for the interaction of training and location. Teachers from both rural and urban districts were conservative in their estimates of the value of acceleration.

A significantly smaller proportion of teachers from rural districts than from urban districts had taken course work in gifted education (chi square = 7.6; $p = .01$). In the rural districts 25% (n = 31) of the teachers said that they had had course work in gifted education compared to 47% (n = 22) of the teachers from urban districts.

DISCUSSION

The results of this study demonstrate that most program options for gifted students are commonly used in both rural and urban districts. Ability grouping, pull-out programs, acceleration, and various extracurricular options are offered in both rural and urban schools. One difference is the extent to which these options are available; most of them are less prevalent in rural areas than in urban districts. Reasons for the disparity include factors mentioned above: (a) the relative novelty of programs for the gifted in rural areas, (b) lack of financial resources, (c) lack of sufficient student enrollment to justify grouping or pull-out options, (d) a dearth of trained staff, and (e) isolation from expertise and cultural opportunities in the rural communities.

Coordinators in both rural and urban areas believed that ability grouping and acceleration are beneficial for the education of gifted and talented students. Coordinators' favorable sentiments about these options appear to be based on their assumptions about the characteristics and needs of gifted students. The vast majority of coordinators from both rural and urban districts considered ability grouping necessary but not sufficient for gifted education in both elementary and secondary grades. If asked, they might not have considered any of the options for gifted education sufficient either. However, it is important to note that, although coordinators of gifted education programs cite issues of instructional efficiency and administrative convenience in regular education programs as support for ability grouping, they never mentioned in the open-ended interviews that bringing gifted students together for instruction was important for their academic or affective development.

Acceleration was more frequently available in urban than in rural districts, but community values and willingness of parents to seek the option probably have more direct influence on the availability of acceleration than apparent attitudes and resources. Rural communities are frequently more conservative, and parents are more reluctant to request changes in the status quo. Since educators are generally conservative in their view of acceleration and since most requests for acceleration arise from parental requests (Southern et al., 1989a), districts which receive fewer parental requests would not develop as large a range of options as districts that received more such requests. Rural and urban teachers shared similar views of the value of acceleration, but accelerative options were less common in the rural districts at both the elementary and secondary levels. Rural schools are less apt to offer cross-age grouping for elementary students, Advanced Placement, subject matter acceleration, or dual high school/university enrollment.

The character of gifted education is inclined to vary between rural and urban districts. Program options that were mentioned by coordinators of rural programs were often extracurricular. Usually they consisted of organized academic contests or competitions (e.g., Odyssey of the Mind). Although extracurricular enrichment options were mentioned by both rural and urban coordinators, such options were rarer in rural districts.

The number of teachers who said that they had received course work in gifted education was significantly lower for rural teachers. Explanations for this finding include: (a) less access to training opportunities, (b) a lower priority for the hiring of teachers who have received training, and (c) a general acceptance of the status quo and a lack of impetus from parents and community to develop programs for the gifted. The results of the study also demonstrated that the training teachers received was associated with more positive beliefs about acceleration. Training appears to have the same effect on teachers in rural districts as on teachers from urban districts.

CONCLUSIONS

The conclusions drawn from this study must be viewed in light of their limitations. The inquiry was confined to a comparison of rural and urban school districts in Ohio. It is possible that other rural areas, ones characterized by greater geographic isolation, less population density, or greater population stability, might have provided different data. In addition, the study did not survey high-level administrators or school board members. Those two groups might have provided different views about programming, grouping, and acceleration. An earlier study by Southern et al. (1989b) reported that coordinators of gifted programs were the least conservative compared with teachers, administrators, and school psychologists. It is reasonable to believe that of all the groups, coordinators would provide the greatest advocacy for programs for the gifted and would be most aware of all district options.

A further limitation to this study may result from the definition of rural employed. Any definition of rural based solely on population density would be somewhat controversial since it would ignore other demographic factors in the population and not take into account relative geographical isolation (under strict adherence to population density guidelines Vail, Colorado, and Kennebunkport, Maine, would be classed as rural). While the federal definition and the definition proposed by the National Rural Development Institute may have institutional credibility, many people might protest the characterization of communities of 5000 as urban. These definitions were adopted in this study because they adequately described the kind of population centers and opportunities present in the school organization structures of the state of Ohio. In interpreting the study, it is important to remember that the definition used reflected factors of district independence and resources, proximity to large urban centers, and geographic factors in Ohio. Other areas of the country may find the results less applicable to local conditions.

Despite the potential limitations, the results do allow some preliminary conclusions to be made. In the first place, it seems clear that gifted programs are not as developed or as varied in rural areas. Rural coordinators seemed more conservative in expressing a need for some options. Most importantly, although rural coordinators held attitudes similar to those of their urban counterparts, they had fewer resources and options.

Acceleration offers one of the most economical ways for rural districts to address the needs of the gifted. Yet it seems that teachers, at least, may not be convinced of its benefits or its freedom from potential harm. In the rural community, it may be even less likely that gifted students have accelerative options open to them.

It was not the province of this study to determine the relative benefits of a rural setting for gifted students. The range of options for gifted students in rural districts is less extensive, but a number of positive outcomes may accrue to students living in small communities. For example, rural settings may offer a nurturing environment. Personal attention and concern by teachers and administrators are more likely in settings where everyone knows everyone. Opportunities for leadership and extracurricular activities may be offered to greater percentages of students in rural schools than in urban ones. It is also clear that many rural communities make great efforts to increase the educational opportunities for capable students. Access to options in the education of gifted students is neither a necessary nor sufficient condition for social adjustment and maximum achievement. Such access does, however, make it easier to meet the unique needs of diverse gifted learners. For the rural communities examined in this study, meeting those needs may be more difficult.

REFERENCES

Cummings, S., Briggs, R., & Mercy, J. (1977). Preacher versus teacher: Local-cosmopolitan conflict over textbook censorship in an Appalachian community. *Rural Sociology, 42* (1), 7–21.

Gallagher, J. J. (1985). *Teaching the gifted child*. Boston: Allyn & Bacon.

Howley, C., & Howley, A. (1988) Gifted programs: Equal access in rural areas. In *Linking programs and resources for rural special education. Proceedings of the Annual National Conference of the American Council on Rural Special Education*. (ERIC Document Reproduction Service No. ED 295 350).

Kleinsasser, A. M. (1988). Equity in education for gifted rural girls. *Rural Special Education Quarterly, 8*(4), 27–30.

Nachtigal, P. (1982). *Rural education: In search of a better way*. Boulder, CO: Westview Press.

National Rural Development Institute. (1986). *Toward a definition of rural and small schools*. Bellingham, WA: National Rural Development Institute.

Pendarvis, E. D., Howley, A. A., & Howley, C. B. (1990). *The abilities of gifted children*. Englewood Cliffs, NJ: Prentice Hall.

Pitts, M. (1988). Developing a gifted program: Suggestions for rural school administrators. *Rural Special Education Quarterly, 8*(4), 23–26.

Robinson, A. (1990). Cooperation or exploitation? The argument against cooperative learning for talented students. *Journal for the Education of the Gifted, 14*, 9–27.

Slavin, R. E. (1990). Ability grouping, cooperative learning and the gifted. *Journal for the Education of the Gifted, 14*, 3–8.

Southern, W. T., & Jones, E. D. (1991). Academic acceleration: Background and issues. In W. T. Southern & E. D. Jones (Eds.), *Academic acceleration of gifted children* (pp. 1–28). New York: Teachers College Press.

Southern, W. T., Jones, E. D., & Fiscus, E. D. (1989a, November). *Academic acceleration: Concerns of gifted students and their parents*. Paper presented at the annual meeting of the National Association for Gifted Children, Cincinnati, OH.

Southern, W. T., Jones, E. D., & Fiscus, E. D. (1989b). Practitioner objections to the academic acceleration of young gifted children. *Gifted Child Quarterly, 33*, 29–35.

Spicker, H. H., Southern, W. T., & Davis, B. (1987). The rural gifted child. *Gifted Child Quarterly, 31*(2), 28–32.

State Board of Education. (1989). *Ohio Educational Directory*. Columbus, OH: Author.

United States Bureau of the Census. (1983). Volume I. Characteristics of the population, Chapter D, PC80-1-D37. 1980 *Census of the population, Ohio*. Washington, DC: Superintendent of Documents, United States Government Printing Office.

Index

Note: References to tables or figures are indicated by *italic type* and the addition of *"t"* or *"f"* respectively.

**CORWIN
PRESS**

The Corwin Press logo—a raven striding across an open book—represents the union of courage and learning. Corwin Press is committed to improving education for all learners by publishing books and other professional development resources for those serving the field of K–12 education. By providing practical, hands-on materials, Corwin Press continues to carry out the promise of its motto: **"Helping Educators Do Their Work Better."**